TESTS COMPLETS POUR LE NOUVEAU TOEIC®

Lin Lougheed

PEARSON
Longman

Publié par Pearson Education France
47 bis, rue des Vinaigriers
75010 PARIS
Tél. : 01 72 74 90 00

ISBN : 978-2-7440-7536-0

Titre original : *Preparation Series for the new TOEIC® Test, More Practice Tests*

Traduction : Hélène Bourgeois

ISBN original : 0-13-199306-2

Table des matières

INTRODUCTION

TESTS COMPLETS

SCRIPTS

SOLUTIONS

GRILLES DE RÉPONSES

CRÉDIT PHOTOS

Ambassade d'Australie, Washington DC.
page 7 (en haut) ; page 45 (en haut) ; page 46 (en haut) ; page 47 (en haut) ; page 48 (en bas) ; page 87 (en bas) ; page 89 (en bas)

Corbis
couverture (à droite) © Darren Modricker ; couverture (à gauche) © Lucidio Studio, Inc. ; page 4 (en haut) © Roger Wood ; page 5 (en bas) © Yang Liu ; 46 (en haut) © Jack Hollingsworth ; page 86 (en bas) © Reuters NewMedia Inc ; page 88 (en bas) © Reuters NewMedia Inc ; page 127 (en bas) © James Leynse

Educational Testing Service, Princeton, New Jersey
pages 3, 43, 85, 125

Fotosearch
page 4 (en bas) ; page 6 (en haut) Image Source

Getty
couverture (milieu) © Triangle Images ; page 5 (en haut) © Digital Vision

Instructional Design International, Inc., Washington, D.C.
page 8 (en haut) ; page 47 (en haut) ; page 48 (en haut) ; page 86 (en haut) ; page 87 (en haut) ; page 88 (en haut) ; page 126 (en bas) ; page 128 (en haut) ; page 130 (les deux)

Korean Information Center, Embassy of the Republic of Korea, Washington, D.C.
page 129

NASA, Washington, D.C.
page 90 (en bas) ; page 126 (en haut)

PictureQuest
page 8 (en bas) © Benelux Press ; page 44 (les deux) ; page 47 (en bas) ; page 90 (en haut) © Bob Llewellyn ; page 127 (en haut) © Esbin-Anderson Photography ; 129 © SuperStock

Sans crédits :
page 6 (en bas) ; page 7 (en bas) ; page 128 (en bas)

Introduction

Conseils pratiques pour se préparer au test TOEIC®

Ce livre vous fournira l'entraînement nécessaire pour obtenir un bon score au nouveau test TOEIC. Lorsque vous ferez les exercices, mettez-vous dans les conditions du test réel. Assurez-vous de disposer du temps nécessaire pour faire chaque section de chaque test. Il n'est pas indispensable de faire l'ensemble d'un test d'un seul coup si vous n'en avez pas le temps. Il est cependant recommandé de ne pas dépasser le temps alloué pour chacune des parties.

Munissez-vous d'un crayon à papier, d'un lecteur de CD et d'un exemplaire de grille de réponses fourni à la fin du livre. Lors du vrai test TOEIC, vous devrez reporter toutes vos réponses sur une grille identique. N'inscrivez rien sur votre livre. Vous pourrez ainsi refaire les tests plusieurs fois. Lorsque vous reportez vos réponses dans la grille, noircissez bien les cases prévues à cet effet. N'inscrivez rien en dehors de ces cases. Si vous ne connaissez pas la réponse à une question, essayez de **deviner**. Vous pourrez ainsi gagner quelques points !

Les solutions des tests sont indiquées à la fin du livre. Chaque réponse est assortie d'une courte explication. Les explications fournies font référence aux points abordés dans l'ouvrage déjà publié chez Longman, *Préparation au nouveau TOEIC*, que vous pouvez également consulter. Le livre que vous avez entre les mains constitue le complément idéal à *Préparation au nouveau TOEIC* dans la mesure où ce dernier propose une méthode d'apprentissage complète (exercices d'entraînement, conseils, tests blancs), *Tests complets pour le nouveau TOEIC* se concentrant sur la pratique au moyen de plusieurs tests blancs. Vous trouverez aussi dans ce livre des éléments d'explication sur la manière de compter vos points aux différentes sections du test et de convertir votre score final. Ces documents vous donneront une idée approximative de votre résultat au test TOEIC. Notez bien qu'il ne s'agit que d'une approximation et non du score TOEIC réel.

Oral

Remarquez l'icône, représentant un casque, qui est utilisée tout au long du livre. Ce symbole signifie que vous aurez besoin d'un lecteur CD pour les sections Oral des tests.

La section Oral est divisée en quatre parties.

	NOMBRE DE QUESTIONS	TEMPS
Partie 1 : Photos	10	45 minutes
Partie 2 : Question-Réponse	30	
Partie 3 : Dialogues	30	
Partie 4 : Tests audio	30	
	TOTAL 100	

Écrit

Pour effectuer les exercices de la section Écrit, vous aurez besoin du livre, d'une grille de réponses et d'un crayon. Cette section est divisée en trois parties.

		NOMBRE DE QUESTIONS	TEMPS
Partie 5 :	Phrases incomplètes	40	75 minutes
Partie 6 :	Texte à compléter	12	
Partie 7 :	Compréhension écrite :		
	• Passages simples	28	
	• Passages doubles	20	
	TOTAL	100	

Consignes du nouveau TOEIC®

CONSIGNES GÉNÉRALES : Les directives qui suivent ont été reproduites avec l'aimable l'autorisation d'ETS (*Educational Testing Service*). Lisez-les attentivement et assurez-vous de les comprendre.

ETS® TOEIC®

Test of English for International Communication

General Directions

This test is designed to measure your English language ability. The test is divided into two sections: Listening and Reading.

You must mark all of your answers on the separate answer sheet. For each question, you should select the best answer from the answer choices given. Then, on your answer sheet, you should find the number of the question and fill in the space that corresponds to the letter of the answer that you have selected. If you decide to change an answer, completely erase your old answer and then mark your new answer.

Ce test a été conçu pour mesurer votre aisance en langue anglaise. Il est divisé en deux sections : oral et écrit.

Vous devez reporter toutes vos réponses sur la grille de réponses qui est fournie séparément. Pour chaque question, vous devrez sélectionner la meilleure réponse parmi les diverses propositions. Puis, sur votre grille de réponses, vous devez trouver le numéro correspondant à la question et noircir la case de la lettre correspondant à la réponse choisie. Si vous décidez de modifier une réponse, merci d'effacer l'ancienne et de reporter la nouvelle.

Tests complets

Test n° 1

Vous trouverez la grille de réponses au test n° 1 à la page 251. Détachez-la du livre et reportez-y vos réponses. Lorsque vous êtes prêt à commencer, mettez le CD et écoutez la partie audio du test n° 1.

LISTENING TEST

In the Listening test, you will be asked to demonstrate how well you understand spoken English. The entire Listening test will last approximately 45 minutes. There are four parts, and directions are given for each part. You must mark your answers on the separate answer sheet. Do not write your answers in the test book.

PARTIE 1

Directions: For each question in this part, you will hear four statements about a picture in your test book. When you hear the statements, you must select the one statement that best describes what you see in the picture. Then find the number of the question on your answer sheet and mark your answer. The statements will not be printed in your test book and will be spoken only one time.

Example *Sample Answer*

(A) (B) ● (D)

Statement (C), "They're standing near the table," is the best description of the picture, so you should select answer (C) and mark it on your answer sheet.

1.

2.

3.

4.

5.

6.

7. 

8. 

9.

10.

PART 2

Directions: You will hear a question or statement and three responses spoken in English. They will not be printed in your test book and will be spoken only one time. Select the best response to the question or statement and mark the letter (A), (B), or (C) on your answer sheet.

Example

Sample Answer

(A) ● (C)

You will hear: Where is the meeting room?

You will also hear: (A) To meet the new director.
(B) It's the first room on the right.
(C) Yes, at two o'clock.

Your best response to the question "Where is the meeting room?" is choice (B), "It's the first room on the right," so (B) is the correct answer. You should mark answer (B) on your answer sheet.

11. Mark your answer on your answer sheet.
12. Mark your answer on your answer sheet.
13. Mark your answer on your answer sheet.
14. Mark your answer on your answer sheet.
15. Mark your answer on your answer sheet.
16. Mark your answer on your answer sheet.
17. Mark your answer on your answer sheet.
18. Mark your answer on your answer sheet.
19. Mark your answer on your answer sheet.
20. Mark your answer on your answer sheet.
21. Mark your answer on your answer sheet.
22. Mark your answer on your answer sheet.
23. Mark your answer on your answer sheet.
24. Mark your answer on your answer sheet.
25. Mark your answer on your answer sheet.
26. Mark your answer on your answer sheet.
27. Mark your answer on your answer sheet.
28. Mark your answer on your answer sheet.
29. Mark your answer on your answer sheet.
30. Mark your answer on your answer sheet.
31. Mark your answer on your answer sheet.
32. Mark your answer on your answer sheet.
33. Mark your answer on your answer sheet.
34. Mark your answer on your answer sheet.
35. Mark your answer on your answer sheet.
36. Mark your answer on your answer sheet.
37. Mark your answer on your answer sheet.
38. Mark your answer on your answer sheet.
39. Mark your answer on your answer sheet.
40. Mark your answer on your answer sheet.

PART 3

Directions: You will hear some conversations between two people. You will be asked to answer three questions about what the speakers say in each conversation. Select the best response to each question and mark the letter (A), (B), (C), or (D) on your answer sheet. The conversations will not be printed in your test book and will be spoken only one time.

41. What does the man want the woman to do?

(A) Type a letter.
(B) Buy him a sweater.
(C) Have lunch with him.
(D) Work this evening.

42. What is the woman doing now?

(A) Eating lunch.
(B) Leaving for the golf course.
(C) Making copies.
(D) Sending e-mail.

43. Where is the man going?

(A) To a restaurant.
(B) To his office.
(C) To the post office.
(D) To the photocopy store.

---

44. When will the phones be installed?

(A) Monday before noon.
(B) Monday afternoon.
(C) Wednesday before noon.
(D) Wednesday afternoon.

45. Why weren't the phones installed last week?

(A) The equipment was out of order.
(B) They couldn't get an appointment.
(C) The order was placed too late.
(D) They didn't bring the right kind of phone.

46. How long have they been waiting for the phones?

(A) Under a week.
(B) One week.
(C) One month.
(D) More than a month.

---

47. How many dozen pens is the man ordering?

(A) Two.
(B) Four.
(C) Six.
(D) Twelve.

48. What colors does he want?

(A) Green and purple.
(B) Green and red.
(C) Red, black, and blue.
(D) Red, black, and purple.

49. How will he pay for the pens?

(A) He will pay by check.
(B) He will pay with cash.
(C) The woman will send him a bill.
(D) The woman will charge it to his account.

---

50. Where does this conversation take place?

(A) At the dinner table.
(B) In a grocery store.
(C) In a bookstore.
(D) At a bakery.

51. What does the man want the woman to do?

(A) Cook a meal.
(B) Stop coughing.
(C) Eat some more.
(D) Sing a song.

52. What does the woman want to do?

(A) Read a book.
(B) Bake a cake.
(C) Drink coffee.
(D) Pick up her mail.

---

53. Who is giving advice?

(A) A travel agent.
(B) A physician.
(C) A teacher.
(D) A golfer.

54. What is the woman's problem?

(A) She lost her job.
(B) She works too much.
(C) She never takes a walk.
(D) She can't decide on a place for a vacation.

55. What will the woman do?

(A) Go to the health club.
(B) Learn to play golf.
(C) Take a vacation.
(D) Hire someone to help her.

---

56. What don't the speakers like?

(A) Spring.
(B) The heat.
(C) The rain.
(D) Standing.

57. How is the weather today?

(A) Sunny.
(B) Cool.
(C) Humid.
(D) Icy.

58. When does this conversation take place?

(A) May.
(B) September.
(C) November.
(D) December.

---

59. What is the woman looking for?

(A) Her raincoat.
(B) Her boots and umbrella.
(C) Her bus ticket.
(D) Her watch.

60. What is the weather like?

(A) Hot.
(B) Cold.
(C) Rainy.
(D) Misty.

61. When will the bus leave?

(A) In 15 minutes.
(B) In 20 minutes.
(C) In 29 minutes.
(D) In 50 minutes.

---

62. Where does the man live?

(A) By the school.
(B) By the police station.
(C) On a mountain.
(D) Near a pool.

63. How does the woman get to work?

(A) On foot.
(B) By train.
(C) By car.
(D) By bus.

64. What time will the woman meet the man tomorrow?

(A) At 7:00.
(B) At 7:30.
(C) At 11:00.
(D) At 11:30.

---

65. Why didn't the woman read this morning's paper?

(A) She didn't have money to buy one.
(B) She didn't have time to buy one.
(C) It wasn't delivered on time.
(D) She read yesterday's instead.

66. What does the man suggest that the woman do?

(A) Buy a newspaper at the newsstand.
(B) Read the front page.
(C) Borrow his newspaper.
(D) Have the newspaper delivered.

67. What does the man want to do?

(A) Read the woman a story.
(B) Tell the woman about the news.
(C) Buy a newspaper for her.
(D) Copy a page from the newspaper.

68. What time did the woman go to bed?

(A) At 7:00.
(B) After 7:00.
(C) At 11:00.
(D) After 11:00.

69. How many hours of sleep does the woman usually get?

(A) Four.
(B) Five.
(C) Eight.
(D) Ten.

70. Why did she get up early?

(A) To do some work.
(B) To work out at the gym.
(C) To finish reading a book.
(D) To get ready for a trip.

PART 4

Directions: You will hear some talks given by a single speaker. You will be asked to answer three questions about what the speaker says in each talk. Select the best response to each question and mark the letter (A), (B), (C), or (D) on your answer sheet. The talks will not be printed in your test book and will be spoken only one time.

71. What is being sold?
(A) Office space.
(B) Office supplies.
(C) Down pillows.
(D) Sailboats.

72. How long does this sale last?
(A) One day.
(B) Three days.
(C) One week.
(D) Eight days.

73. When does the sale end?
(A) Thursday.
(B) Friday.
(C) Saturday.
(D) Sunday.

---

74. What was the weather yesterday?
(A) Rainy.
(B) Foggy.
(C) Sunny.
(D) Clear.

75. When might it snow?
(A) This evening.
(B) Tomorrow morning.
(C) Tomorrow evening.
(D) This weekend.

76. What will the weekend temperature be?
(A) Below freezing.
(B) Right around freezing.
(C) Around 7 degrees.
(D) About 11 degrees.

---

77. What kind of news item is this?
(A) An analysis.
(B) A review.
(C) A correction.
(D) A warning.

78. When might this announcement be heard?
(A) Spring.
(B) Summer.
(C) Fall.
(D) Winter.

79. What causes power failure?
(A) Excessive use.
(B) Lack of demand.
(C) Increased supply.
(D) Poor quality fans.

---

80. Who is probably listening to this announcement?
(A) Ticket agents.
(B) Telephone line technicians.
(C) Airline representatives.
(D) Potential travelers.

81. Why is there a delay?
(A) All the agents are busy.
(B) All flights are late.
(C) The fares are going up.
(D) Representatives are on strike.

82. When should travelers to other countries get to the airport?
(A) Two hours before their flight leaves.
(B) Three hours before their flight leaves.
(C) Four hours before their flight leaves.
(D) Five hours before their flight leaves.

---

83. What kind of people are attending the seminar?

(A) Teachers.
(B) Managers.
(C) Waiters.
(D) Gardeners.

84. Which of the following describes Mr. Margalis?

(A) Inexperienced.
(B) Retired.
(C) Speechless.
(D) Young.

85. Where is the announcement being heard?

(A) In a garden.
(B) In a private office.
(C) In a dining hall.
(D) On a train.

---

86. What is needed to enter?

(A) A special pass.
(B) An authorized signature.
(C) A secure vehicle.
(D) A hunting license.

87. Where can passes be obtained?

(A) Within the secure area.
(B) From authorized personnel.
(C) At the Security Office.
(D) At the License Bureau.

88. What should visitors do when leaving the area?

(A) Sign out.
(B) Pay an exit fee.
(C) Give the pass back.
(D) Keep the pass for future visits.

---

89. What kind of work is advertised?

(A) Full-time.
(B) Part-time.
(C) Overtime.
(D) Volunteer.

90. What qualifications are required?

(A) Law degree.
(B) Medical diploma.
(C) Advertising experience.
(D) Office skills.

91. What are job seekers required to do?

(A) Take a test.
(B) Be available immediately.
(C) Fill out an application form.
(D) Understand employment law.

---

92. What time is the report being presented?

(A) At 8:00.
(B) At 10:00.
(C) At 12:00.
(D) At 2:00.

93. What advice is given?

(A) Wear a hat.
(B) Go to bed early.
(C) Have a nice day.
(D) Take your umbrella.

94. What is the weather now?

(A) Rainy.
(B) Clear skies.
(C) Dark clouds.
(D) Windy.

---

95. What kind of place is Family Security Systems?

(A) A police station.
(B) A travel agency.
(C) An insurance company.
(D) An alarm installation company.

96. For urgent problems, what number should be pressed?

(A) One.
(B) Four.
(C) Five.
(D) Six.

97. How can you register an address change?

(A) Press 4.
(B) Visit the website.
(C) Speak to an agent.
(D) Send it in by mail.

98. Where is this announcement made?

(A) At a school.
(B) At an airport.
(C) At a grocery store.
(D) At a shopping mall.

99. What is today's special?

(A) Chicken.
(B) Beef.
(C) Spaghetti.
(D) Vegetables.

100. What do kids get with their meal?

(A) A toy.
(B) Free dessert.
(C) Extra vegetables.
(D) A seat by the entrance.

Fin du test de compréhension orale. Passez à la partie 5.

READING TEST

In the Reading test, you will read a variety of texts and answer several different types of reading comprehension questions. The entire Reading test will last 75 minutes. There are three parts, and directions are given for each part. You are encouraged to answer as many questions as possible within the time allowed.

You must mark your answers on the separate answer sheet. Do not write your answers in the test book.

PART 5

Directions: A word or phrase is missing in each of the sentences below. Four answer choices are given below each sentence. Select the best answer to complete the sentence. Then mark the letter (A), (B), (C), or (D) on your answer sheet.

101. Both companies are __________ the same business.

(A) in
(B) with
(C) from
(D) through

102. __________ there were so many options, everyone was satisfied.

(A) If
(B) Why
(C) Because
(D) When

103. If they __________ more aware of the trends, they could have avoided bankruptcy.

(A) were
(B) are
(C) have been
(D) had been

104. Make checks __________ to the company.

(A) paid
(B) payable
(C) paying
(D) pay

105. Ms. Bolton is both a strong manager __________ a skilled negotiator.

(A) or
(B) with
(C) and
(D) though

106. __________ the stockbrokers said the market was healthy, they refused to invest more money.

(A) Because
(B) Although
(C) In addition
(D) So

107. The seminar will adjourn __________ five o'clock.

(A) in
(B) on
(C) at
(D) the

108. Marketing is important; __________, we're hiring a new public relations firm.

(A) therefore
(B) even though
(C) nevertheless
(D) but

109. The secretary had the messenger __________ the envelope as soon as possible.

(A) delivering
(B) to deliver
(C) deliver
(D) delivered

110. The board meetings usually __________ on time.

(A) have started
(B) start
(C) are starting
(D) have been starting

111. Everyone was disappointed to hear that the company's proposal was __________.

(A) turned up
(B) turned on
(C) turned away
(D) turned down

112. Even though the exchange rate was high, we __________ from them.

(A) buy
(B) must have bought
(C) had to buy
(D) had better buy

113. __________ Dr. Rossi hired the new assistant, the office has become more organized.

(A) When
(B) Before
(C) While
(D) Since

114. Mr. Cutler will __________ as president.

(A) step out
(B) step down
(C) step from
(D) step through

115. Ms. Silva sent the memo __________ it had been approved.

(A) so
(B) but
(C) after
(D) until

116. It's time to take advantage of current __________ rates.

(A) interesting
(B) interest
(C) interested
(D) interests

117. The manager has to __________ the presentation until next week.

(A) put off
(B) put with
(C) put on
(D) put through

118. When the directors __________ a profit, they'll be satisfied.

(A) will see
(B) are seeing
(C) see
(D) have been seeing

119. Do __________ an estimate before getting it in writing.

(A) not ever accept
(B) never accept
(C) accept never
(D) not accept ever

120. Production went down __________ morale was low.

(A) even though
(B) when
(C) but
(D) to

121. The distributors will collaborate __________ a British company.

(A) with
(B) in
(C) from
(D) of

122. If banks __________ the number of credit cards, the economy would improve.

(A) limiting
(B) limited
(C) had limited
(D) are limiting

123. One suggestion was to __________ gasoline taxes.

(A) raise
(B) have raised
(C) be raising
(D) raising

124. The host will want the total amount __________ before paying the bill.

(A) checked
(B) be checked
(C) checking
(D) check

125. The new sales manager cooperates with her colleagues; __________, she is a valued member.

(A) although
(B) however
(C) for example
(D) therefore

126. __________ our office, Mr. James voted against the proposal.

(A) Representation
(B) Representative
(C) Representing
(D) Representative of

127. Paychecks __________.

(A) are twice distributed a month
(B) twice a month are distributed
(C) are distributed twice a month
(D) a month are distributed twice

128. There has been a decline in local __________ national advertising.

(A) therefore
(B) so
(C) but
(D) and

129. __________ Mrs. Lee was calling her husband's office, he was calling hers.

(A) While
(B) Because
(C) So
(D) Then

130. The CEOs will meet __________ Chicago next month.

(A) at
(B) in
(C) to
(D) from

131. The award was contested by one of the __________.

(A) competitors
(B) competition
(C) competing
(D) competitive

132. The __________ was considered final.

(A) decisive
(B) decided
(C) decision
(D) deciding

133. Mr. Wong once lived __________ New Orleans.

(A) in
(B) at
(C) from
(D) on

134. The report focused on the __________ of the study.

(A) foundlings
(B) finds
(C) findings
(D) found

135. The staff __________ the office had been burglarized.

(A) suspicion
(B) suspense
(C) suspicious
(D) suspected

136. __________ all the references to verify the information.

(A) Look by
(B) Look out
(C) Look up
(D) Look to

137. Mary is __________ an excellent writer.

(A) considerate
(B) considered
(C) considerable
(D) considers

138. They __________ the launch of their new company only a year ago.

(A) announce
(B) are announcing
(C) have announced
(D) announced

139. After re-evaluating the proposal, the agency __________ the contract to us.

(A) awarding
(B) had awarded
(C) awarded
(D) awards

140. My supervisor had me __________ the morning taking inventory.

(A) spend
(B) to spend
(C) spent
(D) spending

PART 6

Directions: Read the texts that follow. A word or phrase is missing in some of the sentences. Four answer choices are given below each of the sentences. Select the best answer to complete the text. Then mark the letter (A), (B), (C), or (D) on your answer sheet.

Questions 141–143 refer to the following letter.

Chandi Akella
Rapid Technology, Inc.
450 Cherry Circle
Detroit, MI 40355

Dear Ms. Akella:

I was interested to read about your company in the online issue of "Technology Today." Perhaps your company's technology can help us.

I own a candy company in Tennessee. We ________ a variety of kinds

141. (A) consume
(B) manufacture
(C) purchase
(D) desire

of candy which are sold all over the USA and in other countries as well. As part of their work, my employees use heavy equipment and move large boxes every day. Sometimes they fall or hurt their backs. As a result, they ________ days of work. Everyone suffers from this situation.

142. (A) avoid
(B) gain
(C) miss
(D) save

These accidents cost my company a lot of money, and my employees suffer from health problems.

Rapid Technology's "cobots" may help. I understand that a "cobot" is like a robot. However, it is a robot that collaborates—or works with—people. So, you call it a "cobot." Is that correct? I understand that people are ________ when they work with cobots. However, the article I read only

143. (A) safer
(B) more safely
(C) safety
(D) more safety

discussed cobots at car companies. Could they also be used at a candy company?

We are very interested in cobots, but we are not sure if they would work here. What do you think? Please reply via mail. Thank you.

Best wishes,

Priscilla Parton
President, Prissy's Candies

Questions 144–146 refer to the following e-mail.

To: IEP Group All
From: Karin O'Flaherty
Subject: Office procedures

Dear Teachers,

Our new school year is starting. I would like to remind everyone about the rules for using our office during this exciting and busy time. Please review these procedures carefully.

1. Door Code: You need a code to unlock the office door. New teachers, your code will arrive this week.
2. Telephone: Everyone shares the same telephone number. If you answer a call for another teacher, please take a message and leave ________ in the teacher's mailbox.

144. (A) them
(B) her
(C) his
(D) it

3. Computers: Please share the computers. Remember to sign ________

145. (A) in
(B) up
(C) out
(D) to

after using the computer. For help with the computer, please call Mario at extension 421.

4. Copying: Copying can be very ________, so please make only a few copies.

146. (A) costly
(B) useful
(C) necessary
(D) complicated

5. Eating: Please eat in the lunchroom. After eating, throw all trash in the bin. Keep this room clean at all times.

We have some new teachers this semester. They are not yet familiar with our office procedures. Please help these new teachers, and welcome them to our program. Thank you.

Best Wishes,
Karin

Karin O'Flaherty
Program Coordinator

Questions 147–149 refer to the following letter.

RDA Company
5943 Alton Lane
Irvine, CA 91628

Office Services, Incorporated
Ms. Misato Sakai
1300 Lincoln Lane
San Francisco, CA 94043

Dear Ms. Sakai:

My boss recommended your company as the fastest at shipping office supplies. I work at RDA Company, and we urgently need some supplies. I hope that you can ship these items __________.

147. (A) quickly
(B) quicker
(C) quickest
(D) quickness

We need two large desks, model 156A, one dark brown and the other black. We also need two chairs for the new desks. We would like the colors to __________ the desks, so please send one dark brown and one black chair.

148. (A) contrast with
(B) differ from
(C) match
(D) cover

We need one new computer, model ABG439, with a medium-sized, flat-screen monitor. Please __________ two speakers.

149. (A) include
(B) included
(C) to include
(D) will include

We also need ten boxes of white, letter-sized paper.

Please send everything immediately. Our new employees need these supplies as soon as possible. Thank you for your assistance.

Regards,

Naser Abdelwali

Naser Abdelwali
Human Resources Director

Questions 150–152 refer to the following letter.

The Little Tea Room
Blumberg 77
Adlkofen, Germany

Dr. Johannes Spieker
Hinterkirchstrasse 15
Frieburg, Germany

Dear Dr. Spieker: January 7, 20__

I wanted to write and personally thank you for your kind effort in helping to tend to one of our ________ at our restaurant in her time of need. Briana

150. (A) doctors
(B) nurses
(C) customers
(D) employees

Hilton, the woman you helped resuscitate on Monday, gave me your name and address when I spoke to her on the phone today. You ________ be glad to

151. (A) had better
(B) could
(C) will
(D) are

know that she is recovering in the hospital and is almost ready to be released.

As it turns out, you assumed correctly that the woman was suffering from a severe and sudden allergic reaction to nuts. She had neglected to inform the waitress that she couldn't eat any food containing nuts. Your skill and presence of mind saved her from suffering a terrible tragedy.

Please bring your family in for a complimentary meal at your earliest convenience so ________ I may thank you in person.

152. (A) that
(B) thus
(C) there
(D) this

Sincerely,

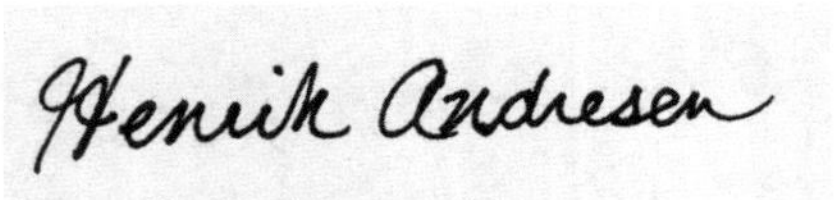

Henrik Andresen, Manager

PART 7

Directions: In this part you will read a selection of texts, such as magazine and newspaper articles, letters, and advertisements. Each text is followed by several questions. Select the best answer for each question and mark the letter (A), (B), (C), or (D) on your answer sheet.

Questions 153–154 refer to the following job announcement.

> **SALES**
>
> California-based company seeking to expand its sales overseas is looking for sales professionals to cover territory in the Pacific Rim region. Successful candidates will have a minimum of two years experience in sales, preferably in the clothing industry, as well as a good professional appearance, excellent communication skills, and a college degree. Conversational knowledge of Japanese or Mandarin Chinese and experience traveling or working in Asia are desirable. Job is based in San Francisco but requires one to two weeks a month of travel. We offer an excellent salary and benefits package including health and life insurance, relocation allowance, and professional development opportunities. Send résumé and two letters of reference to: J. M. Schmidt, 150 State Street, San Francisco, CA 94181. Closing date: June 15.

153. Who would most likely apply for this job?

(A) An engineer
(B) A real estate agent
(C) A professor
(D) A clerk in a clothing store

154. Which of the following is NOT mentioned as a requirement?

(A) Good appearance
(B) Previous experience
(C) A master's degree
(D) Good speaking and writing skills

Questions 155–157 refer to the following article.

These days, everybody buys computer software. Consumers purchase all kinds of software, from games for the kids to highly sophisticated professional programs and everything in between. Computer software has become part of everybody's daily life, and this is just one more thing adding to an ever-growing problem. The excessive packaging on computer software is joining catchy wrappers, durable plastic and cardboard boxes, plastic jugs, and other types of packaging in the trash. Everything we buy is packaged in one way or another. When we get our purchases home, we unwrap them and throw the packaging in the trash. It then ends up in the nation's garbage dumps. Communities all around the country are struggling with the problem of where to put all this waste. Much of this excessive packaging serves only to make the products more attractive to consumers. It catches the eye but does not really protect the goods from damage. Environmentalists are asking consumers to say "No!" to wasteful packaging practices. Please purchase only those products that come with a minimum of packaging or that are packaged in 100% recycled materials.

155. What is this article about?

(A) Recycling
(B) Computer software
(C) The use of garbage dumps
(D) A problem with packaging

156. According to the passage, why are products packaged?

(A) For protection
(B) For attractiveness
(C) For ease of consumption
(D) For environmental safety

157. What happens to most packaging?

(A) It's recycled.
(B) It's discarded.
(C) It's stored on shelves.
(D) It's redesigned.

Questions 158–160 refer to the following table.

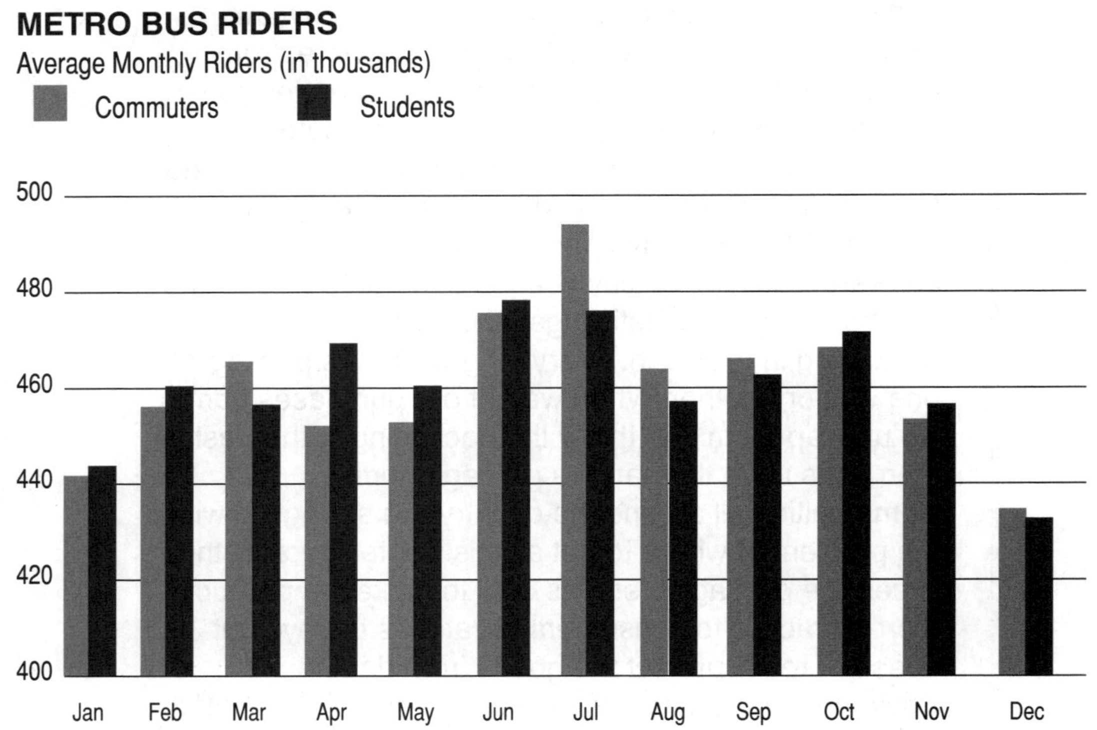

These figures apply to bus trips within the city limits only. City-to-suburb and suburb-to-suburb trips were not included in the study.

158. What does this table compare?

(A) Daily schedules
(B) Means of transportation
(C) Monthly ridership
(D) Riders with drivers

159. Which month had the highest number of commuters?

(A) June
(B) July
(C) September
(D) October

160. In which month were the buses used least?

(A) February
(B) May
(C) August
(D) December

Questions 161–164 refer to the following report.

The Postal System has announced that postal rates are going up yet again. On the first of the year, the price of a first-class stamp will rise by 8 cents. Express mail and priority mail rates will increase by 20 percent. The rates for third-class mail will also go up, while the special book rate will be entirely eliminated. Special services such as Delivery Confirmation, Return Receipt, and Overnight Delivery will also cost more, and it has even been announced that rental rates on post office mail boxes will increase.

Everybody everywhere will be paying more for postal services next year, but one sector will be particularly hard hit. Direct-marketing companies rely on the postal system to carry out their business. These companies include catalog houses as well as sellers of mailing lists. Postal services account for a significant percentage of their costs.

Direct-marketing companies say the proposed increases in postal rates will hurt their industry and will likely even drive some into bankruptcy. "Our business is carried out almost entirely through the mail," says Esther Bergen, president of Mega Marketers, Inc., one of the largest direct-marketing companies in the country. "Of course these increases will hurt us. They will have a huge effect on the way we do business." Direct-marketing companies rely mostly on third-class mail, which is expected to have rate increases as high as 30 percent. Will this mean less junk mail arriving at your doorstep? "Possibly," says Bergen. "But the more likely outcome is that the smaller companies, which will have more difficulty absorbing the costs of the rate increases, will go under, while the larger companies will stay in business and take over the markets now covered by the smaller companies. There will probably be some increases in prices of mail-order products, but not enough to drive the average consumer away."

161. The word "drive" in paragraph 3, line 2, is closest in meaning to

(A) force
(B) operate
(C) transport
(D) remove

162. According to the passage, who will be most affected by this change?

(A) Direct-marketing companies
(B) Greeting card manufacturers
(C) Postal employees
(D) Stamp collectors

163. According to the passage, what rate do most direct-marketing companies use?

(A) Book rate
(B) First class
(C) Third class
(D) Proposed rate

164. What are the catalog houses in this report?

(A) Preferred postal clients
(B) Direct-marketing companies
(C) Financially stable companies
(D) First-class mail users

Questions 165–168 refer to the following information.

1. The One-Call System

In most states, natural gas industry–supported laws require contractors and private landowners to call the local One-Call number before beginning any kind of digging. With forty-eight hours' notice, a pipeline operator will locate the pipeline and mark it clearly. Any damage at all to a pipe—even the slightest scratch—could lead to a leak later on. Whether One-Call has become the law in your state or not, you can help keep pipelines safe by calling the number on the right-of-way markers before you dig.

2. Leak Detection

Most pipelines are operated twenty-four hours a day from a control station, using telephone, satellite, or microwave communications systems. Computers are widely used to monitor conditions along the line every ten to sixty seconds, sounding an alarm if they detect any abnormality or sudden change in pressure. In the event of an alarm, valves can be closed and nearby pipeline crews dispatched within minutes.

3. Emergency Response Preparedness

Although leaks occur infrequently and rarely result in a fire, readiness for any emergency is a crucial responsibility for pipeline companies. Federal and state laws supported by the natural gas industry require pipeline companies and local police and fire departments to maintain a coordinated plan of response and to practice for an emergency by staging drills. These drills and personnel training programs emphasize the need for immediate action and for cooperation between the various rescue agencies and the pipeline company.

4. Public Awareness

The One-Call system, state-of-the-art leak detection equipment, and emergency response procedures have all been put in place with one thing in mind—the safety of you, the public. Please visit the website of the Natural Gas Association to find out more about our safety procedures, tips for using natural gas safely in your home, and information on what to do if you see someone tampering with pipeline right-of-way markers.

165. What is the main focus of this passage?

(A) Safety
(B) Personnel training
(C) Computer monitoring
(D) Industry-supported laws

166. What is One-Call?

(A) A telecommunications firm
(B) An excavating company
(C) A contractor
(D) A pipeline detection safety service

167. What do rescue agencies and pipeline companies coordinate?

(A) Leaks
(B) Drilling
(C) Emergency readiness
(D) Microwave communications

168. The word "dispatched" in paragraph 2, line 4, is closest in meaning to

(A) fired
(B) fixed
(C) sent
(D) hired

Questions 169–171 refer to the following manual.

TROUBLESHOOTING

If your TV does not work, check the following points:

PICTURE	SOUND	POSSIBLE CAUSES	WHAT TO DO
No picture	Noise	Not properly tuned	Adjust tuning
Picture visible	No sound	• Volume control dial turned too low • Earphones inserted	• Turn up volume • Disconnect earphones
Picture all white	Sound heard	Brightness control not set correctly	Adjust brightness control
Picture dark or blurred	Sound heard	Brightness control not set correctly	Adjust brightness control

169. What is this chart used for?

(A) To determine a problem with a TV
(B) To pick a TV program
(C) To compare prices
(D) To wrap packages

170. What does the manual advise if the picture is all white?

(A) Turn down the volume
(B) Adjust the brightness control
(C) Adjust the tuning
(D) Disconnect the earphones

171. When should the tuning be adjusted?

(A) When there is no picture and no sound
(B) When there is a picture but no sound
(C) When the picture is white
(D) When there is noise but no picture

Questions 172–174 refer to the following letter.

April 23, 20__

China Books, Inc.
23405 San Antonio Ave.
San Fernando, CA 94509

To whom it may concern:

I have just received a "Payment Due" notice from your office. This is the second time I have received such a notice. I don't understand why I have received these notices since I paid for my purchase at the time I placed my order. I enclosed a check in the envelope with the order form. The first time I received a notice, I sent you a photocopy of the canceled check as proof of payment. I am now enclosing, for the second time, a photocopy of both sides of canceled check #535 in the amount of $35.95, which I sent to cover payment for the book *In a Modern World*, plus shipping and handling costs. Please note that the date on the check is October 13. The information on the back shows that it was endorsed and deposited into your company's bank account on October 23.

Please call me at (415) 555-4856 to acknowledge receipt of this letter. I wish to avoid any further harassment about this payment. Your company is a wonderful source for hard-to-find books about Asia, and I would like to continue doing business with you. As a professor of Asian Studies, I am a frequent buyer of books dealing with all aspects of Asian culture and history and often recommend your store to my students. However, if we cannot resolve this matter quickly, I will have to take my business elsewhere. I sincerely hope that will not be necessary.

Sincerely,

Margaret Tomkins

Margaret Tomkins

172. Who owes money?

(A) No one
(B) Ms. Tomkins
(C) China Books
(D) The author

173. When was the check written?

(A) April 23
(B) May 30
(C) October 13
(D) October 23

174. According to the letter, which of the following is NOT true?

(A) Ms. Tomkins has paid twice.
(B) This is Ms. Tomkins' second letter.
(C) Ms. Tomkins has received two notices.
(D) The company received the payment.

Questions 175–176 refer to the following report.

When personal computers first began showing up in offices around the world, people believed that this business tool would lead to something called the "paperless office." This was hailed as a great advance in business practices.

The "paperless office" theory went something like this: people would store their information on disks and computers instead of using file folders and paper. As a result, paper use would decrease. This was supposed to help preserve natural resources as well as reduce the world's solid-waste disposal problem.

In some ways this theory has played out in practice. In offices everywhere around the world, files and records are increasingly being stored electronically rather than on paper. But the prediction has not proven to be entirely true. Documents are often printed out in part or in their entirety in order to be reviewed or shared with others. Often multiple versions of a document go through the printout stage, thus actually increasing the use of paper for each document rather than reducing it. In addition, computers have made it easier to generate notices and flyers, of which people readily make multiple copies to distribute to as wide an audience as possible. In some ways, computers have made it easier than ever before to use large quantities of paper.

So, while computers have reduced paper use in some areas, they have increased it in others. The issue of felling forests in order to manufacture paper and the question of how to dispose of so much solid waste still remain problematic.

175. What is the report about?

(A) Selling computers
(B) Desktop publishing
(C) The "paperless office"
(D) World problems

176. What would the "paperless office" have done?

(A) Preserved resources
(B) Confused secretaries
(C) Cut costs
(D) Improved communication

Questions 177–180 refer to the following job announcement.

Public Health
Pakistan

Position Available: Division of Public Health and Clinical Nutrition.
The University of Karachi at Karachi General Hospital (KGH) is recruiting for an assistant clinical professor of medicine for the Division of Public Health and Clinical Nutrition. The candidate will participate in all teaching, clinical, and basic research activities of the division and serve as chief of the public health clinic at KGH. The individual will be expected to develop independently funded clinical research programs dealing with basic public health issues and/or clinical nutrition. Board certification required. Competitive salary in U.S. dollars, airfare, and full board/lodging included. Professional growth and cultural opportunities abound. Send curriculum vitae, summary of clinical research interests, and three letters of reference to Faroque Khan, MD, 572 St. Kilda Road, Sydney 2000, Australia.

177. In line 2, the word "recruiting" is closest in meaning to

(A) hiring
(B) training
(C) helping
(D) funding

178. Which of the following is part of the job description?

(A) Giving blood tests
(B) Supervising research
(C) Repairing equipment
(D) Diagnosing patients

179. Which of the following is a requirement for employment?

(A) Pakistani medical license
(B) Medical board certification
(C) Clinical nutrition training experience
(D) Abstracts of published articles

180. Which of the following is NOT necessary to apply?

(A) Curriculum vitae
(B) References
(C) Clinical research summary
(D) Abstracts of published articles

Questions 181–185 refer to the following purchase order and letter.

PURCHASE ORDER
Ship Prepaid—Add all delivery charges on invoice

Fish Market Restaurant
905 North High Street
Baltimore, MD 21002

Tel: (401) 555-5154
Fax: (401) 555-5177

Vendor:
Super Seafood Suppliers
39908 Cold Spring Circle
Baltimore, MD 21117
Tel: (401) 555-0087
Fax: (401) 555-0097

Ship To: Joey Farina
Restaurant Manager
Address above

Reference: Purchase Order 9855
Date: April 9, 20__

Invoice To: Catherine Cox
Accounting Department
Address above

Delivery Date: April 16, 20__

Item	**Number**	**Quantity**	**Unit Cost**	**Total Cost**
Tuna	S8704T	200 pounds	$4.00	$ 800.00
Lobster	S4399L	150 pounds	8.00	1200.00
Shrimp	S3280S	350 pounds	6.00	2100.00
Salmon	S2956A	300 pounds	8.00	2400.00
Subtotal				6500.00
Shipping/Handling 5%				325.00
TOTAL				$6825.00

Prepared by: *Joey Farina*
Date: *April 8, 20__*

CC: Accounting Department; Purchasing Department; Receiving Department

April 11, 20__

Mr. Joey Farina
Restaurant Manager
Fish Market Restaurant
905 North High Street
Baltimore, MD 21002

Dear Mr. Farina:

I received your purchase order yesterday, and I need to go over a few items with you. Please call me as soon as you receive this letter. April 16 is coming soon and I have not been able to reach you to discuss the order. Have you received my voicemail messages? We normally need ten days between receiving a purchase order and filling it. You must pay an express service charge of $100 in order to have the order filled by April 16.

I've checked with our suppliers, and we can provide 300 pounds of shrimp and 250 pounds of salmon at the present time. We will provide the remainder as soon after April 16 as possible, if that suits you.

Finally, a correction needs to be made to the shipping/handling fee on the purchase order. Our usual charge for this is twice as much as you assumed. I'm enclosing a revised bill for you. With the express service charge, the change in quantity of shrimp and salmon, and the recalculated shipping/handling fee, your new total comes out to $6,480.

Please call or e-mail me today so that we can discuss your order. Thank you for working with Super Seafood Suppliers.

Sincerely yours,

Sandra James

Sandra James
Sales Manager

181. Where does Joey Farina work?

(A) At a fish market
(B) At a seafood restaurant
(C) At a fish canning factory
(D) At a seafood supply house

182. When does Joey Farina want his order delivered?

(A) April 8
(B) April 9
(C) April 11
(D) April 16

183. How long did it take Joey Farina's letter to reach Sandra James?

(A) 1 day
(B) 2 days
(C) 3 days
(D) 4 days

184. What did Joey Farina forget to include in his purchase order?

(A) A shipping address
(B) An order for shrimp and salmon
(C) An express service charge
(D) A shipping and handling fee

185. What is the usual shipping and handling fee charged by Super Seafood Suppliers?

(A) 2%
(B) 2.5%
(C) 5%
(D) 10%

Questions 186–190 refer to the following fax and memo.

FAX COVER SHEET

TECH INTERNATIONAL
Betlemske namesti 11
198 16 Prague
CZECH REPUBLIC
Tel: (204) 12 44
Fax: (204) 12 45

To: All Board Members
From: Jarek Cichy
Marketing Department
Date: November 30, 20__
Pages: This + 5
Ref: Annual Award

Message:

Please review the attached nomination form for our department's nominee for this year's award. Anezka Novotna is my best staff member and is truly deserving of this honor. I am going to Switzerland next week on business and won't return until December 13. I will be checking my e-mail regularly while I'm gone, so please e-mail me if you have any questions about this nominee.

Memo

To: All department staff
From: Jarek Cichy
Re: Annual party—please attend!

As usual, the Board Members are inviting everyone to their annual Appreciation Party held to show their appreciation of the hard work you have all done during the year. This year, as in past years, the Board Members will give out the Employee of the Year award during the party.

I would like to especially encourage each of you to attend the party since this year's Employee of the Year award will be given to the nominee from our department. In addition to the honor and award she will receive from the Board, we're collecting money to buy her a group gift. If everyone contributes just $10, we can buy her the portable DVD player that she wants. See my assistant, Basia, by Thursday at 4:00 to contribute to the gift. I hope to see you all on December 14 at 5:00 P.M.

186. Why did Jarek Cichy send the fax?

(A) To invite employees to a party
(B) To recommend someone for an award
(C) To inform board members of his trip
(D) To ask for money for a gift

187. When will Jarek Cichy return to the office?

(A) The day before the party
(B) The day of the party
(C) Next week
(D) November 30

188. What is the purpose of the party?

(A) To honor all company staff
(B) To give an award
(C) To give out presents
(D) To celebrate the holidays

189. Who will receive an award?

(A) Basia
(B) Jarek Cichy
(C) Anezka Novotna
(D) A board member

190. Where does Basia work?

(A) In Switzerland
(B) On the Board of Directors
(C) In the Marketing Department
(D) In the Accounting Department

Questions 191–195 refer to the following advertisement and form.

Join our company!

BANGALORE TECHNOLOGY CENTRE (BTC)

Now hiring!

One of the world's top 5 electronics companies
Located in Bangalore, India

Excellent benefits!
Educational assistance, health coverage, free gym membership, paid vacation!
BTC is a great place to work, but don't just take our word for it. Look at the testimony from some of our employees:

"I've worked here for 3 years and it's wonderful. I will work here forever!"
—Manov, Engineering Department

"BTC is the perfect employer. You should apply today."
—Rupal, Marketing Team

"Everyone on the BTC staff is a real team worker, and your supervisors really care about you. It's like one big family."
—Mohan, Accounting Department

Tel: (80) 91 22932001
Fax: (80) 91 22932011
E-mail: btc@btc.com
http: www.btc.com

To learn more, go to our website and fill out the "Request for Information" form.

Request for Information

Learn more about the company called the "Best Technology Company" by the Organization of Computer Engineers.

☑ YES! Send me information about the excellent opportunities at BTC, including the great benefits for employees.

☑ YES! I would like to have a BTC employee contact me.

Name: Bert Roberts
Job: Electrical Engineer
Address: Gulf Harbour Drive
Auckland, New Zealand

Interested in working in: Engineering Department

Tell us something about yourself.
Highest level of education: Master's degree in electrical engineering

Work Experience: 5 years as an electrical engineer at Servitrix, Ltd., Auckland, 2 years as an engineering assistant at R&J Company, Auckland

When you have completed the form, click here.

191. What kind of business is BTC?

(A) A marketing firm
(B) An accounting firm
(C) A computer retail store
(D) An electronics company

192. Which of the following benefits is NOT offered by BTC?

(A) Help paying for school
(B) Medical insurance
(C) Time off with pay
(D) Life insurance

193. How did Bert Roberts get this form?

(A) He visited a website.
(B) Manov sent it to him.
(C) He wrote to BTC to request it.
(D) He found it in the newspaper.

194. How many years of work experience does Bert Roberts have?

(A) Two
(B) Three
(C) Five
(D) Seven

195. If Bert Roberts accepts a job with BTC, what will he probably have to do?

(A) Get a master's degree
(B) Add his testimony to the company's advertisements
(C) Move to another country
(D) Join a gym

Questions 196–200 refer to the following agenda and e-mail.

International Environmental Protection Group (IEPG)
Meeting & Awards Ceremony
Thursday, August 1, 20__ 7:00 P.M.
Place: Room 1, Sofitel Hotel

AGENDA

1. Welcome	Birsen Aksay
2. Fall projects & plans	Ari Tabaku
3. Introduction of Nominating Committee	Kazadi Koite
4. Presentation of award Recipient: J. S. Choi, CEO	Jakob Skolnik
5. Reception	

To: Jakob Skolnik
From: Victoria Williams
Subject: yesterday's awards ceremony

Mr. Skolnik,

We were all concerned about your sudden illness yesterday and hope that you are feeling better today. I know that you will feel reassured to learn that last night's awards ceremony went very well despite your absence. We had Kazadi Koite lead both items 3 and 4, and I am happy to report that he did an excellent job. The CEO of B. J. Technology accepted the award for "most environmentally friendly company" on his company's behalf and expressed great delight on receiving it. The reception was enjoyed by all. We had reserved the room for only three hours, and some guests stayed until the last possible moment. More guests attended than we expected, so we barely had enough room for everyone. Perhaps we should ask for a bigger room next year. Rooms 2 and 3 are also small, but either room 4 or room 6 would be a good size, I think. Even though the ceremony and reception were a great success, I have several other ideas for improvements for next year's ceremony. We can discuss them when you return to work. Please rest well. We hope to see you healthy and back at work soon.

Victoria

196. What company does J. S. Choi work for?

(A) IEPG
(B) B. J. Technology
(C) Sofitel Hotels
(D) Williams Inc.

197. Who presented the award?

(A) Jakob Skolnik
(B) Victoria Williams
(C) Kazadi Koite
(D) Ari Tabaku

198. In which room was the reception held?

(A) Room 1
(B) Room 2
(C) Room 3
(D) Room 4

199. What time did the reception end?

(A) 3:00
(B) 6:00
(C) 7:00
(D) 10:00

200. What does Victoria Williams suggest doing next year?

(A) Asking Jakob Skolnik to present the award
(B) Using a larger hotel
(C) Inviting more guests
(D) Reserving a different room

Stop! Fin du test. Si vous avez terminé avant la fin du temps imparti, vous pouvez retourner aux parties 5, 6, 7 afin de vérifier votre travail.

Test n° 2

Vous trouverez la grille de réponses au test n° 2 à la page 253. Détachez-la du livre et reportez-y vos réponses. Lorsque vous êtes prêt à commencer, mettez le CD et écoutez la partie audio du test n° 2.

LISTENING TEST

In the Listening test, you will be asked to demonstrate how well you understand spoken English. The entire Listening test will last approximately 45 minutes. There are four parts, and directions are given for each part. You must mark your answers on the separate answer sheet. Do not write your answers in the test book.

PART 1

Directions: For each question in this part, you will hear four statements about a picture in your test book. When you hear the statements, you must select the one statement that best describes what you see in the picture. Then find the number of the question on your answer sheet and mark your answer. The statements will not be printed in your test book and will be spoken only one time.

Example

Sample Answer

(A) (B) ● (D)

Statement (C), "They're standing near the table," is the best description of the picture, so you should select answer (C) and mark it on your answer sheet.

1.

2.

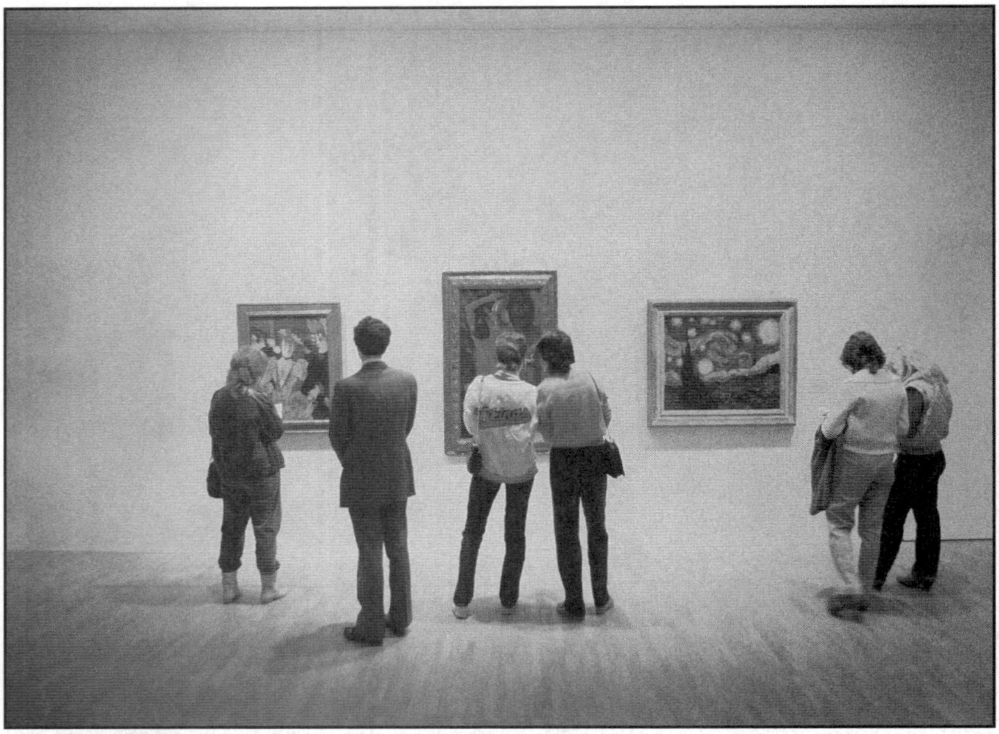

3.

4.

5. 

6. 

7.

8.

9.

DANGER
FLAMMABLE
GAS
92271

10.

ICS
Lot No.
DRUM No.
G T N
ERA
RADIOACTIVE LSA

PART 2

Directions: You will hear a question or statement and three responses spoken in English. They will not be printed in your test book and will be spoken only one time. Select the best response to the question or statement and mark the letter (A), (B), or (C) on your answer sheet.

Example

Sample Answer

(A) ● (C)

You will hear: Where is the meeting room?

You will also hear:
(A) To meet the new director.
(B) It's the first room on the right.
(C) Yes, at two o'clock.

Your best response to the question "Where is the meeting room?" is choice (B), "It's the first room on the right," so (B) is the correct answer. You should mark answer (B) on your answer sheet.

11. Mark your answer on your answer sheet.

12. Mark your answer on your answer sheet.

13. Mark your answer on your answer sheet.

14. Mark your answer on your answer sheet.

15. Mark your answer on your answer sheet.

16. Mark your answer on your answer sheet.

17. Mark your answer on your answer sheet.

18. Mark your answer on your answer sheet.

19. Mark your answer on your answer sheet.

20. Mark your answer on your answer sheet.

21. Mark your answer on your answer sheet.

22. Mark your answer on your answer sheet.

23. Mark your answer on your answer sheet.

24. Mark your answer on your answer sheet.

25. Mark your answer on your answer sheet.

26. Mark your answer on your answer sheet.

27. Mark your answer on your answer sheet.

28. Mark your answer on your answer sheet.

29. Mark your answer on your answer sheet.

30. Mark your answer on your answer sheet.

31. Mark your answer on your answer sheet.

32. Mark your answer on your answer sheet.

33. Mark your answer on your answer sheet.

34. Mark your answer on your answer sheet.

35. Mark your answer on your answer sheet.

36. Mark your answer on your answer sheet.

37. Mark your answer on your answer sheet.

38. Mark your answer on your answer sheet.

39. Mark your answer on your answer sheet.

40. Mark your answer on your answer sheet.

PART 3

Directions: You will hear some conversations between two people. You will be asked to answer three questions about what the speakers say in each conversation. Select the best response to each question and mark the letter (A), (B), (C), or (D) on your answer sheet. The conversations will not be printed in your test book and will be spoken only one time.

41. What time will the woman leave?

(A) 4:00.
(B) 5:00.
(C) 5:30.
(D) 7:00.

42. Where will the woman go?

(A) To the train station.
(B) To the airport.
(C) To the office.
(D) To the bus station.

43. What does the man give the woman?

(A) A toothbrush.
(B) A book.
(C) Some newspapers.
(D) Some writing paper.

---

44. How much money does the man need?

(A) Fourteen dollars.
(B) Fifteen dollars.
(C) Forty dollars.
(D) Fifty dollars.

45. What does he need the money for?

(A) To buy lunch.
(B) To pay a sales tax.
(C) To pay his taxi fare.
(D) To buy some reading material.

46. When does the man say he will pay the money back?

(A) This afternoon.
(B) Tomorrow.
(C) The day after tomorrow.
(D) Next week.

---

47. What kind of movie do both speakers like?

(A) Comedies.
(B) War stories.
(C) Murder mysteries.
(D) Westerns.

48. What time does the next movie start?

(A) 4:00.
(B) 7:00.
(C) 7:30.
(D) 10:30

49. What does the man want to do?

(A) See a war movie.
(B) Stay home.
(C) Watch TV.
(D) Go to a restaurant.

---

50. When will the meeting be held?

(A) Tuesday.
(B) Wednesday.
(C) Thursday.
(D) Friday.

51. Why has the meeting been postponed?

(A) The accountant is ill.
(B) The room is not ready.
(C) Ms. Schmidt is away at a conference.
(D) The speaker is still reading the budget report.

52. How will people be notified about the postponed meeting?

(A) By phone.
(B) By e-mail.
(C) By letter.
(D) In person.

---

53. Why was the woman late today?

(A) She slept late.
(B) She walked slowly.
(C) She took the bus.
(D) She ran out of gas.

54. How does the man get to work?

(A) By bus.
(B) By car.
(C) On foot.
(D) By train.

55. How long does it take the man to get to work?

(A) 14 minutes.
(B) 35 minutes.
(C) 40 minutes.
(D) 45 minutes.

---

56. Where did the man leave his glasses?

(A) On his desk.
(B) In the woman's office.
(C) In his briefcase.
(D) In the car.

57. What does the woman give the man?

(A) A kiss.
(B) Her keys.
(C) A briefcase.
(D) A locket.

58. Where is the woman's car?

(A) In a parking lot.
(B) In front of her office.
(C) Across the street from the park.
(D) In front of the post office.

---

59. What are the speakers talking about?

(A) Eating.
(B) Doing business.
(C) The hot weather.
(D) The city's sidewalks.

60. What does the man sell?

(A) Eggs.
(B) Coolers.
(C) Ice cream.
(D) Air conditioners.

61. Where does the woman work?

(A) At a pool.
(B) At an office.
(C) At a school.
(D) At a restaurant.

---

62. What did the man buy?

(A) A shirt.
(B) A tie.
(C) A suit.
(D) A pair of shoes.

63. Where did he buy it?

(A) In Hong Kong.
(B) At the mall.
(C) Downtown.
(D) At a local department store.

64. What is the woman's opinion of the suit?

(A) It's not very attractive.
(B) It's too expensive.
(C) It's nice-looking.
(D) Its color is great.

---

65. How will the man spend his vacation?

(A) Hiking.
(B) Reading.
(C) Lying in the sun.
(D) Swimming in the sea.

66. How long is his vacation?

(A) Two days.
(B) Eight days.
(C) Two weeks.
(D) Three weeks.

67. When will his vacation begin?

(A) This afternoon.
(B) On Sunday.
(C) On Tuesday.
(D) In a few weeks.

68. How many buses are there?

(A) One.
(B) Two.
(C) Three.
(D) Four.

69. Where will the buses leave from?

(A) The hotel.
(B) The convention center.
(C) The bus station.
(D) The loading dock.

70. How often should the buses leave?

(A) Every five minutes.
(B) Every ten minutes.
(C) Every fifteen minutes.
(D) Every thirty minutes.

PART 4

Directions: You will hear some talks given by a single speaker. You will be asked to answer three questions about what the speaker says in each talk. Select the best response to each question and mark the letter (A), (B), (C), or (D) on your answer sheet. The talks will not be printed in your test book and will be spoken only one time.

71. When will the Revenue Office in City Hall be open?

(A) From 8:00 A.M. to 12:00 on Saturday.
(B) Every day this week.
(C) In the afternoon only.
(D) From 8:00 A.M. to 5:00 P.M., Monday through Friday.

72. What must be filed?

(A) Citizenship papers.
(B) Tax forms.
(C) Time reports.
(D) Housing requests.

73. Why should people come early?

(A) To get a refund.
(B) To become citizens.
(C) To avoid long lines.
(D) To pick up their files.

---

74. Where would this announcement be heard?

(A) At a subway station.
(B) In a hotel.
(C) On an airplane.
(D) At an airport.

75. Which signs should passengers follow for rental cars?

(A) Blue.
(B) Red.
(C) Green.
(D) Yellow.

76. How can passengers get to their cars?

(A) By city bus.
(B) By shuttle.
(C) By subway.
(D) By walking.

---

77. When will the speech be heard?

(A) Before lunch.
(B) After lunch.
(C) Next month.
(D) Next Friday.

78. How often are the luncheons held?

(A) Every Friday.
(B) Every month.
(C) Twice a month.
(D) Once a year.

79. What is Dr. Jenny Chang's profession?

(A) Politician.
(B) Criminal.
(C) Saleswoman.
(D) Author.

---

80. What should employees do if a badge is lost?

(A) Ask the security office for a replacement.
(B) Report to their supervisor.
(C) Request a visitor pass.
(D) Leave the building.

81. How may visitors enter the building?

(A) With an employee escort.
(B) With permission from security personnel.
(C) With an identification badge.
(D) With proper dress.

82. Who must wear identification badges?

(A) All employees.
(B) Potential employees.
(C) Visitors with escorts.
(D) Visitors alone.

---

83. What is opening?

(A) The Civic Center.
(B) A new golf course.
(C) A downtown office.
(D) A residential hotel.

84. What is being offered?

(A) Golf lessons.
(B) City apartments.
(C) New watches.
(D) Club memberships.

85. What is the cost of a one-year membership?

(A) $600.
(B) $650.
(C) $700.
(D) $1,100.

---

86. What is the weather perfect for?

(A) Going to the beach.
(B) Bicycling in the mountains.
(C) Playing golf.
(D) Watching the races.

87. How is the sun described?

(A) Rising.
(B) Hazy.
(C) Shining.
(D) Bright.

88. What will the weather be like on Saturday?

(A) Very hot.
(B) Sunny.
(C) Cloudy.
(D) Rainy.

---

89. How much was the man's estate worth?

(A) Nothing.
(B) Under two thousand dollars.
(C) A million dollars.
(D) Over two million dollars.

90. Who inherited the money?

(A) His children.
(B) His wife.
(C) His dog.
(D) His best friend.

91. When will the funeral be held?

(A) Sunday.
(B) Monday.
(C) Wednesday.
(D) Thursday.

---

92. When is the office open?

(A) Every day of the week.
(B) Only on Monday.
(C) Only on Friday.
(D) Monday through Friday.

93. What service is provided only in the afternoon?

(A) Renewal of driver's licenses.
(B) Applications for new driver's licenses.
(C) Driving tests.
(D) Blood tests.

94. When does the office stop taking customers?

(A) At 12:00.
(B) At 4:00.
(C) At 4:30.
(D) At 5:00.

---

95. What is the caller's complaint?

(A) Her order arrived damaged.
(B) She received something she didn't order.
(C) Her order hasn't arrived yet.
(D) She was charged too much for her order.

96. When did the caller place her order?

(A) One week ago.
(B) Two weeks ago.
(C) Three weeks ago.
(D) Four weeks ago.

97. What does she ask the company to do?

(A) Call her today.
(B) Send her a check.
(C) Deliver the order right away.
(D) Charge the order to her credit card.

98. What did CompCo do today?

(A) It hired new employees.
(B) It gave a training workshop.
(C) It negotiated a deal.
(D) It had a celebration.

99. How many employees currently work at CompCo?

(A) 50
(B) 100
(C) 150
(D) 200

100. What happened when PC Computer Systems closed down?

(A) Many people lost their jobs.
(B) The Intrax Company took its place.
(C) They broke a contract with city leaders.
(D) Other technology businesses left the area.

Fin du test de compréhension orale. Passez à la partie 5.

READING TEST

In the Reading test, you will read a variety of texts and answer several different types of reading comprehension questions. The entire Reading test will last 75 minutes. There are three parts, and directions are given for each part. You are encouraged to answer as many questions as possible within the time allowed.

You must mark your answers on the separate answer sheet. Do not write your answers in the test book.

PART 5

Directions: A word or phrase is missing in each of the sentences below. Four answer choices are given below each sentence. Select the best answer to complete the sentence. Then mark the letter (A), (B), (C), or (D) on your answer sheet.

101. Mr. Doh __________ clients' phone calls.

(A) rarely returns
(B) returns rarely
(C) has returned rarely
(D) rarely had returned

102. Success depends __________ the efforts of the organization.

(A) from
(B) in
(C) on
(D) of

103. There has been strong competition; __________, the new company has made great profits.

(A) instead
(B) nonetheless
(C) then
(D) despite

104. Ms. Shirish will resign her position as chief __________ officer.

(A) operator
(B) operational
(C) operation
(D) operating

105. The weather report predicts it will rain __________ become colder.

(A) neither
(B) nor
(C) and
(D) either

106. The printer __________ paper.

(A) ran into
(B) ran out of
(C) ran without
(D) ran over

107. The electricity went out __________ we were making coffee.

(A) so
(B) because of
(C) while
(D) for

108. __________ all the negotiators, Ms. Neos seems the most reliable.

(A) From
(B) As
(C) Of
(D) But

109. The sales division reported a 64 percent drop __________ the last sales period.

(A) during
(B) with
(C) at
(D) to

110. The company is financially sound; __________, there is no debt.

(A) in spite of
(B) for example
(C) on the other hand
(D) nevertheless

111. Get the invoice __________ upon receipt.

(A) signature
(B) sign
(C) signed
(D) signing

112. __________ time to submit a bid.

(A) Still there is
(B) Is there still
(C) There is still
(D) They're still is

113. Our future will be __________ on what services we can provide.

(A) basic
(B) based
(C) basing
(D) base

114. If there __________ better communication, I would not resign.

(A) were
(B) was
(C) is
(D) will be

115. __________ the critics and answer their questions.

(A) Stand in for
(B) Stand at
(C) Stand with
(D) Stand up to

116. By the end of this century, business __________ greatly.

(A) will be changed
(B) will have changed
(C) changes
(D) changed

117. The __________ market has declined in many parts of the country.

(A) homing
(B) housed
(C) homes
(D) housing

118. __________ saving money, you will purchase a reliable product.

(A) With
(B) So
(C) Besides
(D) Consequently

119. __________ one partner has resigned, others are quitting, too.

(A) Because
(B) Although
(C) If
(D) Before

120. The management makes an assessment __________.

(A) rarely
(B) still
(C) monthly
(D) already

121. The chairman said his __________ would continue his strategies.

(A) successful
(B) successor
(C) success
(D) successive

122. This region __________ as the costliest place to do business.

(A) often is referred
(B) is often referred
(C) is referred often to
(D) is often referred to

123. Since 1990, our customers __________ with our service.

(A) are satisfied
(B) have satisfied
(C) have been satisfying
(D) have been satisfied

124. People either don't have the money __________ they aren't willing to spend it.

(A) and
(B) neither
(C) or
(D) although

125. The group is composed __________ five companies.

(A) in
(B) of
(C) up
(D) from

126. In order to make more money, Mr. Garcia has decided to __________ a second job.

(A) take off
(B) take out
(C) take from
(D) take on

127. A survey of the __________ shows they are satisfied with their jobs.

(A) employment
(B) employs
(C) employees
(D) employing

128. __________ the bad location, the management is confident of success.

(A) Despite
(B) Since
(C) With
(D) As

129. Company officials must disclose their own __________ affairs.

(A) finance
(B) financing
(C) financial
(D) financed

130. The new business has __________ incorporated.

(A) still
(B) once
(C) yet
(D) already

131. The manufacturer listed assets __________ liabilities.

(A) but
(B) nor
(C) and
(D) so

132. The competitor's attempt to __________ the new company was stopped.

(A) take off
(B) take over
(C) take to
(D) take out

133. The new agent has experience __________ not expertise.

(A) but
(B) and
(C) with
(D) however

134. __________ the flight is canceled, the seminar will have to be postponed.

(A) While
(B) If
(C) Although
(D) Besides

135. The proposal was submitted __________ April 28.

(A) at
(B) the
(C) on
(D) from

136. __________ costs have increased dramatically.

(A) Advertising
(B) Advertisements
(C) Advertised
(D) Advertise

137. Ford Motor Company reported a drop __________ quarterly profits.

(A) to
(B) from
(C) in
(D) with

138. The company was __________ by an immigrant.

(A) found
(B) founding
(C) find
(D) founded

139. Mr. Daley is our most skilled speaker; __________, he is unavailable to give the presentation.

(A) besides
(B) nevertheless
(C) for example
(D) while

140. Have Ms. Alva __________ a press release immediately.

(A) writes
(B) to write
(C) writing
(D) write

PART 6

Directions: Read the texts that follow. A word or phrase is missing in some of the sentences. Four answer choices are given below each of the sentences. Select the best answer to complete the text. Then mark the letter (A), (B), (C), or (D) on your answer sheet.

Questions 141–143 refer to the following letter.

Office Works
544 Hudson Street
Boston, MA 34602
Tel: (617) 555-7664 Fax: (617) 555-7670

May 10, 20__

Mary Briddock
Banqueting Director
Wynd's Garden Hotel
219 Center Circle
Boston, MA 03299

Dear Ms. Briddock:

Our company, Office Works, is seeking a place to host a banquet. We will honor our top employees at this event, which will include dinner followed by speeches and the presentation of awards.

At the same time we plan to celebrate an ________ to our

141. (A) addition
(B) additive
(C) addend
(D) addendum

company. We recently purchased the Office Supply Store, and we are now the region's largest seller of office supplies.

We expect approximately 100 guests. We would like to have our event on Saturday, August 15th. If no room is available for that date, we could consider ________ it on the following Saturday, August 22nd.

142. (A) have
(B) to have
(C) having
(D) will have

Could you please mail me your latest price list, descriptive brochure, and menus? I am interested in learning more about ________ facilities and services.

143. (A) my
(B) our
(C) your
(D) their

Thank you.

Lynn Ishii
Events Coordinator

Questions 144–146 refer to the following notice.

GLOBAL AIRLINES POLICY STATEMENT

Baggage

Each passenger may carry two items onto the plane: one small suitcase and one personal item. The personal item may be a purse, laptop computer, or briefcase.

The items should fit under the seat in front of you or in the overhead bin. These bins fill quickly, so in case of overload, the flight attendant may place your suitcase in the back of the plane.

In addition ________ the two carry-on items, each passenger may check

144. (A) of
(B) to
(C) with
(D) from

two suitcases to be transported in the airplane's luggage compartment. These suitcases must meet the airline's size limits. ________ baggage

145. (A) Excess
(B) Excelled
(C) Excepted
(D) Executive

charges apply to oversized and additional pieces. These charges must be paid at the time of check-in.

Please ________ a customer service representative if you have questions

146. (A) contact
(B) contacts
(C) to contact
(D) can contact

about this policy.

Questions 147–149 refer to the following magazine article.

Is dentistry the career for you? Today's dentists have many more opportunities than they used to. In the past, a dentist's life was predictable. Most were men who would leave home for a few years to study at a dental school, then return to their hometown, open up an office, and work there their whole life. Most dentists looked forward to this or something similar. Today, dentists are more mobile. Men and women can ________ dental school in

147. (A) will attend
(B) attending
(C) to attend
(D) attend

different places. Some still return to their hometown to work. Others move on to new cities.

Dentists today may specialize in one or more areas. Two common ones are oral surgery and dental public health. Oral surgery focuses ________ treating diseases and problems through

148. (A) in
(B) at
(C) on
(D) to

operations. Dental public health concentrates on improving the dental health of a community. For example, these dentists ________ to schools to teach children how to brush their teeth.

149. (A) go
(B) went
(C) had gone
(D) would go

Some dentists work only in their specialty areas while others do both general and specialty work.

Questions 150–152 refer to the following e-mail.

To: frontoffice1
From: geraldinebennett
Re: Doing our part

Dear Mr. Cobalt:

I'm writing to you to express my concern about Pascal's reputation as a wasteful company. I'm sure you read the recent letter to the editor in the *Sydney Daily News* regarding our non-recyclable plastic bottles and caps. Since the letter was printed, ________ have received complaints from

150. (A) we
(B) he and I
(C) they
(D) your

hundreds of customers who are threatening to boycott our company if we don't change our practices. We have also received flyers from ________ manufacturing companies offering to help us become a more

151. (A) varies
(B) variety
(C) various
(D) variable

environmentally friendly company. I have looked briefly into some of these options on my own time but would like to ask your permission to do more.

I would like ________ 20 hours of my upcoming workweek to this cause

152. (A) devote
(B) devoting
(C) to devote
(D) devotion

in hopes of coming up with a viable plan for Pascal's future as a company that cares about recycling. I hope you will agree with me that our environment is worth us making an effort. Please respond as soon as possible.

Sincerely,
Geraldine Bennett, Administrative Assistant
Pascal's Pharmaceuticals

PART 7

Directions: In this part you will read a selection of texts, such as magazine and newspaper articles, letters, and advertisements. Each text is followed by several questions. Select the best answer for each question and mark the letter (A), (B), (C), or (D) on your answer sheet.

Questions 153–155 refer to the following fax.

One Devonshire Gardens

7 July, 20__

Fax to: *P. Peterman*
Fax number: *0101-202-555-1218*

Dear Mr. Peterman:

Thank you for your confirmation fax of today. We take great pleasure in confirming your reservation of one superior double room for the evenings of 28 through 30 July. The cost of this room will be £135 a night, inclusive of tax, newspaper, and continental breakfast. The total charge of £405 will be made to the credit card number which you previously provided to us.

I would like to take this opportunity to remind you that we have a fully equipped exercise room, as well as an indoor swimming pool, for the exclusive use of our guests at no extra charge. We also have a restaurant located on the premises at which you may purchase lunch or dinner at your discretion.

Should you require transportation from the airport when you arrive in our city, we can arrange a special airport shuttle for you. Just call the hotel from one of the white courtesy phones located throughout the arrivals terminal. Press 15 to reach the One Devonshire Gardens front desk.

We look forward to welcoming you at One Devonshire Gardens. Please don't hesitate to contact me should you have any questions regarding your reservations or our accommodations.

Yours sincerely,

Debbie Smith
Reservations Manager

153. What kind of room was reserved?

(A) A single
(B) A twin
(C) A double
(D) A suite

154. Which of the following is NOT included in the price of the room?

(A) Breakfast
(B) Tax
(C) A newspaper
(D) Dinner

155. How did Mr. Peterman make a reservation?

(A) By fax
(B) Through an agent
(C) By letter
(D) In person

Questions 156–159 refer to the following job announcement.

Seeking: Assistant Controller

- Large downtown law firm is seeking an Assistant Controller for our Accounting Department.
- Basic responsibilities include control of the accounting systems, supervision of a seven-person team, and assisting with the hiring and training of new employees.
- Qualified applicant should have eight years of accounting experience, as well as a minimum of two to three years in a supervisory position. Experience working in a law firm is desirable.
- Education requirements include an undergraduate degree in accounting. CPA is preferred.
- The successful candidate will have the necessary computer skills and be familiar with the most current automated financial systems.

To apply for this position, send a résumé and three letters of reference to:
Annabelle Smythe
Forbes, Lawrence, and Ross
187 Oakland Boulevard
Detroit, MI 41084
Closing date: November 12

156. What kind of firm is hiring?

(A) A computer company
(B) An accounting office
(C) An advertising agency
(D) A law firm

157. Which of the following is NOT mentioned as a qualification?

(A) Experience as a supervisor
(B) Familiarity with automated financial systems
(C) A law degree
(D) A degree in accounting

158. What kind of applicant would be most attracted to this job?

(A) A lawyer
(B) An accountant
(C) A computer science major
(D) A director of human resources

159. The word "automated" in paragraph 5, line 2, is closest in meaning to

(A) global
(B) modern
(C) common
(D) mechanical

Questions 160–162 refer to the following letter.

Dear Customer,

Congratulations! You have just purchased one of the world's most sophisticated microwave ovens. This appliance has been designed with your convenience in mind. It combines an array of special features with ease of use. State-of-the-art features include a temperature sensor so that you will never again have an overcooked or undercooked meal; a 24-hour timer so that you can prepare your food when you have time and have it ready to eat when you are; an automated defrosting system so that you can prepare frozen food with no extra waiting time; a programmable chime system to let you know when your food is ready; and an automatic self-cleaning system so that your oven is always fresh and ready for use.

All of these features and more are available to you at just the push of a button. It is so simple to use. Each feature is completely explained in this manual. Just follow the step-by-step instructions and you will be cooking delicious meals in no time at all! In addition, recipes for various entrees and desserts are included at the back of the manual to get you started on your new adventures in microwave cooking. This product has been designed to give you many years of trouble-free operation as long as the instructions are followed. If for some reason the product should fail, it is completely guaranteed for one year. A complete explanation of the warranty is included on page 15 of the manual. Additional instructions and recipes are available on our website.

Thank you again for becoming a Kitchen Appliances customer.

Sincerely,

M.S. Fujimoto

M.S. Fujimoto
President
Kitchen Appliances, Inc.

160. Where would this letter most likely be found?

(A) In a microwave manual
(B) In the mail
(C) In an advertisement
(D) In a design store

161. The word "sophisticated" in line 2 is closest in meaning to

(A) popular
(B) advanced
(C) dependable
(D) well-known

162. What must the user do for trouble-free operation?

(A) Exchange the product
(B) Follow instructions
(C) Purchase another model
(D) Redesign the kitchen

Questions 163–165 refer to the following press release.

More than 50,000 electronics retailers and distributors are expected at the McCormick Convention Center in Chicago starting next Saturday. Some 1,300 manufacturers from more than 35 countries will exhibit their latest high-technology equipment, including industrial equipment, office machines, and household appliances. The new products won't appear on retailers' shelves until next fall, but show attendees will be able to purchase them during the show at special prices.

Highlights of the show include the following:

- Demonstrations of robots designed for household use. Watch robots perform everyday household chores. Each day, models from a different group of manufacturers will be shown. Hall of Industry, 3:00–5:00 P.M. daily.
- Talks by product developers representing companies from various countries on topics such as *The Impact of Electronic Technology on Business, Future Developments in Technology, How Electronic Technology Will Solve Our Transportation Problems,* and more. Call the Convention Center or visit our website for the speaker list. Wilson Auditorium, 7:00 P.M. nightly.
- Musical equipment demonstrations. Show attendees will be able to try out the latest synthesizers, guitars, and other electronic musical equipment. Exhibit Hall A, ongoing.
- Inventors of Tomorrow, a special hands-on workshop for children ages 10–13. Free with the price of admission to the show, but due to space limitations, pre-registration is required. Call the Convention Center or visit our website to register. Saturday and Sunday, 2:00 P.M.

Visit the Convention Center website for a complete schedule of demonstrations, workshops, and special events going on throughout the show.

Tickets are available by calling the Convention Center or through the Convention Center website. Special prices are available for multi-day passes.

Contact us by phone: 800-555-0913 or on the web.

The Summer Consumer Electronics Show will continue through June 5.

163. What is the main topic of the press release?

(A) The McCormick Convention Center
(B) Chicago's convention centers
(C) Electronics retailers
(D) The Summer Consumer Electronics Show

164. How many manufacturers are expected?

(A) 1,300
(B) 5,000
(C) 13,000
(D) 50,000

165. What is on display at the Convention Center?

(A) High-technology products
(B) Distribution of networks
(C) Retail outlets
(D) Shelving samples

Questions 166–168 refer to the following table.

Programming for Sunday, March 26

11:30 A.M.

Ch 4 — *Business Review*

A review of this week's business news. This week's special guest is international business analyst Marilyn Kim of the McGuire Institute.

1:00 P.M.

Ch 9, 11 — *Company Profiles*

An in-depth look at significant companies around the world. Featured this week are Limnex, Inc., and Asian Global Industries, two newcomers to the international finance scene.

1:30 P.M.

Ch 4 — *Up Front with Politics and Economics*

Discussion of the latest political decisions affecting business and finance. Host Richard Lee interviews political analysts and finance experts.

2:00 P.M.

Ch 7, 13 — *Business Today*

Recent innovations in business. This week we visit with Tina and Luis Gomez, who will share how they built their small family clothing business into an international company.

3:00 P.M.

Ch 4 — *World View of Business*

News on business around the world, with commentaries by Masafumi Sachimoto and Jacques DeLeon.

4:00 P.M.

Ch 20 — *Making Money*

Successful personal investing. This week's topic: "How to Take Advantage of the Real Estate Market." Plus, tips for financing your child's college education.

166. What do these TV listings feature?

(A) Concerts
(B) Business programs
(C) Travelogues
(D) Sports events

167. What begins on TV at 2:00 P.M.?

(A) *Business Today*
(B) *Company Profiles*
(C) *Making Money*
(D) *Business Review*

168. Which station would someone who has money to invest watch?

(A) Ch 4
(B) Ch 7
(C) Ch 11
(D) Ch 20

Questions 169–170 refer to the following announcement.

As a national leader with over forty years of experience providing TV, radio, and marketing services to the corporate world, Abingdon can offer you outstanding career opportunities.

We are looking for energetic, creative, and committed professionals to join the Abingdon family. If you are looking for a position in a dynamic and stimulating work environment with plenty of room for professional growth, we want to talk to you.

We are currently seeking applications for computer programmers and software developers. We offer a competitive salary and benefits, excellent working conditions, and a chance to make a difference.

Please visit our booth at the National Career Center Job Fair during the week of October 13–18 to find out about the exciting job opportunities awaiting you at Abingdon.

169. What type of announcement is this?

(A) A government proclamation
(B) A job announcement
(C) A television listing
(D) Publicity for the opening of a National Career Center

170. Which of the following people would be most interested in this announcement?

(A) A communications major
(B) A retired radio announcer
(C) A production manager
(D) A computer specialist

Questions 171–174 refer to the following letter.

International Films, Ltd.
124 West Houston St., New York, NY 10012

July 30, 20__

E. Denikos, Inc.
Earos 42
Aghia Paraskevi 15342
Athens, Greece

Dear Mr. Denikos:

I am writing to you at the request of Ms. Evangelia Makestos, who is applying for a position as an assistant in your company.

Ms. Makestos worked for me as an assistant during her summer vacations for the past three years. My colleagues and I found her to be a very competent and reliable employee. Her duties consisted of typing and copying documents, maintaining files, organizing appointment schedules, assisting visitors to the office, and other office tasks as they arose. She was able to handle multiple tasks and to work independently. She always assisted our clients in a knowledgeable, professional, and patient manner. In addition, she developed a high level of ability in the English language during the time she worked and studied in this country. We had hoped to rehire her at our company in a permanent position when she finished her business course here in New York. However, she has decided to go through with her original plan of returning to Greece.

We will miss Ms. Makestos here at International Films, but I am happy to recommend her as a valuable addition to your company staff. Please feel free to contact me at the above address if you have any questions or need further information.

Sincerely,

Elizabeth Hogan

Elizabeth Hogan, Director
International Films, Ltd.

171. What is Ms. Makestos probably doing?

(A) Job hunting
(B) Quitting her job
(C) Moving to New York
(D) Applying to school

172. The word "competent" in paragraph 2, line 2, is closest in meaning to

(A) responsible
(B) friendly
(C) skilled
(D) useful

173. How long did Ms. Makestos work at International Films?

(A) One summer
(B) Three summers
(C) One year
(D) Three years

174. What kind of letter is this?

(A) A letter of complaint
(B) A job inquiry
(C) A letter of recommendation
(D) A request for information

Questions 175–177 refer to the following announcement on the Internet.

Current Issue (#148, March 20–26)
SPP Archive of back issues
Prospects (SPP Culture & Lifestyle Guide)

Moscow DAILY

Subscription Information

To order an international subscription to the English language edition of the *Moscow Daily*, please e-mail Vladimir Alekseev, subscription service manager.

Please include your name and address to receive a subscription coupon.

Yes! I want to subscribe to the ***Moscow Daily*** and have 5 percent of the subscription rate go to the charity of my choice:

Please check one:

- ❏ Protecting Our Natural Resources Organization
- ❏ Clean Oceans Today Association
- ❏ Saving Endangered Species Society

All subscriptions are honored with a money-back guarantee. The first month's issue is complimentary. CONTINUE

- *How to contact us*
- *More about the* Moscow Daily
- *How to subscribe to the printed newspaper*
- *Staff*

Return to Moscow Daily *web home page*

175. Where would this form most likely be seen?

(A) On a computer monitor
(B) On a movie screen
(C) In a phone book
(D) In a newspaper

176. What would happen if the reader were dissatisfied with the newspaper?

(A) The newspaper would send a complimentary issue.
(B) The subscription would be extended.
(C) The reader would be contacted.
(D) The subscription price would be refunded.

177. Which type of charities does the newspaper support?

(A) Disadvantaged children
(B) Disease prevention
(C) Environmental concerns
(D) Art and cultural institutions

Questions 178–180 refer to the following announcement.

TWO TYPES OF TRAINING

There are two common forms of employee training—on-the-job training and off-the-job training. On-the-job training is the most widely used and least expensive form of training. It consists of an employee learning from a supervisor or co-worker how to do the job. On-the-job training could be described as an apprenticeship. It is efficient because it is done at the workplace while the employee is fulfilling work duties. As time goes by, the employee becomes more and more skilled at the job and eventually can train other employees in turn.

Off-the-job training is the most expensive form of training. It consists of an employee being sent away from the workplace to a training program where training is provided. It is less efficient because it requires the employee to take time away from work duties. In addition, depending on where the training site is located, travel and accommodation expenses may be incurred. And of course, fees must be paid to the person or organization providing the training.

When deciding which form of training to provide, an employer must consider such things as the availability of staff with necessary skills and time to provide on-the-job training and the types of off-site training available, in addition to the expense. It may well be decided that off-the-job training is worth the cost. While the requirements are different for on-the-job training as compared to off-the-job training, the purpose of both types is the same—to improve employee efficiency and productivity.

178. Which of the following best describes on-the-job training?

(A) Expensive
(B) Ineffective
(C) Common
(D) Quick

179. What is on-the-job training similar to?

(A) An apprenticeship
(B) Off-the-job training
(C) A supervisory position
(D) A company benefit

180. According to the passage, what is the purpose of training?

(A) To improve employee efficiency
(B) To spend excess capital
(C) To satisfy government requirements
(D) To please a supervisor

Questions 181–185 refer to the following e-mail and directory.

From: Hussein Gitai
To: Olga Montgomery
Subject: Errands for Monday

Olga,

I am out sick today, so there are several errands I'll need you to do for me. I have outlined them below. Please call me at home if this message is not clear.

There are several things to deliver to other floors in the library. All of these items are on my desk, and they must be delivered today. Take the DVDs to Marjorie. At the same time, you can take the black umbrella to the Lost and Found since it's on the same floor. Also, there are some books in Arabic. They go to Level 2. Deliver the biography on Anwar Sadat to Level 3.

I was scheduled to give two presentations today. The first one is a workshop in Room C. Please put a sign on the door saying, "Today's workshop is canceled." I am also scheduled to read a book to the children. Please go to Children's Services and let Adishree know that I can't do it.

Because you are a new employee, I have attached a copy of the library directory to help you find your way around. Thank you again. I hope to recover quickly and see you at work tomorrow.

Hussein

Directory

Audiovisual (DVDs, Videos)	Level 1
Biography	Level 3
Children's Services	Level 5
Fiction	Level 3
Information Desk	Level 1
International Languages	Level 3
Lost and Found Items	Level 1
Music Research Collections	Level 6
Political Science	Level 2
Research Collection, A–M	Level 6
Research Collection, N–Z	Level 6
Security Desk	Level 1
Telephones	Level 1
Workshop Rooms	Level 4

181. Where does Marjorie work?

(A) Level 1
(B) Level 2
(C) Level 3
(D) Level 4

182. To which department should Olga take the Arabic books?

(A) Biography
(B) Fiction
(C) International Languages
(D) Political Science

183. Why should Olga put a sign on a door?

(A) To help children learn to read
(B) To tell library users that a workshop location has changed
(C) To inform people that Hussein can't give a presentation
(D) To let Adishree know that Hussein is out of the office today

184. Why does Olga need a library directory?

(A) She hasn't been working at the library for long.
(B) Several locations have changed recently.
(C) She has never been in the library before.
(D) People often get lost in the library.

185. What does Hussein plan to do tomorrow?

(A) Stay home
(B) Show Olga around the library
(C) Return to work
(D) Read a story to children

Questions 186–190 refer to the following two e-mails.

From: Christina van Dijk
To: Heinz Niebaum
Subject: Meeting next week

Dear Heinz,
I am coming to Germany next Wednesday at 10:00 A.M. I will be at our office in Berlin. I am free on Thursday at 9:00 A.M. to go to Potsdam and meet with you. Are you available then?

I'd like to talk about ordering computer systems from your company. Our offices in Utrecht and Tillburg are expanding and need to upgrade their technology. I'd also like to meet with a trainer from your company so that we can work out a training package. Also, could you bring a training manual with you?

Let me know if you need me to bring anything. Also let me know if 9:00 isn't good for you. Maybe we can work something out later in the day.
Christina

From: Heinz Niebaum
To: Christina van Dijk
Subject: Re: Meeting next week

Christina,
I'm delighted that you're coming to Germany. It will be very convenient for us to meet because I will actually be in Potsdam from Tuesday through Friday, so we'll be able to meet at our office there on the day you suggested. The time you suggested is a bit early for me as I will be meeting with our CEO all morning. Are you available to meet at noon? Perhaps we could meet during lunch.

I will bring the materials that you requested. Theodor Eckert, our training supervisor, will join us. It would be helpful if you could bring some of your company's brochures and a copy of the annual report for us. Thank you.
Heinz

186. What does Christina want to discuss at the meeting with Heinz?

(A) Finding train schedules
(B) Buying computers
(C) Mailing packages
(D) Expanding office space

187. Where will Heinz and Christina meet?

(A) Berlin
(B) Potsdam
(C) Utrecht
(D) Tillburg

188. What day will they meet?

(A) Tuesday
(B) Wednesday
(C) Thursday
(D) Friday

189. Why can't Heinz see Christina at 9:00?

(A) He will be in another city.
(B) He has to pick up Mr. Eckert at the train station.
(C) He will be supervising a training session.
(D) He has to meet with someone else.

190. What will Heinz bring to the meeting with Christina?

(A) Some computers
(B) A training manual
(C) Some brochures
(D) An annual report

Questions 191–195 refer to the following letter and purchase order.

Green Construction Co.
429 Mills Road
Minneapolis, MN 55440-0710
Tel: (763) 555-2100 Fax: (763) 555-2252

July 30, 20__

Sevil Tuncay
Construction Manager
National Bank
349 Taksim Square
Istanbul, Turkey 34400-4488

Dear Ms. Tuncay:

Thank you for contacting us to learn more about our environmentally friendly products. We suggest that you try a sample of our materials first. If you are happy with them, then you can buy more. If your order totals $10,000 or more, then we will reduce your shipping/handling fee by 3%. We prepared a purchase order for you so that you can try a sample of our products.

Our products may seem to cost more up front than other similar products. For example, you pay $200 more for our standard carpet than you would for a similar carpet that is not environmentally friendly. However, you save money in other ways. Because our carpets are made of special materials, they are much easier to clean and maintain.

One motion light is double the price of a regular light. However, motion lights save you money on electricity bills because the light stays on only when people are in the room. Also, the solar panels provide free energy. We suggest that you try the panels in several places on your building.

To buy the materials, please sign the purchase order. You may fax it to us, with your credit card number. We will ship the supplies immediately. Thank you for your business.

Yours truly,

Peter Lindstrom

Peter Lindstrom
Product Consultant

PURCHASE ORDER
Ship Prepaid—Add all delivery charges on invoice

National Bank
349 Taksim Square
Istanbul, Turkey 34400-4488

Tel: (212) 555-9890
Fax: (212) 555-9899

Vendor:
Green Construction Co.
429 Mills Road
Minneapolis, MN 55440-0710
Tel: (763) 555-2100
Fax: (763) 555-2252

Ship To: Melike Paksoy
Purchasing Department
Address above

Reference: Purchase Order 22-385-06T
Date: 25 February 20__

Invoice To: Mert Miller
Accounting Department
Address above

Delivery Date: ASAP

Item	Model	Number	Quantity	Unit Cost	Total Cost
C84	Standard carpet	E569C	2	$500.00	$1000.00
M22	Motion lights	L230M	4	100.00	400.00
S76	Solar panels	L194S	4	200.00	800.00
Subtotal					2200.00
Shipping/Handling 10%					220.00
TOTAL					$2420.00

191. Who is the construction manager at the National Bank?

(A) Sevil Tuncay
(B) Peter Lindstrom
(C) Melike Paksoy
(D) Mert Miller

192. What is special about the products at Green Construction?

(A) They cost less than other companies' products.
(B) They don't harm the natural environment.
(C) They use more electricity than most other products.
(D) They can be ordered by fax.

193. How much does Green Construction charge for shipping on orders over $10,000?

(A) 3%
(B) 7%
(C) 10%
(D) 22%

194. What is the price for a carpet that is not environmentally friendly?

(A) $200
(B) $300
(C) $500
(D) $700

195. What is the price of one regular light?

(A) $40
(B) $50
(C) $100
(D) $400

Questions 196–200 refer to the following agenda and fax.

Central Engineering Company
Board of Directors Meeting
Wednesday, November 15, 20__ 8:30 A.M.–11:30 A.M.
Place: Suite 10

AGENDA

1. Hiring challenges	Jorgen Spelman
2. Management changes	Narelle Dundee
3. Financial report	Madeira Jones
4. Technology upgrades	Jerry Carver

FAX COVER SHEET

CENTRAL ENGINEERING COMPANY
294 Green Street
Brasilia
Brazil

Tel: (55) 61 3420 4015
Fax: (55) 61 3420 4017

To: Ruben Baker
From: Narelle Dundee
Date: November 15, 20__
Pages: 1
Ref: Results of the board meeting
Message:

I hope your business trip is going well. Today's meeting went well for the most part, even though it began 30 minutes late. Jorgen wasn't there at the beginning, so I used his time slot to give my report. Jorgen finally arrived at 9:30 and gave his report. The board members were surprised to hear that job applicants complain about our salary offers. Jerry's report really shocked and upset the board. Fortunately, Madeira's report had the opposite effect. Everyone was happy to hear about our great profits.

The technology upgrades report didn't go so well. Jerry had to leave the meeting before his report because there was an Internet problem in the Electrical Engineering department. Because of this, the presenter for our third agenda item read Jerry's report, and it was a bit confusing. She didn't really know what she was talking about and couldn't answer questions satisfactorily. We decided to ask Jerry to provide written answers to questions raised by board members during the meeting.

Because we started late, we finished a half hour late, but we still had to hurry to finish within the allotted time. We decided to make the next board meeting a half-hour longer to give more time for discussion and questions.

196. What time did the meeting start?

(A) 8:30
(B) 9:00
(C) 9:30
(D) 11:30

197. What was the topic of the first report given?

(A) Hiring challenges
(B) Management changes
(C) Finances
(D) Technology

198. How did people feel about the financial report?

(A) Dissatisfied
(B) Confused
(C) Happy
(D) Shocked

199. Who spoke about technology upgrades?

(A) Jerry Carver
(B) Narelle Dundee
(C) Madeira Jones
(D) Jorgen Spelman

200. How long did the meeting last?

(A) ½ hour
(B) 2½ hours
(C) 3 hours
(D) 3½ hours

Stop! Fin du test. Si vous avez terminé avant la fin du temps imparti, vous pouvez retourner aux parties 5, 6, 7 afin de vérifier votre travail.

Test n° 3

Vous trouverez la grille de réponses au test n° 3 à la page 255. Détachez-la du livre et reportez-y vos réponses. Lorsque vous êtes prêt à commencer, mettez le CD et écoutez la partie audio du test n° 3.

LISTENING TEST

In the Listening test, you will be asked to demonstrate how well you understand spoken English. The entire Listening test will last approximately 45 minutes. There are four parts, and directions are given for each part. You must mark your answers on the separate answer sheet. Do not write your answers in the test book.

PART 1

Directions: For each question in this part, you will hear four statements about a picture in your test book. When you hear the statements, you must select the one statement that best describes what you see in the picture. Then find the number of the question on your answer sheet and mark your answer. The statements will not be printed in your test book and will be spoken only one time.

Example

Sample Answer

(A) (B) ● (D)

Statement (C), "They're standing near the table," is the best description of the picture, so you should select answer (C) and mark it on your answer sheet.

1.

2.

3.

4.

5.

6.

7.

8.

9.

10.

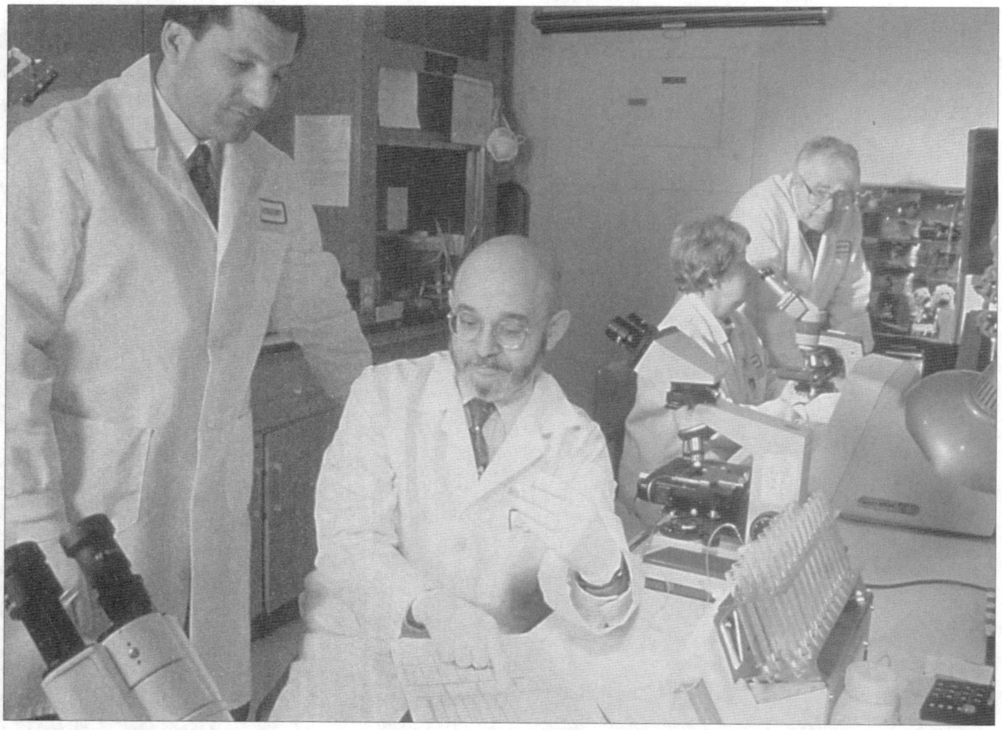

PART 2

Directions: You will hear a question or statement and three responses spoken in English. They will not be printed in your test book and will be spoken only one time. Select the best response to the question or statement and mark the letter (A), (B), or (C) on your answer sheet.

Example

Sample Answer

(A) ● (C)

You will hear: Where is the meeting room?

You will also hear:
(A) To meet the new director.
(B) It's the first room on the right.
(C) Yes, at two o'clock.

Your best response to the question "Where is the meeting room?" is choice (B), "It's the first room on the right," so (B) is the correct answer. You should mark answer (B) on your answer sheet.

11. Mark your answer on your answer sheet.

12. Mark your answer on your answer sheet.

13. Mark your answer on your answer sheet.

14. Mark your answer on your answer sheet.

15. Mark your answer on your answer sheet.

16. Mark your answer on your answer sheet.

17. Mark your answer on your answer sheet.

18. Mark your answer on your answer sheet.

19. Mark your answer on your answer sheet.

20. Mark your answer on your answer sheet.

21. Mark your answer on your answer sheet.

22. Mark your answer on your answer sheet.

23. Mark your answer on your answer sheet.

24. Mark your answer on your answer sheet.

25. Mark your answer on your answer sheet.

26. Mark your answer on your answer sheet.

27. Mark your answer on your answer sheet.

28. Mark your answer on your answer sheet.

29. Mark your answer on your answer sheet.

30. Mark your answer on your answer sheet.

31. Mark your answer on your answer sheet.

32. Mark your answer on your answer sheet.

33. Mark your answer on your answer sheet.

34. Mark your answer on your answer sheet.

35. Mark your answer on your answer sheet.

36. Mark your answer on your answer sheet.

37. Mark your answer on your answer sheet.

38. Mark your answer on your answer sheet.

39. Mark your answer on your answer sheet.

40. Mark your answer on your answer sheet.

PART 3

Directions: You will hear some conversations between two people. You will be asked to answer three questions about what the speakers say in each conversation. Select the best response to each question and mark the letter (A), (B), (C), or (D) on your answer sheet. The conversations will not be printed in your test book and will be spoken only one time.

41. Where did the woman park the car?

(A) On the street.
(B) In the garage.
(C) In the parking lot.
(D) Next door.

42. How much does it cost to park?

(A) Two dollars an hour.
(B) Four dollars an hour.
(C) Five dollars an hour.
(D) Eight dollars an hour.

43. Where are the speakers going?

(A) To a class.
(B) To a movie.
(C) To a concert.
(D) To a soccer game.

---

44. Why didn't the man call the woman?

(A) He was away last week.
(B) He didn't feel well.
(C) He couldn't find the woman's number.
(D) He forgot.

45. What did the woman do last Saturday?

(A) She had a party.
(B) She went on a trip.
(C) She went to the doctor.
(D) She called the man.

46. What will the man do?

(A) Make a cake for the woman.
(B) Take the woman out for dinner.
(C) Buy the woman a birthday present.
(D) Give the woman some sweets.

---

47. What day does this conversation take place?

(A) Monday.
(B) Wednesday.
(C) Thursday.
(D) Saturday.

48. What did the man probably do last night?

(A) Watch TV.
(B) See some friends.
(C) Go out for dinner.
(D) Buy a watch.

49. What time does the woman usually get home?

(A) 1:00.
(B) 4:00.
(C) 6:00.
(D) 7:00.

---

50. What is the man's business?

(A) A farm.
(B) A restaurant.
(C) A flower shop.
(D) A grocery store.

51. How long has he had the business?

(A) Four years.
(B) Thirteen years.
(C) Fourteen years.
(D) Thirty years.

52. Where did he work before?

(A) At a hotel.
(B) At an office.
(C) At a hospital.
(D) At a car dealership.

---

53. Why are the speakers leaving?

(A) They are bored.
(B) The play is over.
(C) They fell asleep.
(D) They were told to leave.

54. How much did they pay for the tickets?

(A) $5.00.
(B) $17.50.
(C) $42.50
(D) $75.00.

55. What does the man want to do next time?

(A) Spend more money.
(B) Go to the movies.
(C) Invite a guest.
(D) Stay home.

---

56. Where are the speakers?

(A) At a tea party.
(B) At a night club.
(C) At a golf course.
(D) At a bowling alley.

57. What advice does the woman give the man?

(A) Swing hard.
(B) Stay calm.
(C) Join a club.
(D) Watch the ball.

58. What does the man want the woman to do?

(A) Hit the ball.
(B) Stop talking.
(C) Make a call.
(D) Stay out all night.

---

59. What time does the man's plane leave?

(A) Noon.
(B) 1:00.
(C) 3:00.
(D) 3:30.

60. How will he get to the airport?

(A) By subway.
(B) By car.
(C) By taxi.
(D) By bus.

61. When will he return?

(A) Sunday morning.
(B) Sunday night.
(C) Monday morning.
(D) Monday night.

---

62. Where does this conversation take place?

(A) By the door.
(B) In an elevator.
(C) In the woman's apartment.
(D) In the furniture department.

63. Which floor does the woman want to go to?

(A) Four.
(B) Seven.
(C) Eight.
(D) Eleven.

64. When will the sale end?

(A) Sunday.
(B) Monday.
(C) Tuesday.
(D) Friday.

---

65. Where does this conversation take place?

(A) At a pool.
(B) At a beach.
(C) At a school.
(D) At a racetrack.

66. What does the woman want to do?

(A) Put on a sweater.
(B) Sit in the sun.
(C) Have a race.
(D) Toss a ball.

67. How does the man feel?

(A) Old.
(B) Wet.
(C) Cold.
(D) Tired.

68. Where are the speakers going?

(A) To a park.
(B) To a hotel.
(C) To a bookstore.
(D) To a restaurant.

69. When do they have to be there?

(A) In fifteen minutes.
(B) In sixteen minutes.
(C) In fifty minutes.
(D) In sixty minutes.

70. What is the man afraid of?

(A) Getting lost.
(B) Being followed.
(C) Driving fast.
(D) Starting the car.

PART 4

Directions: You will hear some talks given by a single speaker. You will be asked to answer three questions about what the speaker says in each talk. Select the best response to each question and mark the letter (A), (B), (C), or (D) on your answer sheet. The talks will not be printed in your test book and will be spoken only one time.

71. What season is it?

(A) Spring.
(B) Summer.
(C) Fall.
(D) Winter.

72. What weather is expected this afternoon

(A) Rain.
(B) Stormy winds.
(C) Cool breezes.
(D) Dry and windless.

73. When will the skies become clear again?

(A) Early in the afternoon.
(B) This evening.
(C) Tomorrow.
(D) Later in the week.

---

74. What day is Dr. Miller's office closed?

(A) Monday.
(B) Wednesday.
(C) Thursday.
(D) Friday.

75. Why would someone call 800-555-3212?

(A) To report an emergency.
(B) To pay a bill.
(C) To reschedule an exam.
(D) To get lab results.

76. How can someone speak with the doctor?

(A) Call back when the office is open.
(B) Call a different number.
(C) Leave a message.
(D) Visit the office on Monday.

---

77. What will the Stonebark Company do on March 1?

(A) Announce a new contest.
(B) Open its first branch in another country.
(C) Give customers a special discount.
(D) Expand its business into Asia.

78. What can Stonebark customers vote for?

(A) Their favorite flavor.
(B) Their favorite café.
(C) The location for a new café.
(D) Their favorite Stonebark employee.

79. What does the announcer say about the future of the Stonebark Company?

(A) It will not grow very fast.
(B) Its coffee will not be very special.
(C) Its future does not look very favorable.
(D) It will probably become popular around the world.

---

80. What does this store do?

(A) Rent computers only.
(B) Rent computers and office furniture.
(C) Rent and sell computers.
(D) Rent and repair computers only.

81. What is the minimum rental period?

(A) Hourly.
(B) Daily.
(C) Monthly.
(D) Yearly.

82. What time does the store close?

(A) 7:30.
(B) 8:30.
(C) 10:30.
(D) 11:30.

---

83. What happened in Japan today?

(A) There was a riot.
(B) There was a tidal wave.
(C) There was a volcanic eruption.
(D) There was an earthquake.

84. When was the last time this happened in the same area?

(A) One month ago.
(B) Two months ago.
(C) Three months ago.
(D) One year ago.

85. How much damage was done to property?

(A) None.
(B) A little.
(C) Extensive.
(D) A great amount.

---

86. Where is the announcement being heard?

(A) At an airport.
(B) On a plane.
(C) At a consulate.
(D) At a bus station.

87. What is the gate number?

(A) 15.
(B) 16.
(C) 58.
(D) 60.

88. Who can go to the head of the line?

(A) People with passports.
(B) People with tickets.
(C) People with small bags.
(D) People with small children.

---

89. How many levels are reserved for employee parking?

(A) One.
(B) Two.
(C) Three.
(D) Four.

90. Which vehicles may park in the red spaces?

(A) Maintenance vehicles.
(B) Employees' cars.
(C) Visitors' cars.
(D) Two trucks.

91. What spaces are reserved for management?

(A) Yellow.
(B) Blue.
(C) White.
(D) Any space.

---

92. Who is listening to this announcement?

(A) Politicians.
(B) Guides.
(C) Diplomats.
(D) Tourists.

93. How is the group traveling?

(A) By van.
(B) By car.
(C) By bus.
(D) By train.

94. How long will the group stay at City Hall?

(A) Two hours.
(B) Three hours.
(C) Four hours.
(D) Five hours

95. What kind of sale is the bookstore having?

(A) Holiday.
(B) End-of-the-month.
(C) Back-to-school.
(D) Going-out-of-business.

96. What item is discounted 50 percent?

(A) Magazines.
(B) Calendars.
(C) CDs and DVDs
(D) Paperback books.

97. What day is the bookstore closed?

(A) Saturday and Sunday.
(B) Sunday only.
(C) Sunday and Monday.
(D) Monday only.

98. What time will the sun set tonight?

(A) 5:00.
(B) 5:45.
(C) 8:00.
(D) 8:30.

99. What are small boats warned about?

(A) A foggy night.
(B) A windy evening.
(C) A rocky shore.
(D) An early sunset.

100. How will the weather be tomorrow afternoon?

(A) Windy.
(B) Snowy.
(C) Sunny.
(D) Rainy.

Fin du test de compréhension orale. Passez à la partie 5.

READING TEST

In the Reading test, you will read a variety of texts and answer several different types of reading comprehension questions. The entire Reading test will last 75 minutes. There are three parts, and directions are given for each part. You are encouraged to answer as many questions as possible within the time allowed.

You must mark your answers on the separate answer sheet. Do not write your answers in the test book.

PART 5

Directions: A word or phrase is missing in each of the sentences below. Four answer choices are given below each sentence. Select the best answer to complete the sentence. Then mark the letter (A), (B), (C), or (D) on your answer sheet.

101. A __________ firm will help us find software.

(A) consultation
(B) consultant
(C) consulting
(D) consult

102. __________ Mr. Jeffries to get the job done.

(A) Count on
(B) Count from
(C) Count in
(D) Count up

103. Ms. Nyguen had submitted her résumé before she __________ the position was filled.

(A) will know
(B) knows
(C) has known
(D) knew

104. If Mr. Donna were looking for a permanent job, our recruiter __________ help.

(A) may
(B) will
(C) can
(D) could

105. The purchaser wanted the equipment __________ by Monday morning.

(A) delivered
(B) delivering
(C) will be delivered
(D) must be delivered

106. The company's quarterly earnings were up; __________ , the officers felt satisfied.

(A) nevertheless
(B) therefore
(C) however
(D) for this purpose

107. __________ substantial layoffs, costs were reduced.

(A) When
(B) Because of
(C) Although
(D) Since

108. Consumer confidence fell __________ April.

(A) next
(B) on
(C) in
(D) the

109. Price quotes __________.

(A) have daily been announced
(B) have been announced daily
(C) daily have been announced
(D) have been daily announced

110. The administration allows Thailand __________ Indonesia trade benefits.

(A) but
(B) nor
(C) and so
(D) and

111. The talks will take place __________ Brussels.

(A) at
(B) the
(C) in
(D) to

112. Many workers can't use computers; __________, training is required.

(A) on the whole
(B) besides
(C) consequently
(D) for example

113. Management let the employees __________ at two o'clock.

(A) leave
(B) left
(C) was leaving
(D) was left

114. If our candidates __________ elected, we'll have a strong board.

(A) are
(B) were
(C) have been
(D) will be

115. It's important that the clients __________ interested.

(A) are seeming
(B) will seem
(C) is seeming
(D) seem

116. Find __________ the details and write a report.

(A) up
(B) about
(C) out
(D) around

117. The meeting __________ going on since eight o'clock this morning.

(A) has been
(B) was
(C) is
(D) will be

118. The consultant __________ his business if he had advertised.

(A) doubled
(B) will double
(C) would double
(D) could have doubled

119. Mr. Dalla would like the invoices __________ directly to Milan.

(A) fax
(B) faxing
(C) be faxed
(D) faxed

120. The members would resign if they __________ asked to do so.

(A) are
(B) were
(C) will be
(D) would be

121. Ambition, talent, __________ desire are ingredients for success.

(A) or
(B) never
(C) yet
(D) and

122. Only five years ago, there __________ a shortage of computer specialists.

(A) was
(B) were
(C) has been
(D) have been

123. The board reported that more funds __________ for training.

(A) was given
(B) could have given
(C) should be given
(D) is given

124. Some employees get their paychecks automatically __________ in their bank accounts.

(A) deposited
(B) depositing
(C) are deposited
(D) deposit

125. Costs should be cut; __________, the number of staff positions will be reduced.

(A) however
(B) therefore
(C) meanwhile
(D) but

126. Office branches are located __________ the metropolitan area.

(A) on
(B) at
(C) about
(D) throughout

127. The company offers a __________ plan for its workers.

(A) retirement
(B) retiring
(C) retire
(D) retired

128. __________ Mr. Hague finished the job interview, he felt relieved.

(A) While
(B) Because of
(C) During
(D) After

129. Ms. Lopez has __________ learned to create zip files.

(A) yet
(B) ever
(C) already
(D) certain

130. The paychecks will be delivered __________ they arrive from the accounting department.

(A) before
(B) soon
(C) when
(D) during

131. The report outlines the products for the first quarter __________ the year.

(A) to
(B) at
(C) from
(D) of

132. The benefits package is impressive; __________, the director promotes only from within the company.

(A) for example
(B) when
(C) despite
(D) nevertheless

133. This company attempts to make its employees __________ like family.

(A) feeling
(B) feels
(C) felt
(D) feel

134. If the bills __________ in five days, the company will seek damages.

(A) weren't paid
(B) won't have paid
(C) aren't paid
(D) don't pay

135. The bank __________ another branch in Houston within the next year.

(A) opened
(B) will be opening
(C) have opened
(D) would open

136. Could you have the assistant __________ my office before he leaves today?

(A) stop off
(B) stop for
(C) stop to
(D) stop by

137. The _________ was settled on Saturday.

(A) dispute
(B) disputing
(C) disputable
(D) disputant

138. Make sure to use an _________ dealer.

(A) authority
(B) authorization
(C) authorized
(D) authoritarian

139. The printer apologized for _________ two names on the program.

(A) leaving for
(B) leaving out
(C) leaving to
(D) leaving from

140. Mr. Fox _________ the results tomorrow afternoon.

(A) will be knowing
(B) will know
(C) will have known
(D) is going to be knowing

PART 6

Directions: Read the texts that follow. A word or phrase is missing in some of the sentences. Four answer choices are given below each of the sentences. Select the best answer to complete the text. Then mark the letter (A), (B), (C), or (D) on your answer sheet.

Questions 141–143 refer to the following memorandum.

From: Cheryl Milkov
To: Gary Bauers
Re: Vacation tasks

I have approved your request to take a vacation from December 20 to January 3. Please take care of the following before you leave.

1. For safety reasons, _________ all floor heaters and appliances, such as coffeemakers,

141. (A) unplug
(B) hook up
(C) activate
(D) refurbish

in your office. Turn off the lights and the computer. Close all windows.

2. Turn in your annual report to me. It should be _________ three and five pages in

142. (A) between
(B) until
(C) from
(D) for

length. Make sure to make a photocopy for yourself.

3. _________ your timesheet to the payroll office.

143. (A) Submission
(B) Submissive
(C) Submits
(D) Submit

4. Ask a co-worker to respond to your urgent phone calls. Leave a message on your voicemail system with your co-worker's phone number and your return date.

5. Add an "out-of-office message" to your e-mail system.

Questions 144–146 refer to the following advertisement.

How would you like to save 50% on a rental car? Contact National Car Rental today!

You pay just half the usual rate on weekend rentals of compact cars. What a deal! But you have to hurry! This special ________ is available

144. (A) celebration
(B) expansion
(C) increase
(D) bargain

only for a short time.

National Car Rental also has luxury cars, trucks, and sports utility vehicles, and all are ________ with air-conditioning, a radio,

145. (A) equip
(B) equipped
(C) equipping
(D) equipment

and a CD player.

With offices at every major airport and in neighborhoods throughout the city, there is always a National Car Rental location close to you. Renting a car from us is easy.

Call now to reserve your ________ and be sure to ask about the

146. (A) suite
(B) vehicle
(C) voucher
(D) accommodation

50% discount. Note that this discount does not include insurance and is only available on certain weekends. Just go to our website to find the National Car Rental office closest to you!

Questions 147–149 refer to the following memorandum.

From: Jun Oh, Benefits Manager
To: Marcus Mains
Re: Special Retirement Opportunity

Thank you for requesting information about the Early Retirement Program. Please review these requirements. If you qualify, act quickly. Applications are due December 1.

Early Retirement Program

1. Employees must meet these ________ :

147. (A) requirements
(B) colleagues
(C) deadlines
(D) advisors

- Be age 50 with 20 years of employment at this company.
- OR have 25 years of employment at this company (age is not a factor). (Retirement funds are reduced by 2% for each year that you are under age 55.)

2. ________ employees should apply by December 1, 20__. The retirement

148. (A) Interest
(B) Interests
(C) Interested
(D) Interesting

program ________ on January 1, 20__.

149. (A) began
(B) will begin
(C) had begun
(D) have begun

3. Attend a workshop to learn more. E-mail my office to request the workshop schedule.

Questions 150–152 refer to the following brochure.

Checklist for Starting Your Own Business

Are you thinking of starting your own business? Before you come up with a name and register your business, it's important to do a bit of homework. While most people think that starting a business is one of the most difficult things to do, this is actually not true. It is fairly easy to get a business started. The difficult part is keeping a business running, especially for the first few years. ________ off on the right foot is very

150. (A) Start
(B) Starting
(C) To start
(D) You start

important, however. This brochure will help you launch your business by following these steps.

Preparation: This section ________ you through the brainstorming

151. (A) guides
(B) controls
(C) promotes
(D) translates

process and helps you write a business plan. Learn to start thinking like an entrepreneur.

Hiring: Who can you trust to help you run a business? Here we will discuss the pros and cons of employing family and friends.

Maintaining Control: So you've got your business name and you've hired your staff. Now, you need to let everyone know who is boss and how ________ going to run.

152. (A) your operation
(B) is your operation
(C) your operation is
(D) will your operation

Expanding: You're following the plan and everything is going great. Are you ready to take your business to the next level? It's time to make a profit.

PART 7

Directions: In this part you will read a selection of texts, such as magazine and newspaper articles, letters, and advertisements. Each text is followed by several questions. Select the best answer for each question and mark the letter (A), (B), (C), or (D) on your answer sheet.

Questions 153–155 refer to the following chart.

CROWDING THE PLANET

This chart shows how much the world's population grew between 1900 and 2000, and how much experts believe it will grow by 2025. The numbers are in billions.

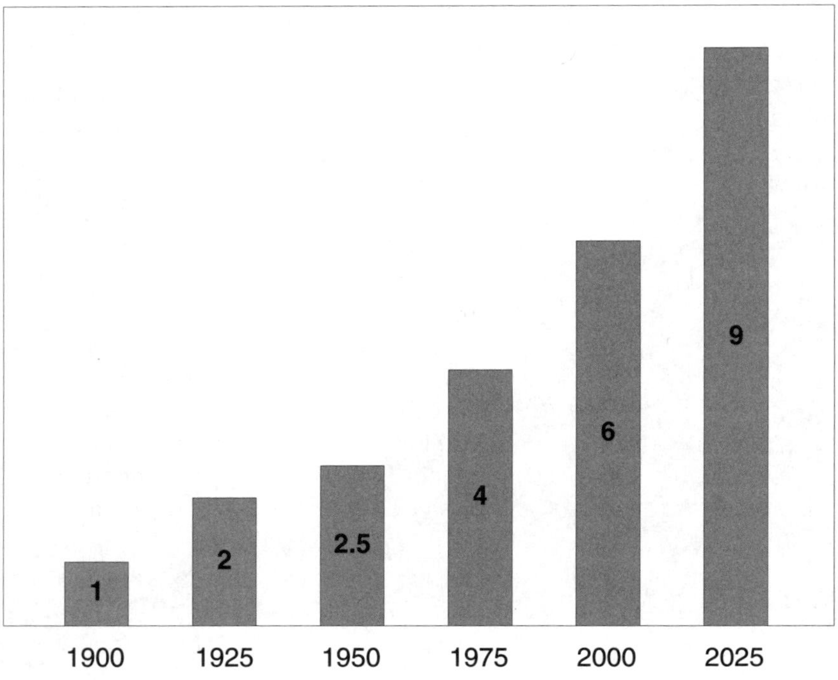

153. What was the world population in 1950?

(A) Half a billion
(B) 2 billion
(C) 2.5 billion
(D) 5 billion

154. In what year did the population reach 4 billion?

(A) 1900
(B) 1925
(C) 1950
(D) 1975

155. When was the population under 2 billion?

(A) In 1900
(B) In 1925
(C) In 1950
(D) In 1975

Questions 156–158 refer to the following article.

When a position becomes vacant, finding a new employee with the skill-set and personality that suit the needs of that particular workplace is a challenge that many companies face. First, the company must outline the tasks and responsibilities involved in the position to be filled. A careful analysis of these will help the company define what skills, abilities, and knowledge an employee must have in order to carry out the job successfully. Often it is the process of writing the job description and vacancy announcement that helps the company define the qualities they seek in a new employee.

Once the requirements of the position are defined, the next challenge is to find the person who can meet those requirements. One of the most common ways to locate a qualified person to fill a vacant position is to look within the organization itself. Is anyone currently working for the company who could do the job? This is often the best way to find qualified people. They are already known to the company, have been successful in it, and are familiar with its people, procedures, and policies.

If there is no available person within the company who is qualified to fill the vacancy, then someone must be sought outside the organization. Some of the most common sources of new employees are educational institutions such as high schools, junior colleges, four-year colleges, and universities. Companies also use newspapers and industry association newsletters to help locate job applicants.

156. What is this article about?

(A) Reading newspapers
(B) Hiring employees
(C) Protecting the organization
(D) Going to high school

157. What is an example of a common outside source?

(A) High schools
(B) Resources within the organization
(C) Spies
(D) Temporary employees

158. According to the passage, what do firms use to help locate applicants?

(A) Yellow pages
(B) Subway ads
(C) Newspaper ads
(D) Word of mouth

Questions 159–161 refer to the following announcement.

AERONAUTIC SYSTEMS, INC., the Berlin-based company also known as AeroSys, has made an agreement with three of the world's major international airlines to provide a satellite system for voice and data communications, a company spokesperson announced last week. This agreement is a major leap forward for the company, which began operations just three years ago and has now gained the business of three of the airline industry's largest companies.

The agreement with Skyways, Air One, and Travelers International will provide communications between aircraft and on-ground systems for operational control and air-traffic services. The agreement was signed last month, and AeroSys will begin providing services to the airlines before the end of the year.

159. Where is AeroSys based?

(A) In London
(B) In New York
(C) In Berlin
(D) In Tokyo

160. According to the passage, what will be provided by the agreement?

(A) Aircraft
(B) A satellite system
(C) On-ground systems
(D) Air traffic services

161. Which of the following is NOT a part of this agreement?

(A) A satellite system
(B) Communication between aircraft
(C) A system of voice and data communication
(D) Ticketing service

Questions 162–165 refer to the following announcement.

San Juan Academy has developed a unique approach to dealing with underachieving students. Instead of doling out punishment for incomplete assignments, or assigning extra hours of tutoring for bad grades, the academy provides failing students with a reward. Through the Computers for Success program, San Juan Academy students who fall behind their classmates in reading and mathematics are given their own computers. For nine weeks, the students get to keep a personal computer with a printer and software in their homes. They can work and play with the computer whenever they like and as often as they like.

Is this a prize for being bad in school? "It may look that way to an outsider," says school principal Edna Seymour, "but this approach is actually well-backed up by research. Studies show that students who are computer literate do much better in school. The figures rise for students who actually have a computer at home, and are even higher for students from homes where most of the family members are comfortable using a computer."

Because of this, when a student is given a computer to take home, families are encouraged to get into the act, too. Students in the Computers for Success program are required, together with their parents and siblings, to attend a weekend computer seminar. This way everyone in the family becomes familiar with the use of the computer. This is an investment in the students' educational future. "It is widely accepted that parental involvement makes all the difference in a child's school success," says Principal Seymour. "We are extending that idea to involve families in our computer literacy program. As part of that program, we make it possible for families to buy refurbished computers at an affordable price. Many of our families have already taken advantage of this opportunity. On the whole, we have been very pleased with the Computers for Success program."

162. Which of the following is NOT part of the program?

(A) Software programs
(B) A printer
(C) A personal computer
(D) Textbooks

163. When can students use the computers?

(A) Only during school time
(B) On weekends only
(C) At lunch break
(D) Anytime they wish

164. What are families of the students encouraged to do?

(A) Become involved
(B) Be actors
(C) Drive away
(D) Donate computers

165. The word "siblings" in paragraph 3, line 3, is closest in meaning to

(A) classmates
(B) brothers and sisters
(C) teachers
(D) friends and neighbors

Questions 166–169 refer to the following article.

We most often think of communication as talking, but it commonly occurs in other forms as well. In addition to words, communication can occur in the form of pictures or through actions.

When we speak or write, we are using words to communicate our ideas and feelings. It is essential for people to use words effectively in order to communicate clearly. Although words may seem straightforward, they are as subject to misinterpretation as any other form of communication.

Pictures can be a quite powerful form of communication. You will understand this if you think of any great work of art. Businesses can successfully use pictures in posters, charts, signs, and packaging. When combining words and pictures, the design should be carefully planned out. The pictures used on posters and charts, as well as in brochures and advertisements, should complement rather than conflict with the words.

Action is an important form of communication that we are often unaware of. As the adage says, "Actions speak louder than words." This medium is most important when dealing face-to-face with employees, colleagues, and clients. A frown, a handshake, a wink, and even silence all have meaning and people will attach significance to these actions. Just as it is important to choose our words carefully, it is also important to be aware of our actions and of how they may be perceived by others.

166. What is the main topic of the article?

(A) Marketing
(B) Communication
(C) Actions
(D) Businesses

167. According to the article, which of the following is used the most?

(A) Words
(B) Posters
(C) Charts
(D) Telephones

168. The word "medium" in paragraph 4, line 3, is closest in meaning to

(A) size
(B) method
(C) situation
(D) movement

169. Which of the following is NOT given as an example of actions?

(A) Silence
(B) A wink
(C) Television
(D) A handshake

Questions 170–171 refer to the following announcement.

Responding to the needs of an aging population, Health Network, Inc. of Melbourne and Futura Computing of Perth Amboy have agreed to cooperate in the development of handheld, computerized products to help the elderly monitor their health. It is widely accepted in the health-care field that patients who participate in monitoring their health status enjoy healthier lives. They are more aware of the factors affecting their health and are better-informed participants in making decisions regarding their health care. It is expected that these products will go a long way toward improving the health of senior citizens.

The cost of these products to the individual consumer will be covered under most insurance plans. They will be made available free or at reduced cost to low-income senior citizens who qualify according to government guidelines.

170. Who would most likely read this announcement?

(A) Lawyers
(B) Health-care professionals
(C) Word processors
(D) Teachers

171. Which of the following could be one of the products?

(A) Dishwashers
(B) Calculators
(C) Blood-pressure monitors
(D) All-weather gloves

Questions 172–173 refer to the following announcement.

Operation of Detroit's trash incinerator, the largest in the nation, was halted last month, less than a year after it was put into service. The huge plant, which was designed to change waste into energy, had been hailed as an innovative means of putting trash to good use. However, soon after the plan began operating, unhealthy levels of mercury began to be detected in the air around the city. It was soon discovered that the culprit was the new incinerator. Entire neighborhoods were threatened by the toxins being discharged into the air. Environmental officials ordered the plant to be shut down last week. They say it is uncertain when, or even whether, the plant will reopen.

172. According to the passage, why was the plant shut down?

(A) There was too much trash.
(B) It was unhealthy.
(C) It was unable to convert waste into energy.
(D) It could not be regulated.

173. What was the function of the plant?

(A) To collect waste
(B) To monitor air quality
(C) To supply Detroit with mercury
(D) To turn trash into energy

Questions 174–177 refer to he following article.

Absenteeism is an ongoing problem in many companies, and the Stummering Corporation was no exception. Absenteeism and late arrival had been issues there for a long time, so management decided to study the problem. During the months of January through June of this year, employee absentee rates and arrival times were monitored. It was discovered that the average employee was showing up for work fifteen minutes late three times a week. In addition, the study showed that the majority of employees were missing a minimum of one day of work per month. Aside from the direct effects this situation was having on productivity, it was also creating a noticeable impact on employee morale. Management knew that this was a serious problem and that something had to be done right away.

Human Resources suggested that management undertake an incentive program. A plan was devised whereby every employee who arrived at work on time every day during the month of August would be eligible for a cash award. Within five days of the announcement, the number of late arrivals had declined to the lowest level the company had ever experienced. The company decided to extend the program so that employees who didn't miss any days of work for the rest of the year (exclusive of approved vacations) would also be eligible for a cash award. As a result, absenteeism declined dramatically. Stummering plans to continue the program into next year and is looking into making it permanent company policy. This successful program could easily be replicated at other companies. It worked for Stummering. It could work for you.

174. What was the problem at the Stummering Corporation?

(A) Management
(B) Absenteeism
(C) Low pay
(D) Unprofessional atmosphere

175. How many times was the average employee late?

(A) Three times a week
(B) Fifteen times a week
(C) Three times between January and June
(D) Fifteen times between January and June

176. What did employees who were on time receive?

(A) A vacation
(B) A cash award
(C) A promotion
(D) A new watch

177. The word "replicated" in paragraph 2, line 10, is closest in meaning to

(A) copied
(B) enjoyed
(C) studied
(D) announced

Questions 178–180 refer to the following letter.

WALTERS CORPORATION
3255 Trenton Avenue, Columbus, OH 43216

November 20, 20__

Mr. Alan Porter
2870 Kennewick Drive
Bloomington, IN 42777

Dear Mr. Porter,

We were pleased to receive your letter and résumé inquiring about the vacant position which we announced in the *Journal of Engineering and Business* last month. Unfortunately, your letter arrived on my desk several days after the closing date of November 1. We received an overwhelming response to our job announcement. There were over 25 applications from qualified accountants. Although you appear to be well qualified for the position we announced, I am sorry to inform you that we have already hired another applicant. However, we were impressed with your background, and we would like to keep your résumé on file. We anticipate hiring again in the spring or summer of next year. We will inform you when another position that matches your qualifications becomes vacant.

We wish you the best of luck in your job search.

Thank you for your interest in the Walters Corporation.

Sincerely,

John Simons
Director of Human Resources

178. What is the main purpose of the letter?

(A) To ask for a job
(B) To reject someone who wanted a job
(C) To ask for references
(D) To learn about the Walters Corporation

179. What did Mr. Porter include with his letter?

(A) His résumé
(B) A report on the Walters Corporation
(C) A gift for Mr. Simons
(D) A job announcement

180. What is Mr. Porter's profession?

(A) Director of Human Resources
(B) Detective
(C) Accountant
(D) Administrative Assistant

Questions 181–185 refer to the following forms.

June 19,20__ TIME: 5:15 A.M. (P.M.)

FOR:

RECEIVED BY: Lev

CALLER: Marina

PHONE NUMBER: (3272) 43-98-58

MESSAGE: She immediately needs 2 computers, 10 packs of ink cartridges, 5 standard phones, and 2 photo: opiers, 1 industrial-sized and 1 personal-sized. She also needs furniture: 2 large wooden desks, 4 small wooden chairs, 1 tall metal filing cabinet, and 1 long metal meeting table. She can wait 7 days for the furniture. Please call her back to confirm fulfillment of this order.

CALL BACK REQUESTED? (YES) NO

DATE/TIME COMPLETED: ___/___/___ ___:___ A.M. P.M.

DATE: June 20, 20__ TIME: 9:20 (A.M.) P.M.

FOR: Marina

RECEIVED BY: Konstantin

CALLER: Alonya

PHONE NUMBER: (095) 555-4503

MESSAGE: Most of those items are here in Moscow. There will be a three-day delay on the large copier. Also, she will have to order the table from Almaty, so it will arrive 1 day after your deadline. Let her know if that's OK. Express shipping is possible. She can explain the charges for that if you are interested. Call her back today to order. She's headed to Berlin tomorrow, then on to Paris later in the week, so this has to be taken care of today.

CALL BACK REQUESTED? (YES) NO

DATE/TIME COMPLETED: ___/___/___ ___:___ A.M. P.M.

181. Who is ordering office supplies?

(A) Lev
(B) Marina
(C) Konstantin
(D) Alonya

182. What kind of filing cabinet does the caller want?

(A) Standard
(B) Personal-sized
(C) Wooden
(D) Metal

183. Where are the ink cartridges now?

(A) Moscow
(B) Almaty
(C) Berlin
(D) Paris

184. When will the table arrive?

(A) In one day
(B) In two days
(C) In seven days
(D) In eight days

185. What will Alonya do tomorrow?

(A) Call Marina
(B) Ship the order
(C) Leave on a trip
(D) Buy a table

Questions 186–190 refer to the following e-mail and table.

From: Guillermo Grimaldi
To: Samantha Young
Subject: Survey Results

We have the results of our Preferred Investments Survey. I have attached the "Types of Investments" table.

There is one change on the survey compared to last year. We divided one major category into two parts. The parts are "buildings" and "property." That's why we don't have a number from last year to use as a comparison.

We talked to 1,000 investors between March 1 and March 15. While most of them put their money into a variety of investments, the survey shows that this year there was a greater variety in the type of investment chosen than last year. More people are purchasing each different type of investment. For example, look at the number of mutual fund investors last year (800) as compared to this year (850).

These results will help our company better decide how to sell our investment products. We predict three types of investment will increase in popularity, and they should be heavily advertised over the next year. Also, we predict that three investments will decrease in popularity. We should decide what to do about those. Are you available on Friday morning? Let's discuss the declining investments.

Types of Investments
March 1–15

	Number of Investors (this year)	Number of Investors (last year)	Prediction*
Annuity	825	815	s
Bonds	1,000	850	s
Cash	1,000	1,000	s
Gold	625	600	d
IRA 900	875	—	d
IRA, Roth	975	900	u
Mutual Fund	850	800	s
Real Estate, buildings	987	—	d
Real Estate, property	700	—	u
Savings	1,000	1,000	s
Stocks, domestic	945	936	s
Stocks, international	965	900	u

*Prediction: d=will go down; s=will stay the same; u=will go up

186. How many investors participated in the survey?

(A) 800
(B) 850
(C) 965
(D) 1,000

187. How many survey participants invested in gold this year?

(A) 600
(B) 625
(C) 900
(D) 875

188. Why are three categories on the table missing numbers from last year?

(A) Nobody invested in those areas last year.
(B) People lost all their money in those investments.
(C) Real estate was not divided into two categories last year.
(D) The survey did not ask about real estate investments.

189. Which types of investment does Mr. Grimaldi want to advertise?

(A) Bonds, cash, and savings
(B) Gold, Roth IRAs, and mutual funds
(C) Annuities, domestic stocks, and real estate
(D) Roth IRAs, real estate, and international stocks

190. Which types of investments does Mr. Grimaldi want to discuss with Ms. Young?

(A) Gold, IRA 900's, and real estate
(B) International and domestic stocks
(C) Cash, savings, and bonds
(D) Mutual funds, Roth IRAs, and annuities

Questions 191–195 refer to the following advertisement and e-mail.

THE 20TH ANNUAL HOME ELECTRONICS SHOW
January 20–24

Join us at the Convention Center to see the latest in home electronics. Companies from around the country will display new model stereos, TVs, and sound systems for home use, as well as the latest in home security devices. Don't miss the special domestic robot demonstrations. See robots clean floors, wash dishes, even take out the garbage!

Admission to the show costs $10 for adults, $5 for children ages 5–12. Children under 5 will not be admitted. An extra $3 fee is charged for some special events. These include:

January 21	Movie: "The Home of Tomorrow"
January 22	Speaker: Roberta Wilkinson, President of Automation, Inc. Topic: The invention team at Automation, Inc.
January 23	Demonstration: Home Security Systems
January 24	Reception with JET Company, the Designers of RoboCleaners

Tickets can be purchased at the Convention Center or online. There is an extra charge of $1 per ticket for online purchases.
Buy your tickets today! Last year's show sold out!

From: Mai Itakura
To: Hank Ellmers
Sent: Wednesday, January 19, 20__ 11:12 P.M.
Subject: Schedule a time to go to the show

Hank,
The Home Electronics Show begins tomorrow and lasts through the weekend. Would you like to go with me? Your daughter Emma might enjoy it, too. It would cost just $25 for the three of us.

We can go tomorrow or later in the week if you prefer. There are some special events that you might enjoy, too. That company that you just bought stock in is giving a presentation on January 22. The company's president is speaking. You will probably want to see the security demonstration, too, since you're a police officer.

E-mail or call me today if you're interested. I'll be near the Convention Center tomorrow, so I can pick up the tickets without paying the extra charge. By the way, there is also an extra charge for the special events. You pay it at the time of each event, so you can decide about that later.
Mai

191. What will robots demonstrate at the convention?

(A) Playing stereos
(B) Watching TV
(C) Doing housework
(D) Operating security systems

192. When can convention visitors see a movie?

(A) January 20
(B) January 21
(C) January 22
(D) January 23

193. How old is Emma?

(A) Younger than five
(B) Between five and twelve
(C) Older than twelve
(D) Eighteen

194. In what company does Hank own stock?

(A) Automation, Inc.
(B) Home Security Systems
(C) JET Company
(D) RoboCleaners

195. How much extra will Hank pay to see the security demonstration?

(A) $1.00
(B) $3.00
(C) $5.00
(D) $10.00

Questions 196–200 refer to the following e-mail messages.

To: Gertrude Gerlak
From: Ping Lai
Subject: Retirement party

Hi Gertrude,
Don't forget that Samir's party is tomorrow night at the Lotus Chinese restaurant at 7:00. I'm giving Rae a ride. Let me know today if you want to ride with us. We plan to leave here at 6:15 so we can get to the restaurant on time to put up some decorations before everyone else arrives. I hope you don't mind helping with that. In fact, we would really appreciate your help since you have such an artistic eye. Rae has a card for Samir already, and she is collecting money for a gift. Let her know if you have any ideas for the gift. Thanks.
Ping

To: Ping Lai
From: Gertrude Gerlak
Subject: Re: Retirement party

Hi Ping,
Yes, I need a ride. Thanks for the offer. I went to the Lotus restaurant last month for my birthday. It's a great place. I don't mind leaving here early, and I'm happy to help with the decorations. Alex needs a ride, too, if you have enough room in your car for all of us. Do you need me to buy any decorations? Why don't we leave thirty minutes earlier than you said? That way we're sure to have enough time to do some really nice decorating. I'll be in a meeting tomorrow afternoon, but it should be over well before we have to leave. I think a digital camera would be a great gift. Tell Rae I'll pick one up tomorrow during my lunch hour. I know where I can get a great price on one. She can give me the money later.
Gertrude

196. Why are Ping and Gertrude going to a restaurant tomorrow?

(A) For a birthday party
(B) For a work meeting
(C) For a retirement party
(D) For a monthly get-together

197. How many people want to ride with Ping?

(A) One
(B) Two
(C) Three
(D) Four

198. What time does Gertrude want to leave for the party?

(A) 5:45
(B) 6:15
(C) 6:30
(D) 7:00

199. Who will receive a digital camera?

(A) Rae
(B) Ping
(C) Alex
(D) Samir

200. Why will Rae give money to Gertrude?

(A) To pay for dinner
(B) To pay for the gift
(C) To pay for decorations
(D) To pay for a ride

Stop! Fin du test. Si vous avez terminé avant la fin du temps imparti, vous pouvez retourner aux parties 5, 6, 7 afin de vérifier votre travail.

Test n° 4

Vous trouverez la grille de réponses au test n° 4 à la page 257. Détachez-la du livre et reportez-y vos réponses. Lorsque vous êtes prêt à commencer, mettez le CD et écoutez la partie audio du test n° 4.

LISTENING TEST

In the Listening test, you will be asked to demonstrate how well you understand spoken English. The entire Listening test will last approximately 45 minutes. There are four parts, and directions are given for each part. You must mark your answers on the separate answer sheet. Do not write your answers in the test book.

PART 1

Directions: For each question in this part, you will hear four statements about a picture in your test book. When you hear the statements, you must select the one statement that best describes what you see in the picture. Then find the number of the question on your answer sheet and mark your answer. The statements will not be printed in your test book and will be spoken only one time.

Example

Sample Answer

(A) (B) ● (D)

Statement (C), "They're standing near the table," is the best description of the picture, so you should select answer (C) and mark it on your answer sheet.

1.

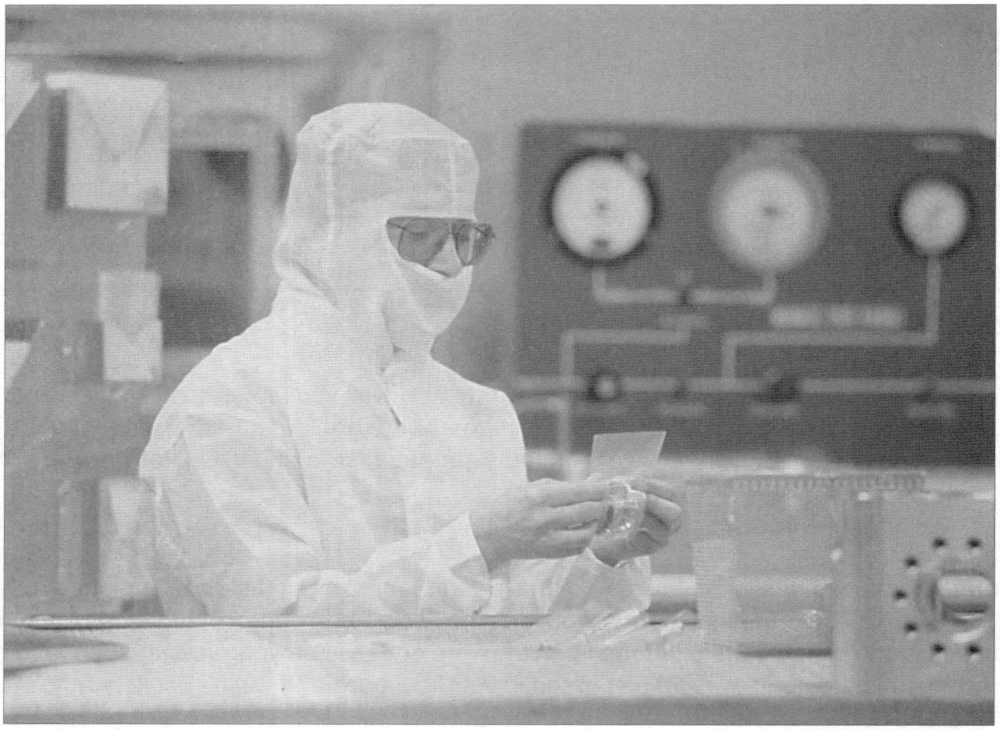

2.

3. 

4. 

5.

6.

7.

8.

9.

10.

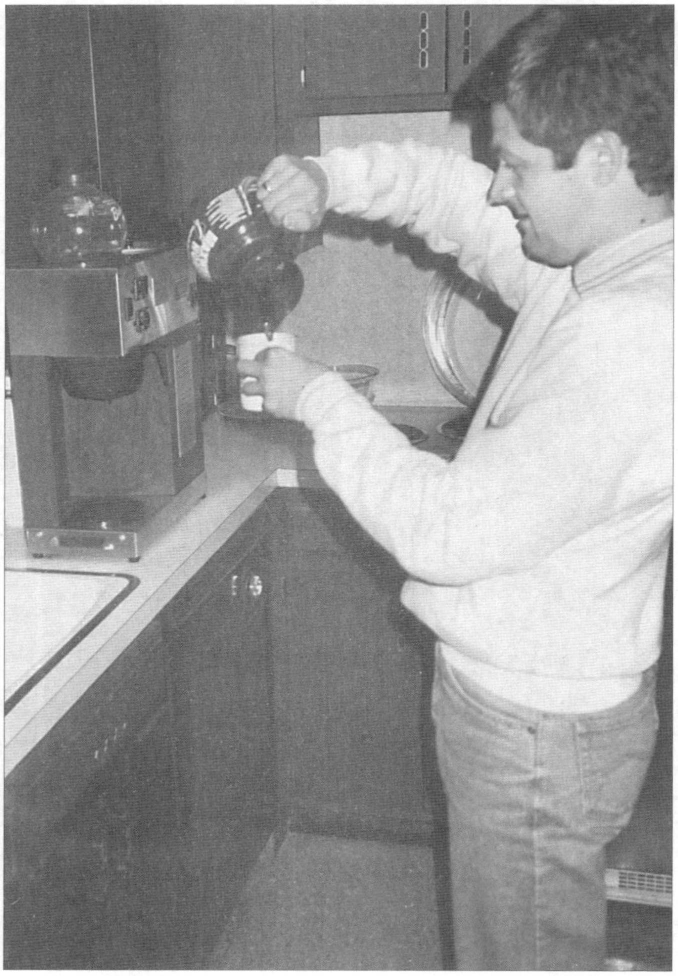

PART 2

Directions: You will hear a question or statement and three responses spoken in English. They will not be printed in your test book and will be spoken only one time. Select the best response to the question or statement and mark the letter (A), (B), or (C) on your answer sheet.

Example

Sample Answer

(A) ● (C)

You will hear: Where is the meeting room?

You will also hear: (A) To meet the new director.
(B) It's the first room on the right.
(C) Yes, at two o'clock.

Your best response to the question "Where is the meeting room?" is choice (B), "It's the first room on the right," so (B) is the correct answer. You should mark answer (B) on your answer sheet.

11. Mark your answer on your answer sheet.

12. Mark your answer on your answer sheet.

13. Mark your answer on your answer sheet.

14. Mark your answer on your answer sheet.

15. Mark your answer on your answer sheet.

16. Mark your answer on your answer sheet.

17. Mark your answer on your answer sheet.

18. Mark your answer on your answer sheet.

19. Mark your answer on your answer sheet.

20. Mark your answer on your answer sheet.

21. Mark your answer on your answer sheet.

22. Mark your answer on your answer sheet.

23. Mark your answer on your answer sheet.

24. Mark your answer on your answer sheet.

25. Mark your answer on your answer sheet.

26. Mark your answer on your answer sheet.

27. Mark your answer on your answer sheet.

28. Mark your answer on your answer sheet.

29. Mark your answer on your answer sheet.

30. Mark your answer on your answer sheet.

31. Mark your answer on your answer sheet.

32. Mark your answer on your answer sheet.

33. Mark your answer on your answer sheet.

34. Mark your answer on your answer sheet.

35. Mark your answer on your answer sheet.

36. Mark your answer on your answer sheet.

37. Mark your answer on your answer sheet.

38. Mark your answer on your answer sheet.

39. Mark your answer on your answer sheet.

40. Mark your answer on your answer sheet.

PART 3

Directions: You will hear some conversations between two people. You will be asked to answer three questions about what the speakers say in each conversation. Select the best response to each question and mark the letter (A), (B), (C), or (D) on your answer sheet. The conversations will not be printed in your test book and will be spoken only one time.

41. What is the man looking for?

(A) Papers.
(B) Cups.
(C) Ink bottles.
(D) Pen caps.

42. Where are the things that he is looking for?

(A) In the cabinet.
(B) Under the sink.
(C) Over the sink.
(D) In the closet.

43. What does the man want to do?

(A) Drink some tea.
(B) Write a letter.
(C) Go to the coffee shop.
(D) Buy some sugar.

---

44. Where does this conversation take place?

(A) At home
(B) At a bank.
(C) At a hotel.
(D) At an airport.

45. What time does the man have to leave?

(A) 2:00.
(B) 5:00.
(C) 5:30.
(D) 10:00.

46. When will the man pay his bill?

(A) Now.
(B) At noon.
(C) Tonight.
(D) In the morning.

---

47. How does the man get to work?

(A) He walks.
(B) He takes a bus.
(C) He rides a train.
(D) He drives a car.

48. How many times has he been late this month?

(A) Two.
(B) Three.
(C) Four.
(D) Eight.

49. What will he do tomorrow?

(A) Stay until 9:00.
(B) Get to work on time.
(C) Talk to the boss.
(D) Take a rest.

---

50. What does the woman want to borrow?

(A) Money for lunch.
(B) A screwdriver.
(C) A paperback book.
(D) A toolbox.

51. When will she return it?

(A) Before lunch.
(B) After lunch.
(C) In the afternoon.
(D) Tonight.

52. Where will she put it?

(A) In the closet.
(B) On the chair.
(C) On the man's desk.
(D) In the man's backpack.

---

53. How long is the man's vacation?
(A) One week.
(B) Two weeks.
(C) Three weeks.
(D) Four weeks.

54. When will he take his vacation?
(A) August.
(B) September.
(C) November.
(D) December.

55. What will he do on his vacation?
(A) Clean the house.
(B) Swim.
(C) Visit different cities.
(D) Sit on the beach.

---

56. What is the woman buying?
(A) Shoes.
(B) Shirts.
(C) Skirts.
(D) Hats.

57. Which color does she choose?
(A) Green.
(B) White.
(C) Blue.
(D) Gray.

58. How much does she have to pay?
(A) $16.
(B) $32.
(C) $25.
(D) $50.

---

59. In which direction does the man want to go?
(A) Left.
(B) Right.
(C) Forward.
(D) Backward.

60. What time is it now?
(A) 6:10.
(B) 6:15.
(C) 6:45.
(D) 7:00.

61. Where are the speakers going?
(A) To a ball game.
(B) To lunch.
(C) To a concert.
(D) To the park.

---

62. Where are the brochures?
(A) In Singapore.
(B) In the supply room.
(C) In the mail.
(D) At the printer.

63. When does the woman need the brochures?
(A) This morning.
(B) This afternoon.
(C) Tonight.
(D) Tomorrow morning.

64. How many brochures does the woman need?
(A) Twenty.
(B) One hundred.
(C) Two hundred.
(D) One thousand.

---

65. What time was the meeting today?

(A) 2:00.
(B) 3:00.
(C) 6:00.
(D) 9:00.

66. Why wasn't the woman at the meeting?

(A) She had to make a call.
(B) She forgot about it.
(C) She was busy.
(D) She was sick.

67. When is the next meeting?

(A) Tuesday.
(B) Wednesday.
(C) Thursday.
(D) Friday.

68. What is the man doing now?

(A) Going to work.
(B) Driving his car.
(C) Eating breakfast.
(D) Reading a letter.

69. How is the weather now?

(A) Sunny.
(B) Rainy.
(C) Cool.
(D) Icy.

70. How will the woman get to school?

(A) By car.
(B) By bus.
(C) On foot.
(D) By train.

PART 4

Directions: You will hear some talks given by a single speaker. You will be asked to answer three questions about what the speaker says in each talk. Select the best response to each question and mark the letter (A), (B), (C), or (D) on your answer sheet. The talks will not be printed in your test book and will be spoken only one time.

71. Why is the airport closed?

(A) Because of heavy traffic.
(B) Because of heavy fog.
(C) Because of strong winds.
(D) Because of falling snow.

72. When will the airport reopen?

(A) By this morning.
(B) By noon.
(C) By early evening.
(D) By late evening.

73. What should passengers on today's flights do?

(A) Go to the airport.
(B) Leave the airport.
(C) Call their airline.
(D) Call the Weather Center.

74. What time does the train arrive in New York?

(A) 9:30.
(B) 2:40.
(C) 6:00.
(D) 6:15.

75. How many stops does the train make?

(A) None.
(B) One.
(C) Two.
(D) Six.

76. Who is not allowed on the train?

(A) Passengers who are late.
(B) Passengers with excess luggage.
(C) Passengers without reservations.
(D) Passengers who don't pay by check.

77. What does this message state?

(A) That there is a convention in town.
(B) That city hotel rooms are all booked.
(C) That hotels have closed.
(D) That there are long lines for tourist attractions.

78. What time frame is mentioned?

(A) All of August.
(B) The first week of August.
(C) The middle of August.
(D) The last two weeks of August.

79. Why would someone leave his or her name?

(A) To get on a mailing list.
(B) To cancel a room reservation.
(C) To apply for any available job.
(D) To be put on a waiting list.

80. Where is this announcement being heard?

(A) In a restaurant.
(B) In a school room.
(C) In a meeting room.
(D) At a train station.

81. What time will the session resume?

(A) 10:15.
(B) 10:30.
(C) 10:45.
(D) 11:00.

82. What did the participants just finish?

(A) The question-and-answer period.
(B) A coffee break.
(C) Their résumé.
(D) Ms. Johnson's report.

83. What is the problem?

(A) High waters.
(B) Lack of food.
(C) More homes than families.
(D) Expensive property.

84. How many people have died?

(A) None.
(B) Twenty.
(C) Thousands.
(D) Millions.

85. When will the president visit the area?

(A) On Sunday.
(B) On Monday.
(C) On Friday.
(D) On Saturday.

---

86. What does Carlos do?

(A) Builds new homes.
(B) Paints houses.
(C) Designs interiors.
(D) Provides servants.

87. Who will provide references?

(A) The painters.
(B) The neighbors.
(C) The decorators.
(D) The real estate agents.

88. How long has Carlos been in business?

(A) Four years.
(B) Eight years.
(C) Thirteen years.
(D) Thirty years.

---

89. Who is listening to this announcement?

(A) A football team.
(B) Hospital patients.
(C) Airplane passengers.
(D) A theater audience.

90. How many minutes is the delay?

(A) Five.
(B) Fifteen.
(C) Twenty-five.
(D) Fifty.

91. What does the speaker ask the listeners to do?

(A) Eat.
(B) Smoke.
(C) Sign a document.
(D) Turn off their phones.

---

92. What kind of organization is this?

(A) Sports.
(B) Music.
(C) Youth.
(D) Scholastic.

93. How can a caller get directions to the Center?

(A) Press 2.
(B) Press 4.
(C) Press 9.
(D) Wait until the end of the message.

94. What happens if a caller presses 1?

(A) He can leave a message.
(B) He can get a monthly schedule.
(C) He can find out about tickets.
(D) He can get on the mailing list.

---

95. When will the snowstorm begin?

(A) Wednesday evening.
(B) Friday evening.
(C) Saturday morning.
(D) Saturday afternoon.

96. How much snow will fall?

(A) 2 to 4 inches.
(B) 8 inches.
(C) Less than 10 inches.
(D) 10 to 12 inches.

97. What are listeners advised to do?

(A) Travel.
(B) Stay home.
(C) Turn out the lights.
(D) Drink plenty of water.

98. At what time will the first group speaker speak?

(A) 8:45.
(B) 9:15.
(C) 9:30.
(D) 12:00.

99. Where will dinner be served?

(A) In the main meeting room.
(B) In the Red River Room.
(C) In the Blue Mountain Room.
(D) In the club room.

100. What is the new evening activity?

(A) A mountain walk.
(B) A presentation.
(C) A play.
(D) A dance.

Fin du test de compréhension orale. Passez à la partie 5.

READING TEST

In the Reading test, you will read a variety of texts and answer several different types of reading comprehension questions. The entire Reading test will last 75 minutes. There are three parts, and directions are given for each part. You are encouraged to answer as many questions as possible within the time allowed.

You must mark your answers on the separate answer sheet. Do not write your answers in the test book.

PART 5

Directions: A word or phrase is missing in each of the sentences below. Four answer choices are given below each sentence. Select the best answer to complete the sentence. Then mark the letter (A), (B), (C), or (D) on your answer sheet.

101. Salary increases will not be higher than the cost of _________ .

(A) life
(B) live
(C) living
(D) lived

102. Feel free to _________ the engineer for more assistance.

(A) call on
(B) call to
(C) call forward
(D) call at

103. Mr. Goa _________ the proposal before he looked at the guidelines.

(A) writes
(B) had written
(C) has written
(D) will write

104. If the project is a success, the office _________ more help.

(A) would hire
(B) hired
(C) can hire
(D) could have hired

105. The office manager wants the computers _________ by tomorrow.

(A) will be installed
(B) installing
(C) install
(D) installed

106. Suggestions were requested; _________ , none were offered.

(A) in spite of
(B) therefore
(C) however
(D) for this purpose

107. _________ the workers put in a lot of effort, profits were not high.

(A) Whatever
(B) Why
(C) Even though
(D) However

108. Ms. Ravi has already conducted market research _________ two new products.

(A) around
(B) from
(C) on
(D) near

109. Transactions _________ .

(A) have weekly been documented
(B) have been documented weekly
(C) weekly have been documented
(D) have been weekly documented

110. Clients are invited to write _________ call for additional information.

(A) but
(B) or
(C) not
(D) either

111. An answering machine takes messages __________ Sundays.

(A) from
(B) at
(C) in
(D) on

112. The solution cannot be determined __________ the problem is identified.

(A) if
(B) when
(C) until
(D) which

113. The director had her assistant __________ the memo.

(A) signing
(B) signed
(C) will sign
(D) sign

114. If you __________ a touch-tone phone, you won't need an operator.

(A) had
(B) are having
(C) have
(D) will have

115. Our company __________ Metro Messenger Service since 1998.

(A) use
(B) used
(C) had used
(D) has been using

116. The new employees will __________ during training sessions.

(A) catch out
(B) catch on
(C) catch in
(D) catch down

117. The __________ result will be announced next week.

(A) finalized
(B) finally
(C) finalist
(D) final

118. The financing deal is expected to __________ in a matter of weeks.

(A) go up
(B) go out
(C) go through
(D) go beyond

119. The supervisor wants the inventory __________ by next Thursday.

(A) will be finished
(B) finish
(C) finished
(D) finishing

120. I would ask for a special meeting if I __________ her.

(A) was
(B) were
(C) am
(D) would be

121. The company appreciates not only the president's ambition __________ his ideas.

(A) or
(B) but also
(C) with
(D) and if

122. A new collection of programs __________ in the conference room.

(A) are presenting
(B) are presented
(C) present
(D) is being presented

123. The supplier said the department __________ more stock in the future.

(A) has been ordered
(B) order
(C) should order
(D) ordered

124. Some managers wouldn't let the assistants __________ early yesterday.

(A) leave
(B) leaves
(C) leaving
(D) left

125. Sales performance has been poor; __________, the store will close soon.

(A) nevertheless
(B) therefore
(C) on the whole
(D) but

126. Ms. Jacobs is one __________ our best agents.

(A) from
(B) by
(C) of
(D) than

127. Please refer to your personal __________ number.

(A) identify
(B) identities
(C) identification
(D) identified

128. __________ you transfer your account, sign on the dotted line.

(A) While
(B) Because
(C) During
(D) Before

129. No one has turned on the air conditioner __________.

(A) yet
(B) never
(C) already
(D) soon

130. Akinori remained calm __________ his anticipation.

(A) while
(B) in spite of
(C) with
(D) as

131. All bank branches are open __________ 8:30 A.M. to 4:00 P.M.

(A) in
(B) at
(C) from
(D) by

132. We need more details, __________, who, when, what, and where.

(A) for example
(B) moreover
(C) however
(D) accordingly

133. My boss gets her messages __________ by a computer.

(A) take
(B) takes
(C) taken
(D) taking

134. If the company __________ in debt, the accountant would be the first to know.

(A) were
(B) are
(C) would be
(D) will be

135. Who __________ how many offices we have contacted for the survey?

(A) knows
(B) know
(C) is knowing
(D) are knowing

136. There is a rumor that the London office is trying to __________ the Edinburgh office.

(A) take out
(B) take away
(C) take over
(D) take off

137. Before the meeting, a __________ was held to verify information.

(A) brief
(B) briefing
(C) briefly
(D) briefed

138. It is not __________ to argue about small details.

(A) advise
(B) advice
(C) advisable
(D) advised

139. __________ these data before publishing them.

(A) Verification
(B) Verify
(C) Verified
(D) Verifying

140. Either the product __________ the advertisement should be changed.

(A) or
(B) and
(C) but
(D) nor

PART 6

Directions: Read the texts that follow. A word or phrase is missing in some of the sentences. Four answer choices are given below each of the sentences. Select the best answer to complete the text. Then mark the letter (A), (B), (C), or (D) on your answer sheet.

Questions 141–143 refer to the following letter.

The Accounting Firm
P.O. Box 90900
Pretoria
0083 South Africa

Alice Michaels
Michaels Enterprises
190 Church Street
Pretoria
0083 South Africa

Dear Mrs. Michaels, November 7, 20__

I received your e-mail last week, stating that you will not require my services for the upcoming tax year. _________ came as a surprise to me, as I have always provided you

141. (A) Theirs
(B) These
(C) Those
(D) This

with timely service. My records show that your company received a large refund from the government last year.

I understand that you, like many small business owners, _________ to use a

142. (A) have decide
(B) have decision
(C) have decided
(D) have been decided

do-it-yourself tax kit this year. While this method may seem less expensive because it saves money on an accountant's fees, there are hidden costs. It takes a lot of time to gather all the data needed to prepare your own taxes. My firm, on the other hand, already has this information on file, and we know the best ways to save you money on your taxes.

I hope you will think _________ your decision to forego professional accounting

143. (A) up
(B) of
(C) over
(D) after

services this year. If you do change your mind about this, I would be more than happy to provide you with the same efficient and accurate service that I have in years past.

Sincerely,

Peter Jones

Questions 144–146 refer to the following e-mail.

To: Reiko Ono
From: Junko Lee
Re: Transfer

Hi Reiko,

I heard the news this morning about your transfer. I was sad to learn that you will be moving to the Yokohama warehouse. It seems like half of the staff is leaving for one reason or another. I considered _________, too, but my

144. (A) transfer
(B) to transfer
(C) transferring
(D) will transfer

husband would never agree to it.

If you need any help packing or making arrangements in Yokohama, let me know. I have many relatives in Yokohama if you and your husband need anywhere to stay for a short time _________ you are looking for a new home. Of course, those

145. (A) while
(B) after
(C) during
(D) before

arrangements may already have been made by the company.

I will miss our conversations in the staff room. You always tell the best stories about your family members, and I feel like I know them personally. I'm sure you will be busy this month, but I'd love to get together for lunch or dinner before you go if you can spare the _________. Tuesdays or Thursdays are the best days for

146. (A) food
(B) place
(C) guests
(D) time

me. If you can't make lunch or dinner, I hope we can at least make one last date for coffee.

Talk to you soon,
Junko

Questions 147–149 refer to the following article.

Korea Daily

International Edition

Maple Home and Life Insurance to Cut 1,500 jobs

The oldest insurance agency in Busan is planning to eliminate at least 1,500 jobs by the end of the year. The mass layoff has already ________, with the first

147. (A) begin
(B) began
(C) begun
(D) beginning

400 people receiving their termination slips last Friday. Maple Home and Life is one of five financial services companies in Korea that has decided to downsize this year. "________ labor costs is the only way we can avoid bankruptcy," said

148. (A) Creating
(B) Building
(C) Operating
(D) Cutting

the company's vice-president.

Financial analyst Yoon Kwang-ung says that an unexpected amount of insurance claims due ________ a season of forest fires, occurring in a weakening

149. (A) to
(B) from
(C) at
(D) in

economy, has caused the mass layoff. But employees are not satisfied with these and other excuses they are hearing in the media. "We want answers. And we won't leave until we get them," said Hwang Woo-suk, who plans to march in a protest outside the insurance office tomorrow.

Questions 150–152 refer to the following letter.

Challenge Media
40, Rue de Suez
13004 Marseille France

Patrice Lerch
Healthy Cereals, Inc.
9, rue Ronchaux
25000 Besançon France

Dear Ms. Lerch: April 5, 20__

We received your request to ________ with our Marseille newspaper

150. (A) write
(B) advertise
(C) photograph
(D) invest

group and are pleased to offer you a full-page spread in three of our papers for the week of April 19. *The Marseille Sun* is a daily paper with distribution in Marseille and surrounding areas. *The Circle* and *The Marseille Bite* are our two local weekly papers. All three of ________ papers cater to middle-class families and business workers.

151. (A) these
(B) theirs
(C) its
(D) ours

Challenge Media charges one flat fee for advertising in all three papers. As well as full-page spreads, you can purchase additional 2-inch squares of advertising in our classified section of *The Marseille Sun.* These options ________ in the price we have quoted you. Please see our website

152. (A) don't include
(B) can't include
(C) aren't included
(D) haven't included

for further information on our classified section (challengemedia.com).

To confirm your order, please call our advertising department at 04.91.88.66. before next Friday.

Thank you for choosing Challenge Media for all of your advertising needs.

Sincerely,

Annie Chateau, Managing Director

PART 7

Directions: In this part you will read a selection of texts, such as magazine and newspaper articles, letters, and advertisements. Each text is follwed by several questions. Select the best answer for each question and mark the letter (A), (B), (C), or (D) on your answer sheet.

Questions 153–156 refer to the following memo.

Memorandum

To: Juan Gomez
From: Maria Johnson, Building Engineer
Date: 17 Jan. 20__
Re: Thermostat located in your office

It has come to our attention that the thermostat located in your office is frequently being turned off. Please be aware that although this thermostat is located in your office, it actually controls the temperature on the entire second floor. When it is turned off, it affects not only your office, but all the surrounding offices as well. We ask that you not touch the thermostat. The other second-floor tenants are complaining about the lack of heat in their offices.

If you wish to adjust the temperature in your office at any time, please speak with me or with one of my assistants. We would be happy to help you create an environment that is comfortable for you and your office staff, but please remember that we need to consider the comfort of everyone in the building. Thank you for your cooperation.

153. What is the problem?

(A) Someone keeps turning off the thermostat.
(B) There is no thermostat on the second floor.
(C) The other tenants want a thermostat.
(D) The second floor has enough heat.

154. When should the thermostat be turned off?

(A) In the evenings
(B) When it gets cold out
(C) Never
(D) When it gets hot

155. The word "adjust" in paragraph 2, line 1 is closest in meaning to

(A) pay for
(B) change
(C) look at
(D) open

156. What should Mr. Gomez do?

(A) Change offices
(B) Turn off the heat
(C) Leave the thermostat alone
(D) Complain to the other tenants

Questions 157–159 refer to the following advertisement.

White Shoe Kleen-Kit

White shoes are a handsome addition to any summer wardrobe, but they have always been difficult to keep clean . . . until now. Wright and Perry, the same company that has been providing you with top quality shoe finishes and other fine shoe care products for years, has developed a solution to the problem of cleaning white shoes. Thorough research and careful testing of trial products have resulted in Kleen-Kit, the fantastic new two-step, two-minute product that will keep YOUR white shoes sparkling white. Our special formula not only cleans your shoes to their whitest, it also protects them from dirt and water and preserves the leather, giving your shoes longer life.

If you own a pair of white shoes, or plan to enjoy that extra sparkle that they can add to your wardrobe, this kit is a must. It solves the problem you have always had . . . of keeping white shoes white. And, at a price you can afford.

Kleen-Kit sells for only $7 each, or $5 with each shoe order. Kleen-Kit is available at most shoe retail outlets and anywhere shoe-care products are sold.

Not convinced? Ask your local shoe dealer for a free trial sample or request one from our website. Your shoes will be sparkling white in no time!

157. What is this advertisement promoting?

(A) White shoes
(B) Shoe cleaner
(C) Shoe repair
(D) Company supplies

158. How long does it take to use the kit?

(A) Two minutes
(B) Five minutes
(C) Seven minutes
(D) Ten minutes

159. What problem does the product solve?

(A) Improving Wright shoe sales
(B) Finishing first
(C) Staying handsome
(D) Keeping white shoes white

Questions 160–162 refer to the following e-mail.

From: Ms. J. Gibbons
To: All employees
Date: July 17, 20__
Subject: Required hours

All employees are reminded that the Smithson Company observes a 35-hour workweek, normally from 9:00 A.M. to 5:00 P.M., Monday through Friday, with a one-hour lunch period. In addition, after careful consideration and planning, the Smithson Company has recently implemented a flex-time policy. This means that individual employees, with good reason, may establish different work schedules with their supervisor's approval. The employee must explain the reasons for requesting flex-time as well as demonstrate that a variation of work hours will not be detrimental in any way to the work of the other people on that employee's team. Whatever changes may be made to an individual's schedule, 35 hours per week is still expected of all full-time employees.

Flex-time does not mean that an employee can work any hours he or she chooses at any time. In order to make schedule changes under the flex-time policy, an approval form must be submitted to your supervisor two weeks in advance of the proposed schedule change date. The form must be signed and filed by your supervisor before you can start following a new schedule. Forms are available from the Human Resources Office. Employees who adjust their schedule without completing a form and getting formal supervisor approval are subject to loss of pay, even if they work a full 35 hours in a week.

160. What is the topic of the e-mail?
(A) Schedules
(B) Hiring
(C) Observations
(D) Lunches

161. How many hours a week do the employees work?
(A) 17 hours
(B) 25 hours
(C) 35 hours
(D) 40 hours

162. Who must approve any change?
(A) The employee
(B) The employee's supervisor
(C) The human resources director
(D) The vice-president

Questions 163–167 refer to the following memo.

MEMORANDUM

To: All employees
From: George Hendriks, Chief of Security
Date: May 30, 20__
Re: Office Visitors

Employees are reminded that a number of our contracts with clients are of a confidential nature. In order to ensure the maintenance of this confidentiality, visitors will not be allowed within the office area unless they are accompanied by a member of the staff.

Please let your visitors know that they will be asked to sign in at the reception desk when they enter the building. The receptionist will call your office to admit them and give them a visitor's pass. You must come to the reception area and escort your visitors to your office. Unescorted visitors will be asked by security to leave the building.

Thank you for your cooperation with this matter.

163. Who will read this memo?

(A) Clients
(B) Company employees
(C) Visitors
(D) Security staff

164. Why must visitors not be alone?

(A) They may get lost.
(B) They have appointments with staff members.
(C) Company projects are confidential.
(D) They are special guests.

165. What must visitors do when they arrive?

(A) Call the office they are visiting
(B) Admit themselves
(C) Leave before closing
(D) Sign in

166. How will employees know when their visitors have arrived?

(A) The visitors will call ahead.
(B) The receptionist will call the employee's office.
(C) The employee must wait in the reception area.
(D) The visitor will be sent to the employee's office.

167. The word "escort" in paragraph 2, line 4, is closest in meaning to

(A) accompany
(B) remove
(C) invite
(D) hide

Questions 168–171 refer to the following article.

Business travelers find that some jobs take them away from home for longer than a few days at a time. Those who find themselves at a new job site for weeks or even months often find it more comfortable and economical to stay at an apartment-hotel rather than a traditional style hotel. The comfort and convenience of these short-term residences are making them more and more popular among frequent business travelers. They provide advantages that more luxurious traditional hotels do not. Apartment-hotels offer both small and full-size apartments that are available to rent on a weekly or monthly basis. Apartments are fully furnished with everything from sofas and writing desks to dishes and silverware. They also usually include cable TV service and Internet access. Best of all, they are run like hotels, with cleaning and linen services, exercise rooms and restaurants, and a desk clerk to take messages and help tenants with questions about the city. In addition, the prices are much more reasonable than the rates normally charged at a traditional hotel. One of the reasons that many apartment-hotels are economically priced is that they are often not found in a city's downtown area. This is not necessarily a disadvantage, however. They are usually conveniently located near public transportation, so the expense of a rental car is not always necessary. In short, apartment-hotels offer a convenient alternative to the business traveler, as they are more cost-effective than traditional hotels and more comfortable than hastily furnished apartments. Many business travelers find that apartment-hotels are as comfortable as it is possible to be away from home.

168. Why are these residences called "apartment-hotels"?

(A) They have characteristics of apartments and hotels.
(B) They contain full-sized apartments.
(C) They look like hotels.
(D) They have only short-term tenants.

169. Who would be likely to use an apartment-hotel?

(A) A businessperson on an overnight trip
(B) A family of tourists
(C) An engineer on a ten-week project away from home
(D) A consultant in town for a convention

170. What is NOT mentioned as an advantage of apartment-hotels?

(A) They are furnished.
(B) They have cleaning service.
(C) They are centrally located.
(D) They have a desk clerk on duty.

171. How do apartment-hotels compare with standard hotels?

(A) The rooms are larger.
(B) They are not as comfortable.
(C) There are fewer services offered.
(D) They are less expensive for a long stay.

Questions 172–174 refer to the following article.

Surveys have found that wages and benefits are not always the major determining factor for employees who are looking to move between jobs. David Bikowski is a case in point. Last year he was laid off from his production job at a factory where he had worked for close to eight years. After several months of searching for a new job, he found employment at another factory in a nearby town. Although he would earn $100 a week less in the new position than he did at his old one, he took the job. He has a family to support and couldn't afford to stay out of work much longer. Just a few months after starting at his new position, he received an offer to return to his old job at his old salary. Bikowski decided to turn the offer down. Why? Because, he says, he finds that his new workplace is much less stressful than the old one. "We've been able to get by on what I've been earning at Strathmore (his new employer), and I know I'll be getting the usual raises as time goes on," he explains. "And it's better for my family in ways that money can't pay for. I'm more relaxed when I get home, I have better quality time with my kids. That's worth more than money to me." Bikowski represents a growing sentiment among the country's workforce. More and more workers are looking for less stressful lives, sociologists say. Work conditions are often given equal weight with wages and benefits when job decisions are made.

172. Why did David Bikowski leave his job?

(A) He wanted a promotion.
(B) He was fired.
(C) He wanted more money.
(D) He was laid off.

173. How does Mr. Bikowski's present salary compare to his salary at his previous job?

(A) It is $100 less a week.
(B) It is $100 less a month.
(C) It is $100 more a week.
(D) It is $100 more a month.

174. According to the article, why did Mr. Bikowski stay at his new job?

(A) The salary is better.
(B) The new job is less stressful.
(C) He has become a supervisor.
(D) He prefers working close to home.

Questions 175–178 refer to the following letter.

GUESS CONSULTING

121 Market St., New York, NY 10012

J. P. Thompson, Esq.
14, Rue du Mont Blanc
1201 Geneva, Switzerland

Dear Mr. Thompson:

I have enclosed a copy of the evaluation that I was hired to prepare for the project "Improving Employee Performance." You will see that the evaluation is divided into three sections, as we agreed upon in our discussion: Employee Relations, Physical Environment, and Training Opportunities. The appendices include all forms and outlines of other methods used to gather information for the evaluation. I have attempted to present everything in as clear a manner as possible. If, however, you have any questions or desire any additional information, please don't hesitate to contact me.

I have enjoyed working with your law firm on this project and look forward to working with you again in the future.

Sincerely,

Amanda Guess

Amanda Guess
Consultant

175. What is the main purpose of the letter?

(A) To submit a report
(B) To inquire about future job possibilities
(C) To request future projects
(D) To ensure prompt payment

176. Which of the following would Mr. Thompson like to improve?

(A) Ms. Guess's writing
(B) Employee performance
(C) The salary
(D) The evaluation

177. According to the letter, which of the following is NOT true?

(A) Ms. Guess would like more projects.
(B) Ms. Guess will discuss her evaluation.
(C) Ms. Guess is a consultant.
(D) Ms. Guess didn't complete the project.

178. What is Mr. Thompson's profession?

(A) Lawyer
(B) Personnel director
(C) Consultant
(D) Landlord

Questions 179–180 refer to the following advertisement.

179. How many time zones can be displayed?

(A) Five
(B) Twelve
(C) Eighteen
(D) Twenty-four

180. How long is the warranty?

(A) Eighteen months
(B) Five years
(C) Eighteen years
(D) Lifetime

Questions 181–185 refer to the following letter and e-mail.

Health Center
29 Adelaide St. E.
Toronto, Ontario
Canada
M5A 1N0

Vanessa Wendel
1907 Street Notre-Dame
Montreal, Quebec
Canada
H3A 5T8

Dear Ms. Wendel: January 2nd, 20__

I understand that you are in charge of the fundraising events for the Heart and Stroke Research Fund of Central Canada. My colleague, Jessica, suggested that I contact you about getting some brochures for our office. We need information on the half marathon that is taking place in Toronto on the weekend of July 1st–3rd.

When I looked at the Heart and Stroke website, I noticed that your name was among the female runners who finished in the top ten last year. Jessica was surprised to hear that in addition to managing the fundraiser, you also participated in the race. You must be in excellent shape! Are you running this year?

I would appreciate your sending some brochures for the center. I'd like to know more about the race myself. I've been thinking about entering, but I'm not sure if I am ready to run a half marathon. I think I should start with a ten-kilometer run. Currently I run about 20 kilometers each week.

Hope to hear from you soon.

Best Wishes,

Kandy Miller

Kandy Miller, Front Office Manager

To: Kandy Miller
From: Vanessa Wendel
Subject: Marathon Brochures

Hi Kandy,

Thank you for your letter. It was fun participating in the race last year. At first when my co-workers decided to do the run I wasn't interested. However, within a few weeks of their training I noticed how much more energy they had. That's when I decided to join them. It was a good experience, but unfortunately I will not be running in this year's event. I pulled a muscle in my leg when I was golfing this summer. You should give this run a try, though. It took me about 6 months to train for the half marathon. It will probably take you half of that since you have some running experience already.

I sent some brochures to the Health Center today. Thank you for your support of our cause. Last year we raised $400,000 in Toronto, and this year our goal is to double that amount.

Thanks again,
Vanessa

Vanessa Wendel
Fundraising Supervisor

181. Why did Miller write this letter?

(A) To request sponsorship money
(B) To explain about a fundraiser
(C) To order some brochures
(D) To ask for advice about exercise

182. How far will participants in the July race have to run?

(A) A full marathon
(B) A half marathon
(C) 10 kilometers
(D) 20 kilometers

183. Why isn't Wendel running at this year's event?

(A) She has a golf engagement.
(B) She has a sore leg.
(C) She has low energy.
(D) She has a running injury.

184. If Miller started training immediately, when would she be ready for the run according to Wendel?

(A) By January
(B) By March
(C) In 6 months
(D) Around July 3rd

185. How much money do they want to raise at the Toronto running event this year?

(A) $200,000
(B) $400,000
(C) $800,000
(D) $1,200,000

Questions 186–190 refer to the following e-mail and advertisement.

To: Katherine Smith
From: Althea Jenkins
Subject: Job opening

Hi Kathy,

I saw this ad today and thought you would be interested. You have exactly the work experience they are looking for, and the office is close to your apartment. That new car you were talking about buying wouldn't be necessary. The position is with a reputable company, too. My cousin Don Wade is the chair of the board. It's too bad you can't make it to my brother's wedding. Don will be there, and I could have introduced you.

If you decide to apply, let me know. I can at least send Don an e-mail and give a personal reference to him for you. He is usually in charge of conducting the interviews.

On the other hand, I haven't heard from you in a few weeks, so maybe you have already found some work. If you do apply, don't forget to attach your résumé after you fill in the online application.

Take care,
Althea

You are reviewing JOB BANK item #334885. To apply to this ad and attach an electronic résumé, click here.

Job Opening
Pharmacy Assistant
Part-time

Harrison's Pharmaceutical Company and Store—Auckland

Job Description:

- Provide clerical support to four pharmacists who have rotating shifts
- Measure, mix, and package prescription drugs*
- Take care of computer inventory and restocking
- Update customer files

Note: This position does not involve patient counseling or taking telephone prescriptions.

Qualifications and requirements:

✔ 2 years' experience under a licensed pharmacist
✔ Pharmacy Assistance License A
✔ Certificate from an accredited Pharmacy Assistant Program

Hours: Monday–Friday 9 A.M.–1 P.M.
Salary: Negotiable
Health Benefits: Not applicable

*Some deliveries may be required. No car is necessary.

How to apply for this job:
Please send a cover letter and résumé to the above JOB BANK number. We will respond within 10 days if we are interested in setting up an interview. Please copy and paste your résumé into the blank file provided. Do not send e-mail attachments.

186. Which is true about Althea's brother?

(A) He is the chair of a board.
(B) He is getting married.
(C) He noticed this ad.
(D) He needs to find a job.

187. What is Althea unsure of?

(A) Whether or not Kathy still needs a job
(B) When Kathy wants to go back to work
(C) Where Kathy and her kids live
(D) Whether or not Wade will be at the wedding

188. What does Kathy NOT need in order to apply for this job?

(A) A Pharmacy Assistant's license.
(B) A vehicle for making deliveries.
(C) Experience in a pharmacy.
(D) A license to work in a pharmacy.

189. Why does Althea think Kathy is suitable for this job?

(A) Kathy is buying a new car anyway.
(B) Kathy knows some of the staff members already.
(C) Kathy has two years' experience working in a pharmacy.
(D Kathy only wants to work part time.

190. What advice does Althea give that Kathy must ignore if she wants the job?

(A) Look at the JOB BANK ad.
(B) Fill out the online application.
(C) Attend Althea's brother's wedding.
(D) Attach her résumé to her e-mail.

Questions 191–195 refer to the following notice and telephone message.

NOTICE

The four parking garages for Mansfield Towers will be closed at various times during the last three weeks of June for cleaning and repainting. Please make alternative arrangements for parking during this period. Make sure to inform the receptionist in the lobby if you are expecting clients from out of town in June. We will issue temporary parking passes for the garage at 5th and Main for our clients. These passes can be purchased for a fee of $2.00 a day during the month of June, but are reserved for regular clients, not employees. There are five spots available for these clients, and these will be assigned on a reservation basis only.

Note: Parking on Green St. or Howe Ave. is strictly prohibited. Cars that are illegally parked will be ticketed and towed. For information about other local parking garages call the city help line at 800-555-9000.

DATE: June 2 TIME: ______ (A.M.) P.M.

FOR: Niels Henrikson
RECEIVED BY: Dagmar
CALLER: Eva Pederson

MESSAGE: Eva Pederson called this morning. She read a notice in the lobby today, and is concerned about parking for the upcoming conference in mid June. She said that at least 50 potential clients have already committed to the conference and about 30 more have not yet responded to the invitation. She is expecting at least 60 people or more. She wants to know where these people are going to park since the parking garage will be closed. Eva thinks the Calvin St. parking garage is open on the weekends, but it's at least a ten-minute walk to the conference room. This doesn't give a very good first impression considering these may one day be important clients. Call her with any ideas.

CALL BACK REQUESTED? (YES) NO
URGENT: (YES) NO

191. Where in Mansfield Towers was this notice posted?

(A) In the parking garage
(B) In the lobby
(C) In the conference room
(D) In the elevator

192. What ideas might Henrikson offer to Pederson if he checks the notice?

(A) They could call the city for parking advice.
(B) They could make a reservation with the receptionist.
(C) They could ask clients not to forget their passes.
(D) They could each give up an employee pass.

193. Why are none of the people attending the conference allowed to park at the 5th and Main garage?

(A) They didn't make reservations on time.
(B) They aren't current clients.
(C) They only have temporary passes.
(D) They are from out of town.

194. When is the conference taking place?

(A) Over a weekend
(B) The first week of June
(C) In the middle of July
(D) In ten minutes

195. How many attendees does Pederson expect at the conference?

(A) less than 30
(B) less than 50
(C) about 60
(D) over 80

Questions 196–200 refer to the following advertisement and e-mail.

Taipei Discount Package Deals

You are viewing our online Hotel and Air Packages

Travel valid from September 10 to December 1*

Tokyo Comfort Zone Inn

Room includes:

- Four-star rating
- 1 single bed
- Internet access and satellite television

Location:

Ten-minute walk from Tokyo International Airport

Free shuttle bus available.

Conditions:

From October 2 to 4 there is a black-out period for this deal. No reservations will be taken during this time.

Click here to bookmark this site.

TAIPEI DISCOUNT PACKAGE DEALS

Managed by TP Discount Travel Agency, Ltd.

Travel Agent License No: 22009

To: Geo Friends
From: Kit-ken Lim
Re: Itinerary

To Whom It May Concern,
Below you will find my travel itinerary. Again, I'm sorry that I wasn't able to book my trip for the weekend of the 3rd as you requested. That weekend would have been perfect for me as well. I leave Tokyo at 4 P.M. on the 10th. Unless I hear from you before I leave, I will assume that one of you will meet me at the airport with a sign. I have never been to Tokyo before, so I would prefer not to have to hire a taxi or find my own way to the hotel. I look forward to discussing franchise opportunities and to meeting all of you. I will have my checkbook with me in case we work out a deal right away.
Thank you,
Kit-ken Lim
P.S. I'll be wearing a green hat and a long black coat.

To: Kit-ken Lim
From: Geo Friends
Re: Itinerary

Name: Kit-ken Lim
Departure: Chiang Kai-shek. 9:30 A.M. October 7th
Arrival: Tokyo. 1 P.M. October 7th
Hotel Accommodations: Tokyo Comfort Zone Inn; 3 nights
Style of occupancy: Double
Total cost including taxes: Not applicable.
*Paid in full using air travel points

196. Why does Lim apologize in his e-mail?

(A) A black-out period changed his travel plans.
(B) He was busy on the weekend of the 3rd.
(C) He forgot to book his return flight.
(D) It is his first time traveling to Tokyo.

197. How does Lim plan to get to the hotel from the airport?

(A) He will take a shuttle bus.
(B) He will hire a taxi.
(C) He will walk the short distance.
(D) He will be picked up.

198. What type of travel was booked?

(A) A business trip
(B) A vacation
(C) A group tour
(D) A study trip

199. How does Lim's reservation differ from the original ad?

(A) He decided to stay in a 4-star hotel.
(B) He requested a room with a television.
(C) He switched to a double room.
(D) He chose a different travel agency.

200. How was this trip paid for?

(A) With travel points
(B) With a credit card
(C) With cash
(D) With a check

Stop ! Fin du test. Si vous avez terminé avant la fin du temps imparti, vous pouvez retourner aux parties 5, 6, 7 afin de vérifier votre travail.

Scripts

Script
Test n° 1

Part 1 (pages 3–8)

Example:

(A) They're leaving the room.
(B) They're turning on the machine.
(C) They're standing near the table.
(D) They're reading the newspaper.

1. (A) The fuel truck is by the jet.
(B) The crane is flying low.
(C) The plan is to buy fuel.
(D) The playing field is wet.

2. (A) The driver is behind the wheel.
(B) The electrician is around the corner.
(C) The technician is at the controls.
(D) The chef is near the stove.

3. (A) The audience is listening to a concert.
(B) The speaker is addressing the group.
(C) The workers are returning to their jobs.
(D) The musicians are watching the conductor.

4. (A) They're rubbing their fingers.
(B) They're stretching their legs.
(C) They're leading a band.
(D) They're shaking hands.

5. (A) The conductor is on the train.
(B) The captain is on course.
(C) The teacher is behind the desk.
(D) The trainer is in front of the group.

6. (A) The closets are full of clothes.
(B) The drawers contain supplies.
(C) The storage bins are open.
(D) The boxes are empty.

7. (A) The fireplace is tall and narrow.
(B) The smoke fumes are coming from the chimney.
(C) The skyscraper is on fire.
(D) The construction worker was fired.

8. (A) They're making coffee.
(B) They're having a discussion.
(C) They're washing their cups.
(D) They're using a calculator.

9. (A) He's buying an umbrella.
(B) He's clearing the table.
(C) He's serving the diners.
(D) He's waiting by the restroom.

10. (A) The trainer is setting his watch.
(B) The tourist is checking his bag.
(C) The pilot is washing his hands.
(D) The traveler is waiting for a train.

Part 2 (page 9)

Example:

Where is the meeting room?
(A) To meet the new director.
(B) It's the first room on the right.
(C) Yes, at two o'clock.

11. Where shall we sit?
(A) How about the front row?
(B) Before the show starts.
(C) It's on the table.

12. This is a great restaurant.
(A) It is. I eat here often.
(B) I need a rest, too.
(C) It's not that late.

13. How much does this suit cost?
(A) It costs a hundred thirty dollars.
(B) The suit fits very well.
(C) There are two suits in the closet.

14. Who took the telephone message?
(A) I'll phone you tomorrow.
(B) I looked for the telephone.
(C) My secretary took the message.

15. What time are you eating dinner?
(A) I'll have dinner about 6 P.M.
(B) We dined early yesterday.
(C) I always eat a big dinner.

16. Has the mail arrived yet?
(A) Yes, we came by jet.
(B) No, it has failed.
(C) Yes, it came an hour ago.

17. Look at how cloudy the sky is.
(A) Yes, it's very crowded here.
(B) No, I don't know who that guy is.
(C) It'll probably rain soon.

18. Who did you expect to come?
(A) I'll accept your proposal.
(B) I hoped my aunt would come.
(C) I suspect it came early.

19. Where is the accountant's office?
(A) It's at the end of the hall.
(B) There are five accountants.
(C) The accountant is on the phone.

20. How many students are in the class?
(A) The class meets every day.
(B) There are about fifteen.
(C) My students have to learn English.

21. Which magazines does she read?
(A) The magazine is on the table.
(B) She read it last week.
(C) She only reads business magazines.

22. I'm sorry. Mr. Williams isn't in the office today.
(A) Then I'll call him back another time.
(B) Yes, he works here.
(C) It's not a big office.

23. Will the report be finished by eight o'clock?
(A) It's five o'clock.
(B) No, it won't be finished until later.
(C) Yes, the reporter will be late.

24. Why do you get up so early?
(A) Because I have to be at work at 6 A.M.
(B) I always get what I want.
(C) You had to leave early, didn't you?

25. Would you like soup with your dinner?
(A) I'm not getting thinner.
(B) I ate dinner at 7 P.M.
(C) No, I'd prefer a salad.

26. When did you learn how to swim?
(A) I learned when I was young.
(B) I swim in the evening.
(C) I wondered how you learned.

27. How much did you pay for this car?
(A) Because it was used.
(B) I paid about three thousand dollars.
(C) The car needs repairs.

28. Why did you change your shirt?
(A) The shirt cost forty-five dollars.
(B) I don't have any change.
(C) Because I spilled coffee on it.

29. What was the movie about?
(A) It's about 6 P.M.
(B) He moved here last August.
(C) It was a western film.

30. I love my new job!
(A) I'm so happy to hear that.
(B) I've never been in love.
(C) I put it up above.

31. When did the doctor leave?
(A) She left at noon.
(B) The boat docked at 8 P.M.
(C) There was no one left.

32. Why hasn't this letter been typed?
(A) She's not my type.
(B) We didn't have time to type it.
(C) It's too little.

33. Who has a black ink pen?
(A) Here, you can use my pen.
(B) She opened a black book.
(C) Blacken the circles completely.

34. Were you born at home?
(A) No, I was born in a hospital.
(B) The barn is behind the house.
(C) No, I'm never bored at home.

35. What's for breakfast?
(A) It's usually at 6:30.
(B) We're having cold cereal and fruit.
(C) I'm hungry.

36. How many pages are in the book?
(A) He's six years of age.
(B) All the pages are white.
(C) There are about three hundred pages.

37. We're almost out of envelopes.
(A) Write the address on the front.
(B) He'll be out all day.
(C) I'll pick some up at the store this afternoon.

38. Who earned the most money last year?
(A) The money is earning interest.
(B) The manager earned the most.
(C) The students learned English last year.

39. When will dinner be served?
(A) The guests were served roast beef.
(B) We ate in the diner.
(C) It'll be served at 7:30.

40. Which bus should we take?
(A) Take the number 14 bus.
(B) We took the first one.
(C) He should talk to us.

PART 3 (PAGES 10–12)

Questions 41 through 43 refer to the following conversation.

Woman I'd be happy to type your letter for you, but can it wait until after lunch? I'm in the middle of something right now.
Man Of course it can wait, just as long as it's mailed this evening.
Woman That won't be any problem. I have to finish copying this report, then I'll grab a bite to eat, then I'll do it. It'll be done by early afternoon.
Man Thanks. I really appreciate it. If you need me, I'll be in my office.

Questions 44 through 46 refer to the following conversation.

Man I just talked to the phone company. They promised to have the new phones installed by Wednesday before noon.
Woman Last week they said they would have it done by Monday afternoon, but it wasn't.
Man Well, you remember there was a mix-up with the order. They were here on time, but they brought the wrong kind of phone.
Woman Yes, that was a big disappointment. I'm beginning to think this phone company isn't very reliable. We've been waiting over a month to get those phones in place. I can't believe that it's taking so long.

Questions 47 through 49 refer to the following conversation.

Man I need twelve dozen ballpoint pens.
Woman Do you want any specific color?
Man Oh, I hadn't thought about that. Well, all right, I'll take six dozen red pens, four dozen black, and two dozen purple.
Woman I'll have to check for the purple. . . . Hmmm, according to our inventory list we have some in the back. I'll have someone bring them out. Your total for 12 dozen pens comes to seventy-five dollars exactly, including tax.
Man Let me see what I have in my wallet. Oh, yes, here's a one-hundred dollar bill.

Questions 50 through 52 refer to the following conversation.

Woman The meal was delicious. It really hit the spot. You're a great cook.
Man But you hardly touched a thing. You should at least have some more dessert. I made it especially for you because I know it's your favorite.
Woman Thank you, but I couldn't, really. I already had two pieces of cake. Not to mention the three courses that preceded that. But I'd love a cup of that delicious coffee you make.
Man I'll be happy to make it for you. I'll have it ready in just a few minutes. You take cream and sugar, right?
Woman Just sugar, thanks. And take your time, please. I'm happy to just sit here and relax for a while.

Questions 53 through 55 refer to the following conversation.

Man You have got to learn to relax. You need to take a vacation or play a little golf or take up gardening.

Woman I'd like to take your advice, Doctor, but I have to work. I have a lot of responsibilities.

Man I'm sure you do. We all do, but if you keep up with this crazy pace, you may never work again. You're ruining your health. You need to find a way to ease up a little.

Woman Well, maybe I could take on an assistant to help me out some with work.

Questions 56 through 58 refer to the following conversation.

Woman Spring is my favorite season. I just love the cool rains. They're so refreshing, and everything is so green and new. It always makes me feel so happy.

Man I know. I love it, too. It's really a beautiful time. I really dislike the summer months, though.

Woman I know. I can't stand the heat and humidity. I'm useless when the weather gets like that. But, you know, I think a sunny September day like today is nice, too. Very pleasant.

Man Yes, this is also a great time of year. The temperatures are quite comfortable, and the colors are so bright.

Questions 59 through 61 refer to the following conversation.

Man Come on! Aren't you ready to go yet? I've already got my raincoat on, and I'm standing by the door. Let's go already.

Woman I can't find my boots and umbrella. Can't you take a minute to help me look for them? I really don't want to go out on a day like this without them. You know how easily I get sick.

Man Come on. You've got a raincoat. That'll keep you dry. We're going to miss the bus if you don't hurry.

Woman Relax. We've got plenty of time. The bus won't leave for another 15 minutes, and I'm not leaving the house without an umbrella.

Questions 62 through 64 refer to the following conversation.

Woman Don't you live by the police station?

Man I used to live by the police station, but I didn't really like the neighborhood, so last year I moved to Mountain View Street. Now I live in a very nice house right by the school.

Woman Oh, that's right. Your house is that small yellow one on the corner, isn't it? The one with the spectacular garden. I pass it every day on my drive to work.

Man You do? Then maybe you can give me a lift sometime when the weather's bad. Normally I walk to work, and I really enjoy getting the exercise, but I'd rather not do it when it rains.

Woman I'm sorry. I thought you took the bus. Look, it's supposed to rain tomorrow. I'll pick you up at 7:30, OK?

Questions 65 through 67 refer to the following conversation.

Woman I didn't read this morning's paper or yesterday's, either. I didn't have time to get to the newsstand to buy one.

Man You should have it delivered. Then it would be waiting for you in your office every morning, and you would always be on top of the news.

Woman Well, it would be in my office every morning, but I still wouldn't have time to read it.

Man Well, let me tell you about the story I read on today's front page. I think you'll find it quite interesting.

Questions 68 through 70 refer to the following conversation.

Woman I'm exhausted. I didn't get to bed last night until after eleven.

Man Really? That's not so late, not unless you got up very early, of course.

Woman I did get up early. I got up at four. I usually get eight hours of sleep, but last night I got only five. That's not enough for me.

Man No, that wouldn't be enough for me, either. Why did you get up so early? Were you getting ready for a trip or something?

Woman No, I wanted to get to the office early because I had some extra work to finish. Even though it means getting up in the dark, I'd rather do that than stay at the office until late at night.

PART 4 (PAGES 13–15)

Questions 71 through 73 refer to the following advertisement.

Have you been looking for an affordable way to stock your office supply closet with quality products? Then don't miss this unique opportunity. You've always relied on Office Supplies Incorporated to provide you with the best products at the best prices. Now we are announcing our biggest sale of the year with fantastic savings on all items big and small, from pens to photocopy machines. Our doors open at eight A.M. tomorrow, and everything in the entire store will be reduced by 50 percent for three big days, Thursday through Saturday. Sale ends Saturday at six P.M., so hurry on down. Don't miss out on this great chance to save, save, save!

Questions 74 through 76 refer to the following weather report.

Good morning and welcome to another cold, gray day. That's right, folks, it looks like yesterday's weather will be with us again today. We'll have more freezing rain all day with a chance of snow later on this evening. This dreary weather will likely be with us for a few more days, though the weekend forecast is looking up. The low-pressure system should be moving out of our area by late Friday. Then we can expect sunny skies all weekend with a high temperature of around 11 degrees Celsius. So don't despair. Better weather is just around the corner. Tune in again at noon for an updated report on today's weather.

Questions 77 through 79 refer to the following news item.

This urgent item just in. The electricity company warns citizens living in the tri-state region that due to unusually high temperatures, the demand for electricity may exceed the supply. Air conditioners and fans are in constant use during this hot summer weather, putting an enormous strain on electricity supply. This increase in demand for electricity may result in power failures in scattered areas throughout the region. In order to help avoid blackouts, citizens are asked to keep their air conditioners set at temperatures no lower than 80 degrees Fahrenheit and to run them only intermittently during the hottest part of the day. In addition, any non-essential use of electrical appliances should be avoided during the middle of the day. If a power failure occurring in your neighborhood should cause a potentially life-threatening emergency, call the electricity company's emergency hotline at 555-9745. Emergency workers are standing by in your area ready to respond where needed.

Questions 80 through 82 refer to the following recorded announcement.

Thank you for calling Jet Stream Airlines. Please excuse this short delay. Due to our special low bargain fares, all our agents are busy assisting other callers. All calls will be answered in turn. Please stay on the line, and an airline representative will be with you shortly. Here's a tip for busy travelers. When planning your trip, don't forget to allow plenty of time to arrive at the airport. Improved airport security means longer lines when passing through security control. Domestic travelers should plan to arrive two hours before their scheduled departure time, while international travelers should arrive three hours ahead of time.

Questions 83 through 85 refer to the following announcement.

Good afternoon. I want to welcome you all to our management improvement luncheon. We have a delicious meal to look forward to. The catering staff here at the club always makes our noon events special. We also have a fantastic speaker with us today. Mr. Andrew Margalis worked as a management trainer for twenty years before he retired. He has given seminars all over the country and in several places abroad. Now he works only in his garden, but I am pleased that he has honored us by agreeing to be here today. He will share his experiences as a manager and lead us through some exercises designed to help us evaluate our effectiveness with our staff. And now, without further ado, I give you Andrew Margalis.

Questions 86 through 88 refer to the following business report.

This area is for authorized personnel only. You must have a special pass to enter the area. Passes may be obtained at the Security Office upon presentation of a valid driver's license. You must keep your pass with you at all times during your visit and be prepared to present it to a uniformed security officer upon request. It should be hung around your neck or pinned to the front of your clothing in order to keep it plainly visible. In addition, you must obey the safety rules posted on signs throughout the area, and stay away from restricted areas. Return your pass to Room 3 before exiting the area. A new pass will be issued each time you wish to enter this area.

Questions 89 through 91 refer to the following advertisement.

Attention all job seekers! Are you unemployed? Are you looking for part-time work? Do you have office skills that would be useful in a doctor's office, a law firm, or an advertising agency? Your search is over. If you have basic computer skills, know how to answer a telephone, and have a neat, professional appearance, we have a position for you. Call Temps Company and let our agents find you a job that matches your qualifications. All our available positions are with well-established downtown business firms. We have job openings in law firms, doctor's offices, marketing firms, and more. All job applicants must visit our office to take a skills test. The results will be available immediately. Call us today to make an appointment. You could be working at your new job tomorrow.

Questions 92 through 94 refer to the following weather report.

Good morning. It's eight o'clock on a beautiful cool morning in the Windy City. This is Dan Richards with your early morning weather report. Remember to take your umbrella to work with you today. Don't be fooled by the nice clear skies and sunshine we are having right now. Dark clouds will be moving in later this morning, and rain showers are expected this afternoon. The rain will continue through the evening with heavy downpours at times and possibly thunder.

Questions 95 through 97 refer to the following message.

You have reached the offices of Family Security Systems, the company that takes care of all your insurance needs. We are open from 9:00 to 5:00 Monday through Friday. If this is an emergency, please press 1. An agent is available to assist you immediately 24 hours a day. To speak to someone about an existing policy, press 4. To sign up for a new policy, press 5. To register a change in your mailing address using our automated system, press 6. You may also change your address and check your policy on our company's website. Please have your policy number and PIN available when logging on to the website. Thank you for calling Family Security Systems.

Questions 98 through 100 refer to the following announcement.

Attention, shoppers. Don't forget to pay a visit to the Mall Garden Restaurant, located near the front entrance. Take a few minutes to relax from your busy day of shopping while you enjoy a drink, a snack, or a meal. Today's special is chicken á là king. Our world-famous roast beef, spaghetti roma, and oven-roasted vegetables are also available for your dining pleasure. The selection of scrumptious desserts and super-tall sodas are sure to bring out the kid in you. The special children's menu includes a free toy with every meal. Our famous teatime special is served every afternoon between two and four-thirty. So stop by our restaurant today. It's a place the whole family enjoys. While you're there, ask the hostess about having your next birthday party or other special event at the Mall Garden Restaurant. It is fast becoming <u>the</u> place to entertain.

Script
Test n° 2

Part 1 (pages 43–48)

Example:

(A) They're leaving the room.
(B) They're turning on the machine.
(C) They're standing near the table.
(D) They're reading the newspaper.

1. (A) He's going to put his bag in the car.
(B) He's opening a cabinet.
(C) He's carrying a trunk.
(D) He's washing a car.

2. (A) They're looking at the paintings.
(B) They're painting a picture.
(C) They're having their picture taken.
(D) They're taking a picture.

3. (A) The crew prepares for the event.
(B) The technician adjusts the equipment.
(C) The plumber fixes the sink.
(D) The mail carrier sorts the mail.

4. (A) He's making a presentation.
(B) He's handing out presents.
(C) He's putting on his jacket.
(D) He's training his horses.

5. (A) They're waving to one another.
(B) They're taking fans.
(C) They're sanding the floor.
(D) They're standing on the steps.

6. (A) The worker is going up the stairs.
(B) The gas tank in the car is full.
(C) The cargo ship sank.
(D) The man is sending the letter.

7. (A) The gardeners are planting a tree.
(B) The firefighters are filling their buckets.
(C) The workers are checking the equipment.
(D) The dentists are cleaning their drills.

8. (A) The flight attendants are getting off the plane.
(B) The pie ought to be ready to take out.
(C) The pilots are preparing to take off.
(D) The musicians are tuning their instruments.

9. (A) The oven operates with gas.
(B) Two men are making repairs.
(C) Both men are sitting down.
(D) Their tools are put away.

10. (A) He's in the middle of a crowd.
(B) He's typing his work order.
(C) He's adding oil to his car engine.
(D) He's surrounded by oil drums.

Part 2 (page 49)

Example:

Where is the meeting room?
(A) To meet the new director.
(B) It's the first room on the right.
(C) Yes, at two o'clock.

11. Where are the stamps?
(A) The post office is closed.
(B) The stamps are in the top drawer.
(C) The letter was not stamped.

12. Why did you leave work so early?
(A) Because you worked so late.
(B) I'm always the first person here.
(C) I left early to go to the doctor.

13. What is your first chore today?
(A) I'm thirsty, too.
(B) First, I'll open the mail.
(C) Today is a short workday.

14. How often do you take a vacation?
(A) I took one of them.
(B) Four to five times an hour.
(C) I take a vacation twice a year.

15. Whose coffee cup is this?
(A) That cup is his.
(B) This is good coffee.
(C) Yes, I like coffee.

16. Will we be on time?
(A) Yes, actually we're early.
(B) No, I don't have a watch.
(C) No, he came at 4:30.

17. How well do you speak Chinese?
(A) She's feeling better.
(B) I know only a few words.
(C) We love Chinese food.

18. Why didn't you study for the test?
(A) They're good students.
(B) Because it was a test.
(C) I was too tired to study.

19. What are they going to do tomorrow?
(A) They're playing golf now.
(B) They plan to stay home tomorrow.
(C) He said he'll go the day after.

20. Where's the ticket counter?
(A) She counted five tickets.
(B) I lost my ticket.
(C) It's on the ground floor.

21. What's for lunch?
(A) Around the corner.
(B) At noon.
(C) Beef and noodles.

22. The weather report said rain all weekend.
(A) Then we'll have to cancel our plans for the beach.
(B) The trains don't run on the weekend.
(C) I'll finish the report soon.

23. How many movies do you see each month?
(A) I'll see that movie next month.
(B) I moved overseas.
(C) About four. I usually go once a week.

24. Which chair is more comfortable?
(A) You should put the chair next to the table.
(B) The brown chair is very comfortable.
(C) We don't care any more.

25. I need to mail this package to California.
(A) There are some letters on your desk.
(B) I can take it to the post office for you.
(C) We already packed our suitcases.

26. Who rented the apartment upstairs?
(A) The renters moved out.
(B) There are stairs in the apartment.
(C) A young couple rented it.

27. What did the hotel clerk say?
(A) I stayed at the hotel.
(B) He said no rooms were available.
(C) The clerk filed the letters.

28. How did you find a computer programmer?
(A) I advertised for one in the paper.
(B) The computer is on the desk.
(C) We watched the program.

29. This is the suit I bought in New York.
(A) I never eat fruit.
(B) Yes, I think he lives in New York.
(C) It looks very nice on you.

30. When was the package mailed?
(A) He packed it yesterday.
(B) It was mailed last week.
(C) The mail comes in the morning.

31. I only get one week's vacation at my new job.
(A) He works at a travel agency.
(B) That's not very much time.
(C) I found a new job.

32. How much money did the company earn last year?
(A) We made three hundred thousand dollars.
(B) Money earns interest during the year.
(C) We spent a lot of money.

33. When can we take a coffee break?
(A) Usually we can take one whenever we want.
(B) We bought coffee and bread.
(C) The coffeepot broke yesterday.

34. Who turned off the photocopier?
(A) We copied the photos.
(B) I turned it off when I finished.
(C) The photographer turned in the photos.

35. Which room is for nonsmokers?
(A) Smoking is not allowed anywhere in the library.
(B) The rooms are full of smoke.
(C) No one is in the room.

36. How large is the auditorium?
(A) It can seat 500 people.
(B) My video player is larger.
(C) The auditorium is often closed.

37. How many bags can I take on the plane?
(A) Take the bag next to mine.
(B) There are two planes.
(C) You can take only one.

38. I didn't get enough sleep last night.
(A) You should go to bed earlier.
(B) You can keep it.
(C) Tonight's the last night.

39. What kind of insurance do you have?
(A) We have health insurance.
(B) The insurance agent is very kind.
(C) Because it's necessary.

40. How long does it take to travel from New York to Tokyo?
(A) None of us likes to travel.
(B) In big cities, we take the subway.
(C) It takes fourteen hours by plane.

PART 3 (PAGES 50–52)

Questions 41 through 43 refer to the following conversation.

Woman My plane is at seven, so I'll have to leave the office around five-thirty. That should give me enough time to get to the airport, don't you think?

Man Actually, I think you should leave earlier. Rush hour starts at five. The traffic will be really heavy by five-thirty.

Woman Yes, you're right. Maybe I'd better plan to leave at four.

Man That's a much better idea. And, look, you'll need something to read on that long flight. Take these newspapers with you. I've already read them.

Questions 44 through 46 refer to the following conversation.

Man Do you have any cash on you by any chance?

Woman Well, yes, I went to the bank this afternoon, but I only have about forty dollars.

Man Great. That's plenty. Could you lend me fifteen until tomorrow? I'm in a rush to get to a meeting, and I need some cash to pay for a taxi.

Woman Well, all right, but promise you'll pay me back tomorrow, not next week or the week after.

Questions 47 through 49 refer to the following conversation.

Woman I really don't want to see a Western or a murder movie. I'm tired of violent movies. Isn't there a comedy playing? That's something we'd both enjoy.

Man Let's see . . . the next movie starts at 7:30. Oh, but it's a war story. More violence.

Woman Then let's just stay home. I'm sure we can find something good on TV to watch.

Man No, I don't want to do that. I'm tired of staying home. I want to go out. Let's have dinner at that place around the corner. We haven't been there in a while.

Questions 50 through 52 refer to the following conversation.

Man Please let everyone know that Wednesday's meeting has been postponed for two days. And please do it as soon as possible. They should know about this right away.

Woman So you want me to tell them that it'll be on Friday instead?

Man Yes. I'm sorry to have to do this at the last minute, but I just found out that Ms. Schmidt is still out sick, and we can't have a budget meeting without our accountant. What would be the point?

Woman I guess you're right about that. I'll make sure the conference room will be ready. And I'll call everyone about the meeting to make sure they get the information on time. It's more reliable that way than by e-mail.

Questions 53 through 55 refer to the following conversation.

Woman I'm sorry I'm late again. I ran out of gas. Can you believe it?

Man You should take the bus. Then you wouldn't have to worry about gas or flat tires or anything like that. Or, even better, get up earlier and walk. That's what I do. I walk to work every morning.

Woman Well, I tried taking the bus yesterday, and I got here even later than I do when I drive because it has to stop at every bus stop. It takes forever.

Man See? Walking's the fastest way. It only takes me 45 minutes to get to work. And I always arrive feeling relaxed and energized.

Woman Well, it would take me a lot longer than it takes you. I'd have to train before I could walk that fast, and anyhow, I live a lot farther away than you do.

Questions 56 through 58 refer to the following conversation.

Man Oh, no. I don't have my glasses. I think I must have left them on the desk in your office.

Woman I'll wait for you here while you go back and look for them. Here, you'll need my keys. My office is locked.

Man OK, thanks. Hold onto my briefcase for me, and don't wait here. I'll catch up with you at the car. It will only take me a minute.

Woman All right. I'm parked right across the street, in front of the post office.

Questions 59 through 61 refer to the following conversation.

Man It sure is hot today. You could fry an egg on the sidewalk. I can't remember the last time it was this hot in April.

Woman I know. It's usually cooler this time of year.

Man Well, I can't complain. Since I sell ice cream, this heat's good for business. I've been doing really well all week.

Woman That's good for you. And I get to stay cool by working in an air-conditioned office all day, so that's something.

Questions 62 through 64 refer to the following conversation.

Woman What a handsome suit. I've never seen you wear it before. Did you buy it somewhere around here?

Man No, I bought it when I was in Hong Kong last spring. The shoes, shirt, and tie I already had. Do you think they look good together?

Woman They look very nice. The whole outfit looks great. That color tie really goes well with the suit. Did you get it in Hong Kong, too? It's really unusual looking.

Man No, I don't remember where I got the tie, but I make a point of buying all my suits when I go out of town. The suits at these local department stores are too expensive and, in my opinion, not very attractive.

Woman I know what you mean. I don't much like going shopping around here, either. The choices are not very good.

Questions 65 through 67 refer to the following conversation.

Man I'm going hiking in the mountains for my vacation.

Woman Hiking? That's energetic of you. After working as hard as you do, I would think you would want to spend a few weeks just lying on a sunny beach reading a good book.

Man I'm tired of lazy vacations by the sea. I like to be active when I take a vacation. I'm really looking forward to three weeks walking in the mountains.

Woman Wow! That's a long time. Are you leaving soon?

Man Yes, on Sunday. Just two days away. I can't wait.

Questions 68 through 70 refer to the following conversation.

Woman I think we've got the transportation plan worked out. We have four buses to take people from the hotel to the convention center. That should be enough, don't you think?

Man Yes, I think so. It takes five minutes to load one bus and ten minutes to make the trip, so we could plan to have one bus leave every fifteen minutes.

Woman That sounds like a good schedule. Each bus could make the round trip in thirty minutes, and no one would have to wait too long for a ride. Then we won't have to worry about anybody's ruffled feelings.

PART 4 (PAGES 53–55)

Questions 71 through 73 refer to the following news item.

City Hall officials have announced that City Hall will be open on Saturday this week in order to accommodate citizens who are filing their tax forms at the last minute. The Revenue Office will be open in the morning only, from eight A.M. until noon. Long lines are expected, so it is suggested that you arrive early in order to avoid them. You can also avoid lines by filing before Saturday. Send your tax return in by mail before the end of this week. Tax returns sent by mail must be postmarked on or before Saturday of this week in order to avoid late penalties.

Questions 74 through 76 refer to the following announcement.

Attention passengers. If you need ground transportation, look for the different colored signs as you exit the baggage claim area. Follow the blue signs for rental cars and hotel shuttles. Follow the red signs for access to public transportation, including the subway, city buses, and airport shuttles to other terminals. Fare and schedule information for public transportation is available just as you exit the terminal building. If you have left your car in an airport parking lot, follow the green signs for a shuttle to the east parking lot, or the orange signs for a shuttle to the west parking lot.

Questions 77 through 79 refer to the following announcement.

I would like to thank you all for turning out for this event on this beautiful Friday, and I hope you all enjoyed your lunch. I would like to extend a special thank you to the Barclay Hotel and especially to its fantastic kitchen staff for sponsoring our monthly luncheons. They never fail to provide us with a special dining experience. And now it's time to introduce our guest speaker for this afternoon. Please welcome Dr. Jenny Chang, author of the best-selling novel *Politics Isn't a Crime,* who will speak to us about her experiences doing research for this book.

Questions 80 through 82 refer to the following announcement.

All employees are required to wear an identification badge at all times. Lost badges must be reported immediately to your supervisor. A replacement badge will be requested for you, and a temporary badge will be issued for the interim. In cases of repeated badge loss, a replacement fee may be charged at the discretion of the security office. Please remember that all visitors must be accompanied at all times by employees with identification badges. Visitors without escorts will be asked by security personnel to leave the building. Help us enforce this security standard by reporting any unescorted persons to the security office. Thank you for your cooperation.

Questions 83 through 85 refer to the following advertisement.

The Spartan Golf Club announces the opening of its newest golf course. This modern course designed by professional golfers is only fifteen minutes from the city center. It is a complete eighteen-hole course with two full-time golf pros available for individual and group instruction. Like other Spartan Club courses, our newest one provides fully equipped locker rooms, a pro shop, and a café serving lunch and dinner daily. Only a few memberships are still available, so visit our downtown office soon to find out how you can join. Sign up for a full-year membership and save. A six-month membership is six hundred and fifty dollars, and a full year costs just eleven hundred dollars.

Questions 86 through 88 refer to the following weather report.

Good morning and welcome to another beautiful day. We've got perfect beach weather again today. The sun is shining, and it's going to be hot, hot, hot. If you haven't done so yet, then today's the day to take advantage of those ocean breezes, take in some sun, and play in the surf. Enjoy the good weather while you can, because it won't last long. A cold front moving into the area toward the end of the week will bring cloudy skies on Friday and nothing but rain, rain, rain on Saturday and Sunday. Since you'll be dusting off those old umbrellas in a few days, get out there today and enjoy the sun.

Questions 89 through 91 refer to the following news item.

Wilton K. Smith, the local business entrepreneur who was well-known to town residents for his many eccentricities, died at his home last night. He was ninety-three years old. Mr. Smith is survived by his son, Wilton K. Smith Jr., and two grandchildren. Don't expect his survivors to take over his business, however. Mr. Smith was estranged from his son and grandchildren for many years, and he left his entire estate to his dog, a spaniel named Charles. Man's best friend inherited over two million dollars. Will he continue his deceased owner's business, or invest it all in dog food? That remains to be seen. Funeral services for Mr. Smith will be held next Sunday at one o'clock at Brown's Funeral Home on Third Street. The dog is expected to attend.

Questions 92 through 94 refer to the following recorded announcement.

The Office of Motor Vehicles, providing services related to driver's licenses, motor vehicle registration, and motor vehicle inspection, is located at 124 State Street, right next to City Hall and within walking distance of bus routes 42 and 55. The office is open Monday through Friday, except for major holidays. If you want to renew your driver's license, you must come in between the hours of noon and four P.M. and report to the License Renewal Window. A twenty-five dollar fee will be charged. If you want to apply for a new license and take the written and driving tests, you may come in anytime between eight A.M. and four P.M. An appointment is not necessary. The fee for a new license is fifty dollars. Licensing fees are payable by credit card, personal check, or money order. Cash is not accepted.

Questions 95 through 97 refer to the following message.

Good morning. I'm calling regarding a problem with my order. I haven't received it yet. My name is Gina Rotelli and my order number is SBB-934. I made a big order of office equipment, including one computer monitor, one box of disks, and three ink cartridges for my laser printer. I also ordered two packages of printer paper and, let me see, oh yes, a box of manila envelopes and fifty ball-point pens. I was promised delivery within two weeks of the date I placed the order, but it still hasn't arrived. I placed it four weeks ago, on July 17th, to be exact. I paid for the items with my credit card, and the amount has been charged to my credit card bill. I don't want to pay the bill until this has been cleared up, so please check on this and call me today. My number is 555-0703. Thank you.

Questions 98 through 100 refer to the following news report.

The innovative computer company CompCo celebrated its opening today at its new facilities in the Montrose Park neighborhood of the city. As part of the celebration, CompCo gave a tour of its facilities to local dignitaries and hosted a banquet inside its new training center. CompCo has hired 100 employees who will start work at their new positions this week, and plans to hire fifty more before the end of the year. This is wonderful news for our city, which is still struggling after the closure of PC Computer Systems three years ago. Two hundred employees lost their jobs when PC left our city. The loss of businesses like PC has had a significant impact on the local economy. The city leaders are working to attract more technology businesses to the area and are currently negotiating a deal with the Intrax Company. The opening of CompCo is an optimistic start to reviving industry in our city.

Script
Test n° 3

PART 1 (PAGES 85–90)

Example:

(A) They're leaving the room.
(B) They're turning on the machine.
(C) They're standing near the table.
(D) They're reading the newspaper.

1. (A) The man is fishing.
(B) The sea is salty.
(C) The fish are for sale.
(D) The snow is turning to ice.

2. (A) They're serving drinks.
(B) They're picking their seats.
(C) They're cleaning the aisle.
(D) They're selling uniforms.

3. (A) Three people are on the plane.
(B) The people are getting off the train.
(C) The workers are out of stationery.
(D) No one is wearing a hat.

4. (A) He's using a knife and fork.
(B) He's operating heavy equipment.
(C) He's shredding paper.
(D) He's driving to work.

5. (A) The tables are set outdoors.
(B) The guests are at the banquet.
(C) The picnic is on the lawn.
(D) The chairs are against the wall.

6. (A) The travelers are checking in for their flight.
(B) The passengers are passing through security.
(C) The baggage handlers are weighing the bags.
(D) The tourists are boarding the train.

7. (A) The cars are in the parking lot.
(B) The bees are in the park.
(C) The barking dog is by the road.
(D) The motorist is at the stop sign.

8. (A) The car is being manufactured.
(B) The windows are being cleaned.
(C) The radio is being installed.
(D) The line is being drawn.

9. (A) They're turning off the TV.
(B) They're watching the monitor.
(C) They're buying a television set.
(D) They're looking through a catalog.

10. (A) The technicians are testing their telescopes.
(B) The scientists are working in the laboratory.
(C) The physicians are performing an operation.
(D) The soldiers are cleaning their uniforms.

PART 2 (PAGE 91)

Example:

Where is the meeting room?
(A) To meet the new director.
(B) It's the first room on the right.
(C) Yes, at two o'clock.

11. What time is she coming?
(A) It's six o'clock now.
(B) She'll be here any minute.
(C) She's combing her hair.

12. Where is the bank?
(A) The check is in the mail.
(B) It's next to the post office.
(C) The banquet is at the hotel.

13. When are you leaving for work?
(A) I'll leave after breakfast.
(B) I plan to retire next month.
(C) I've been working for ten years.

14. Who's on the telephone?
(A) That's Maria talking to her mother.
(B) It's my phone.
(C) I told everyone last week.

15. Why are we taking a bus?
(A) All of us have gone once.
(B) It's cheaper than a taxi.
(C) We walk too much.

16. What type of music is this?
(A) I didn't find any mistakes.
(B) She types fast.
(C) It's classical music.

17. How many oranges do you want?
(A) About five of us ordered wine.
(B) Give me half a dozen, please.
(C) I made arrangements for fifty people.

18. Where were you yesterday?
(A) You were gone yesterday.
(B) I was home all day.
(C) I'm going tomorrow.

19. Which of these books haven't you read?
(A) I haven't read the ones in French.
(B) I only read in the evening.
(C) Here are the books you must read.

20. What day did the guest arrive?
(A) The day after tomorrow.
(B) She arrived yesterday.
(C) You'll never guess who called.

21. When will the performance begin?
(A) The foreman will begin working tomorrow.
(B) The performance is too long.
(C) It always begins a few minutes late.

22. How often do we need to change the oil in the car?
(A) Every 3 months or every 3,000 miles.
(B) I changed it last week.
(C) I want to change the color of my car.

23. Who received the package in the mail?
(A) He looks young for his age.
(B) The receptionist opened the mail.
(C) The package was for me.

24. Can your assistant type this letter for me?
(A) I prefer handwritten letters.
(B) My assistant will send you a letter.
(C) He's too busy to type it now.

25. How many chairs are around the table?
(A) The four of us will sit down.
(B) There are only two chairs.
(C) The table is round.

26. It's really cold in here.
(A) Put on a sweater.
(B) He's not that old.
(C) I keep it in here.

27. I don't have enough change for the bus fare.
(A) The weather will be fair all week.
(B) I can lend you some money.
(C) It isn't a long ride.

28. Where is your class meeting?
(A) We're all eating in the cafeteria.
(B) No, it's not made of glass.
(C) The class is meeting in room 300.

29. My apartment is on the tenth floor.
(A) This is the right department.
(B) His door is the one on the left.
(C) You must get a good view from there.

30. Why is the radio on?
(A) It's on the bookcase.
(B) We want to hear the news.
(C) Because no one is ready.

31. How many pencils are in the drawer?
(A) It's in the bottom drawer.
(B) She's drawing with a pen.
(C) There are about a dozen.

32. Where is the golf course?
(A) I play golf in the morning.
(B) The course is two miles from here.
(C) Because it's near the Gulf of Thailand.

33. When did the plane take off?
(A) It took off on time.
(B) Take off that shirt now.
(C) We'll leave shortly.

34. What's the fastest way to get downtown?
(A) Traffic is slow during rush hour.
(B) The tallest building is downtown.
(C) At this time of day, I'd take the subway.

35. How far is the restaurant from here?
(A) I'm not hungry.
(B) It's about two blocks.
(C) Because it serves good food.

36. Why are you so tired?
(A) I didn't sleep last night.
(B) The tire needs air.
(C) We're required to wear ties at work.

37. The elevator is broken again.
(A) We'll have to take the stairs.
(B) He hasn't spoken yet.
(C) Yes, there are eleven.

38. The food in this restaurant is very expensive.
(A) I turned in my expense report yesterday.
(B) Yes, but it's really delicious.
(C) The waitress will bring you some water.

39. Whose desk is near the window?
(A) My desk is by the door.
(B) The one by the window is Bob's desk.
(C) I'll close the window.

40. What shall we do first?
(A) I was the last one here.
(B) I need a towel.
(C) Let's clean up the office first.

PART 3 (PAGES 92–94)

Questions 41 through 43 refer to the following conversation.

Woman There wasn't room in the lot next door, so I parked in the garage across the street, but I can't believe how expensive it is. They're charging me five dollars an hour.

Man That's really not much for parking around here. Most places charge more than that. Anyhow, let's get moving. It's late.

Woman What time does the concert start?

Man The musicians will start playing in about two minutes. Come on. Walk fast! I want to get there before the music begins.

Questions 44 through 46 refer to the following conversation.

Woman You didn't call last week like you promised. I hope you weren't sick.

Man No, I'm sorry. It must have just slipped my mind.

Woman Well, if you had called, I would have invited you to my party last Saturday.

Man Oh, that's right. It was your birthday! And I missed your party. Let me make it up to you. I'll take you out to dinner tonight. We'll go to that new French restaurant downtown.

Woman Why, thank you. That's very sweet of you. It sounds lovely.

Questions 47 through 49 refer to the following conversation.

Man Were you home last night? Did you watch TV?

Woman No, I was out having dinner with some friends. Did I miss a good program?

Man Yes, there's a great comedy on every Wednesday at six. You know, that one that everyone is always talking about. It's really funny.

Woman I know the one you mean, but I've never had the chance to see it. Six o'clock is a bit early for me to watch TV. I usually don't get home until seven.

Questions 50 through 52 refer to the following conversation.

Man We only grow vegetables here. It's a small place, and we don't really have room to expand into other crops like fruit trees or flowers. But it's a nice little business.

Woman Yes, it seems like you've got a good thing going here. How long have you been running this place?

Man For 13 years. Farming's not an easy life, but it sure beats getting in the car and driving to an office every day like I used to do.

Woman You don't have to tell me! I'm starting to get sick of that life, too. Living out here in the country is starting to look like a much healthier lifestyle to me.

Questions 53 through 55 refer to the following conversation.

Man This is the most boring play I have ever seen. Who told us to come see it?

Woman I really don't remember, but we don't have to stay to the end if you don't like it. We can leave if you really want to.

Man All right. Let's leave now before I fall asleep and start snoring.

Woman All right, all right, calm down, we'll go. Though I really think it's a shame to waste these seventy-five dollar tickets.

Man What? You paid that much for us to see this play? Next time, why don't we just rent a movie for two-fifty and stay home. I'm sure I'll enjoy that a lot more.

Questions 56 through 58 refer to the following conversation.

Woman All right, now. Before you step up to the tee, take one practice swing.

Man I know. And keep my eye on the ball. I remember everything you've told me.

Woman Good. And don't throw your club. That won't help matters at all. If you miss the ball, just stay calm and try again. You don't want to lose your concentration, so it's really important to stay calm.

Man All right, all right. I get it. Will you be quiet now so I can try hitting the ball?

Questions 59 through 61 refer to the following conversation.

Man I guess I should leave for the airport soon. My plane takes off at three-thirty, and I'm supposed to be there at least an hour ahead of time.

Woman You'd better get going, then. It's almost one o'clock. If you leave now, the subway should get you there in plenty of time.

Man Yes, but I don't think I want to go on the subway with all my luggage. I'll take a taxi instead. It'll cost more, but I think it's better.

Woman You're right. It'll be much easier for you that way. You'll be back Sunday morning, right? I can pick you up at the airport then if you want me to.

Questions 62 through 64 refer to the following conversation.

Woman Is this elevator going up or down?

Man It's going up. What floor would you like, please?

Woman I need the furniture department on floor 7. And hurry. There's a great sale there today, and I don't want to miss it. I'm planning to refurnish my whole apartment.

Man Relax. The sale lasts all week. It started on Monday and won't be over until Friday, and you'll be there in less than a minute.

Questions 65 through 67 refer to the following conversation.

Man Come on, stop it, don't get me wet. I'm really not in the mood for a swim.

Woman You'll like it once you get in. I promise. Come on, I'll race you across the pool.

Man I really don't want to. I'm too cold to get in the water. You go ahead without me.

Woman Oh, just try it once. It's fun. Once you start moving, you'll warm up.

Man I mean it. I don't want to. Go on and enjoy yourself and I'll meet you back at the car.

Questions 68 through 70 refer to the following conversation.

Woman You two go in your car. I know where the restaurant is, so you can follow me.

Man OK, but don't drive too fast. I don't want to lose you on the road. We don't have to be there for another fifteen minutes, anyhow.

Woman Don't worry. I'll drive really slowly so you won't get lost. There's no parking at the restaurant, so you should try to park in front of the bookstore. You can usually find a space there.

Man I don't want to park on the street. Isn't there a garage at the hotel?

Woman Yes, I think there is, but there's a charge for parking there, and I'm sure it isn't cheap. But go ahead and put your car there if you want.

PART 4 (PAGES 95–97)

Questions 71 through 73 refer to the following weather report.

It's another hot and humid summer day. We can expect warm and sunny weather for most of the morning, but be prepared for the clouds that will roll in before noon. There will be rain showers starting in the early afternoon, but don't despair, the skies will clear up again by early evening, and we should enjoy pleasantly cool temperatures overnight. That will be a welcome relief from the high temperatures we have been experiencing lately. There will be more of the same weather tomorrow and for the rest of the week, with sunny mornings and cloudy, rainy afternoons. So enjoy the few hours of early sunshine while you can.

Questions 74 through 76 refer to the following recorded announcement.

You have reached the dental office of Dr. Richard Miller. If this is an emergency, please hang up and dial 800-555-3212, and an emergency operator will assist you. Our office hours are from eight thirty A.M. until four P.M. Monday through Thursday. The office is closed on Friday. If you wish to make an appointment, please call again during our regular office hours. If you wish to leave a message for Dr. Miller, please wait for the beep, then begin recording your message. If you wish to speak directly with the doctor, please leave a message and he will call you back as soon as possible.

Questions 77 through 79 refer to the following news report.

The popular café Stonebark has announced that it will be expanding its business into other countries. The first overseas branch will open in Melbourne on March 1st. More Stonebark openings will soon follow in other locations throughout Australia and New Zealand. Stonebark also plans to open cafés in several Asian countries before the end of the year. In order to generate more interest in their business, Stonebark has announced a monthly contest for its customers. Starting in April, Stonebark customers will be able to visit the company's website to vote for their favorite Stonebark coffee flavor. Each month, the winning flavor will be featured at discount prices in Stonebark cafés throughout the country. Stonebark is the fastest-growing specialty coffee chain in the country and is well posed to become an international favorite in the near future, as well.

Questions 80 through 82 refer to the following advertisement.

Rent-A-Computer lets you rent a computer by the day, month, or year, so that you can have your computer for the exact amount of time that you need it. We carry all brands and models of computers. Whether you need a computer for home, school, or office use, we can help you find the one that best suits your needs. Short-term leasing contracts are available, too. Need help getting your computer set up? All our contracts include initial set up and a free troubleshooting hotline. Do you want to own your own computer? We also sell refurbished computers at a price you can afford. Visit us at the Crystaltown Mall to find out what we can do for you, and take a computer home with you today. We're open Monday through Saturday from 10:30 A.M. until 8:30 P.M.

Questions 83 through 85 refer to the following news item.

Seismologists report that an earthquake was recorded in the northern islands of Japan today at approximately 6:30 A.M. Tremors were felt as far away as Hawaii. This is the third earthquake that has occurred in that area since the beginning of this year. The last one occurred just two months ago. Fortunately, no one was reported hurt, and there was little damage to property. According to scientists, this recent series of minor tremors indicate that a more serious incident could occur in that area in the near future.

Questions 86 through 88 refer to the following announcement.

Friendly Skies flight 58 departing for Honolulu and San Francisco is now ready for boarding. All passengers who have not already done so should proceed through passport control and report immediately to gate 16. Please have your ticket ready to show the gate attendant. Remember, you may have one small carry-on bag only. Passengers with extra baggage will be required to check it with the gate attendant before boarding the plane. Passengers with small children may go to the head of the line.

Questions 89 through 91 refer to the following announcement.

Attention employees. Employee parking is permitted on the second and third levels of the parking garage. You must have a parking sticker clearly displayed on the front left windshield of your car in order to park there. Parking stickers are available free of charge from the security office upon presentation of your employee identification card. Cars without parking stickers or with improperly displayed stickers will be ticketed and towed. Please take note of the following: the yellow spaces near the door are reserved for management, and the blue spaces are for all other employees. The red spaces are reserved for maintenance vehicles. Employees or visitors parking in the red spaces with or without parking stickers will have their cars ticketed and towed.

Questions 92 through 94 refer to the following announcement.

On your visit, you will see the Monument of Independence. Coming up on your left is the United Nations Building, our next stop. While touring the building, please stay with your guide, and please be back on the bus by two o'clock. It is important to return on time. We will not be able to wait for latecomers. If you are left behind, you will be responsible for returning to the hotel on your own. The bus will leave at exactly two o'clock in order to arrive at our next stop, the historic City Hall building, by 2:30. We will spend three hours there enjoying the architecture and learning about the building's history. There will also be time for browsing the gift shop. We will leave City Hall at exactly 5:30 for dinner at the renowned downtown restaurant Bavaria.

Questions 95 through 97 refer to the following advertisement.

Barry's Bookstore is going out of business. This is our final month, and everything in the store must go! Come in today for the most amazing bargains you've ever seen. You'll find our lowest prices ever on school texts, books, magazines, calendars, CDs, DVDs, and more. All paperback books are half off. So hurry on down to Barry's before we are gone forever. We're located downtown, at the corner of Queen Street and Trafalgar Road, one block from the Queen Street subway station. Our special holiday hours are nine A.M. to nine P.M. Monday through Friday, and nine A.M. to midnight on Saturday. Closed on Sunday.

Questions 98 through 100 refer to the following weather report.

This is your local weather update with meteorologist Chris Lee. We can look forward to a beautiful evening, with warm temperatures and a lovely sunset. Sunset will occur at 8:30, and the beach is the perfect place to watch it. It's better to stay on shore, though. There is a fog warning out for small boats tonight. A light fog will roll in just after sunset and stay with us all night. The sun rises tomorrow morning at 5:45. Light winds in the morning will blow the fog out to sea, so we'll enjoy sunshine and more warm temperatures tomorrow afternoon. Take advantage of the nice weather now because rain is predicted for later in the week.

Script
Test n° 4

Part 1 (pages 125–130)

Example:

(A) They're leaving the room.
(B) They're turning on the machine.
(C) They're standing near the table.
(D) They're reading the newspaper.

1. (A) She's wearing protective clothing.
(B) She's buying a new hat.
(C) She's storing food in jars.
(D) She's dressing for a party.

2. (A) The water glass is empty.
(B) The swimmers are racing.
(C) The man is cleaning the pool.
(D) The guest is relaxing by the pool.

3. (A) The man is putting the suitcase into the trunk.
(B) The woman is walking behind the man.
(C) The couple is getting out of the car.
(D) The bags are being weighed.

4. (A) She's closing the notebook.
(B) She's filling out a form.
(C) She's checking the bookshelves.
(D) She's cleaning the table.

5. (A) The cord is being cut.
(B) The telephone booth is on the corner.
(C) The woman is on the phone.
(D) The tourist is studying the map.

6. (A) The panes are in the frames.
(B) The planes are at their gates.
(C) The trains are in the station.
(D) The cranes are on the wharf.

7. (A) He's trying to catch a mouse.
(B) He's holding a pad of paper.
(C) He's examining his eyes.
(D) He's working at his computer.

8. (A) The ferry is crossing the water.
(B) The passengers are boarding at the pier.
(C) The sailboat is in the harbor.
(D) The tanker is in dry dock.

9. (A) The customers are waiting for a table.
(B) The people are reading their newspapers.
(C) The library is open at night.
(D) The menus are being printed.

10. (A) He's pouring a cup of coffee.
(B) He's emptying his pockets.
(C) He's spilling the liquid.
(D) He's brewing a pot of coffee.

Part 2 (page 131)

Example:

Where is the meeting room?
(A) To meet the new director.
(B) It's the first room on the right.
(C) Yes, at two o'clock.

11. What time will the bank open?
(A) It opens at 8 A.M.
(B) The door is open.
(C) The bank has a large clock.

12. I come to this park a lot.
(A) I always use this parking lot.
(B) Me too. I like to be outside.
(C) I don't go out when it's dark.

13. Why are you walking so quickly?
(A) Sue talks very fast.
(B) I'm late for a meeting.
(C) They enjoy walking.

14. Who may I say is calling?
(A) My name is Ralph Smith.
(B) You're calling my mother.
(C) You didn't tell me who called.

15. When do you expect your visitor?
(A) Her visit was too short.
(B) He should arrive any minute.
(C) I'll visit there next week.

16. Whose car shall we take?
(A) It's shallow.
(B) We took the bus.
(C) Let's take my car.

17. How hungry are you?
(A) Not very, but I could eat.
(B) I've never been to Hungary.
(C) Because I haven't eaten.

18. Mr. Sato called while you were out.
(A) Thanks. I'll call him back later.
(B) The phone needs repairs.
(C) I put the file over there.

19. Do I have any messages?
(A) Yes, your wife called at noon.
(B) I had a massage.
(C) No one has seen us for ages.

20. Why is the ground wet?
(A) He hasn't grown up yet.
(B) It rained all morning.
(C) Because it's round.

21. Where are the invoices?
(A) They're in the files.
(B) Her voice is low.
(C) The invoice is paid.

22. Why don't you take a vacation?
(A) I'll take them with me.
(B) I'm too busy at work.
(C) I take public transportation.

23. It's supposed to rain tomorrow.
(A) I never take the train.
(B) Yes, we can talk again tomorrow.
(C) Then it won't be a good day for the beach.

24. What color will you paint the walls?
(A) I think green's a good color.
(B) Because he painted it blue.
(C) He read the poster on the wall.

25. Do any of you like sugar with your coffee?
(A) He doesn't like cigars.
(B) We all like sugar with our coffee.
(C) Sugar's very sweet.

26. How much time will it take to finish the building?
(A) The architect thinks about three more months.
(B) The building is thirty stories high.
(C) We'll be here about six o'clock.

27. Whose newspaper is on the table?
(A) The table is by the window.
(B) It's our new table.
(C) That newspaper belongs to me.

28. Did the mail come yet?
(A) No, we'll eat later.
(B) Yes, the mail is on your desk.
(C) Nobody came this morning.

29. Ms. Green's plane arrives at three o'clock this afternoon.
(A) I'll pick her up at the airport.
(B) I already have my ticket.
(C) I think she looks the same.

30. Why are you working late?
(A) You never work at night.
(B) Because my work is finished.
(C) I have to finish this report.

31. Where should the applicants wait?
(A) Let them sit in my office.
(B) We applied for a job here.
(C) They waited for over an hour.

32. Can you recommend a good hotel?
(A) I don't have a reservation.
(B) That's not good enough.
(C) I like the new hotel by the river.

33. Which do you prefer, a pen or a pencil?
(A) My pencil needs sharpening.
(B) I prefer to write with a pen.
(C) This pen writes well.

34. This copy machine is always breaking down.
(A) It's time for a coffee break.
(B) Maybe we should buy a new one.
(C) There's one in town.

35. How many employees do you have?
(A) I have nine employees.
(B) My employees work very hard.
(C) Because we pay well.

36. Where did you leave your coat?
(A) I left it on the bus.
(B) I bought my coat last year.
(C) Leave your coat at the door.

37. When will the weather get warmer?
(A) They'll get her one tomorrow.
(B) Whenever she wants.
(C) Not until summer.

38. Who's copying the report?
(A) The reporter asked the questions.
(B) The clerk is making five copies.
(C) The copyright date is 2003.

39. Is your chair comfortable?
(A) No, it's very uncomfortable.
(B) Yes, the chairman is available.
(C) He's neither fair nor capable.

40. How far is your office from here?
(A) Not bad, thank you.
(B) It's only about a mile.
(C) I can hear very well.

PART 3 (PAGES 132–134)

Questions 41 through 43 refer to the following conversation.

Man Could you tell me where you keep the paper cups? I've looked everywhere, but I can't seem to find them.

Woman There should be some in the cabinet over the sink. That's where we usually keep them.

Man I already looked there. You must be all out of cups. I guess I'll have to go down to the coffee shop and get a cup of tea there.

Woman Oh, you wanted hot drink cups, not water cups. I have some right here in the supply closet. There's sugar in here, too, if you want it, and there's milk in the refrigerator.

Man OK, great. Thanks. Now, is there something I can use to heat the water up in?

Questions 44 through 46 refer to the following conversation.

Woman Here's your key, Mr. Smith. You're in room three ten on the third floor. The elevator is just over there. Oh, and check-out time tomorrow is at noon.

Man That won't be a problem. I'll need to leave here by 5:30 in the morning to catch an early flight.

Woman Will you need a wake-up call, then?

Man Yes, please. Could you have someone call me at 4:45? And since I'm leaving so early, I'll just go ahead and settle my bill now.

Questions 47 through 49 refer to the following conversation.

Man I know I'm late. I'm sorry. I left home early, but traffic was tied up all over the city because of the weather, and my bus was late again.

Woman That may be, but this has really gone too far. It's the third time this month that you've been late. It's getting to be a bad habit with you.

Man I know. I'm sorry. I'll come on time tomorrow, even if it means getting up at five. I promise I'll be on time for the rest of the week.

Woman Let's hope so because if this happens again, we'll have to do something about it.

Questions 50 through 52 refer to the following conversation.

Woman I need a screwdriver. Do you mind if I borrow yours?

Man Go right ahead. It's in my toolbox in the closet, but please don't forget to return it soon. I don't want to lose it, and I'll need to use it later, anyhow.

Woman Don't worry. You'll have it back before lunch. I just need it for a few minutes to tighten up some screws on this bookshelf.

Man Just put it on my desk when you're done. I'll use it to fix that squeaky chair before I go home tonight.

Questions 53 through 55 refer to the following conversation.

Man We always start our vacation the first week of August, and we spend the whole month out of town. We've been doing this for years.

Woman You're lucky you can take such a nice long vacation. Two or three weeks really isn't enough, is it?

Man No, it isn't. We're renting a house by the lake this time. I'm really looking forward to swimming everyday.

Woman Well, to each his own, I guess. I like to spend my vacations traveling to different cities. I like to be in a different place each day.

Man I find it more relaxing to stay in just one place. I remember when I was young, we always spent vacations at the lake. That's why I like to go there now.

Questions 56 through 58 refer to the following conversation.

Woman Could you help me choose some long-sleeved shirts for my husband? He takes a size sixteen. It's for his birthday, so I'd like to find something really nice.

Man Would you be interested in these? They're one-hundred percent cotton, and look how nice the details are. They're on sale this week for just 25 dollars apiece. That's a real bargain for shirts as nicely made as these.

Woman They're just right. That stitching around the cuffs and collars is very nice. I'll take two of the gray ones.

Questions 59 through 61 refer to the following conversation.

Man OK, now get in the left lane because you'll have to turn left at the next intersection. That's the street that goes toward the concert hall.

Woman But I can't turn left there. It's one way going to the right. Don't you see the sign?

Man Well, now what are we going to do? We don't have time to be driving around in circles. It's already 6:45, and the concert starts in 15 minutes. I told you we should've left home earlier.

Woman Well, look, there's an open space right here on the corner. Let's just park here and walk. It's not far. We can walk it in ten minutes easily.

Questions 62 through 64 refer to the following conversation.

Woman We ordered those new program brochures over a week ago, didn't we? Haven't they come back from the printer yet?

Man Yes, they have. They got here this morning. They're in those two white boxes on the floor of the supply room.

Woman Good. They got here just in time. I have to mail a hundred of them to Singapore this afternoon so that they'll have them in time for their conference.

Man Well, you'll find plenty there. We ordered a thousand.

Questions 65 through 67 refer to the following conversation.

Man Wendy, it's three o'clock. The meeting was at two. Do you realize that's the second meeting you've missed this week? What's going on with you?

Woman Why didn't you call me this morning to remind me that it was today? You know what a terrible memory I have, and I have so much on my mind right now with this project deadline.

Man I called six times, but I couldn't get through. Your line was busy all morning. Anyhow, the next meeting is on Friday, and you'd better be there.

Woman I will be if you call me Thursday to remind me about it.

Questions 68 through 70 refer to the following conversation.

Man Do you need me to do something for you? I'm still eating breakfast.

Woman Well, after you finish eating, can you drive me to school?

Man I don't see why you can't walk. It's a warm sunny day, and you could use the fresh air and exercise.

Woman Yes, it's a nice day now, but it might rain later. I heard it on the weather report.

Man Well, then, you'll just walk to school now, and if it rains later, you can always take a bus home.

PART 4 (PAGES 135–137)

Questions 71 through 73 refer to the following weather report.

In a noon bulletin, the Weather Center at the Municipal Airport reported that the airport had been closed this morning due to the heavy fog that rolled in overnight. The fog is expected to lift by early evening when cooler air moves into the area, and planes will be allowed to take off and land then. Many of today's flights have been canceled. Passengers who have tickets on a flight today should call their airline before leaving for the airport to find out whether their flight has been canceled. More poor weather conditions are expected over the next few days, and all people with air travel plans this week are advised to contact their airline to find out the status of their flights.

Questions 74 through 76 refer to the following announcement.

Attention passengers. The 6:50 A.M. nonstop express train from Union Station Washington to Penn Station New York is now ready for boarding. This is a two-hour forty-minute trip and the train is due to arrive in Penn Station at nine-thirty A.M. All passengers with tickets for the six-fifty nonstop express train to New York, please line up at Gate Ten. This is an all-reserved train. Passengers without prepaid reservations will not be allowed to board. Passengers may check their excess luggage at the gate at no extra charge. Please have your ticket ready to show to the gate attendant.

Questions 77 through 79 refer to the following message.

Thank you for calling the City Convention Bureau's hotel hotline, providing out-of-town visitors with local hotel information and a reservation service with participating hotels. We are sorry to inform our callers that all hotels are full for the period from August 15 through August 30. We regret the inconvenience. If you would like to be put on a hotel waiting list, at the sound of the tone please leave your name, phone number, dates you plan to visit the city, and the number of people in your party. We will contact you if a room that fits your needs becomes available. Thank you.

Questions 80 through 82 refer to the following announcement.

Thank you, Ms. Johnson, for your very informative report. It covered the topic quite thoroughly. I know many of you have questions for Ms. Johnson, but it's about 10:30 now, and we still have several points to cover before we break for lunch. So, before we continue with the next part of our board meeting and the question-and-answer period, why don't we take a short coffee break? Coffee and tea and fruit and pastries are available in the next room. We'll resume in fifteen minutes, and following a short question and answer period with Ms. Johnson, we'll hear Mr. Kim's report on the Harbor Project. I believe he has a slideshow to go along with his report, so it should be quite interesting.

Questions 83 through 85 refer to the following news item.

Following last Monday's heavy storm in the Wilmington Valley, flood waters from the Wilmington River have risen over twenty feet. Thousands of families have been evacuated from the region and are living with relatives and in shelters throughout the state. Fortunately, no loss of life has been reported, but property damage is estimated to be in the millions. The downtown districts of both Riverside and Wilmington Falls are completely flooded, and the areas have been closed to all visitors. It is doubtful whether the evacuees will be able to return to their homes any time soon. The president will tour the area on Friday. He will speak to the nation about the situation during his regular Saturday address.

Questions 86 through 88 refer to the following advertisement.

Is your house looking drab? Does it need a makeover? Carlos's Painting and Decorating can make your home look like new. We specialize in both interior and exterior painting. We also provide decorative painting services such as stenciling and marblizing. We help you choose colors and designs to suit your needs and tastes, and we supply all the paint. Let Carlos's Painting and Decorating turn your house into someplace special. Ask your neighbors; they probably use us. You can count on our experience. We've been painting homes in this city for 13 years. Don't wait. Call us today.

Questions 89 through 91 refer to the following special announcement.

Ladies and gentlemen, this is your captain speaking. Because of the large number of planes waiting to take off, twenty-five to be exact, we can expect to sit on the runway for a good fifteen minutes or so. I ask you all to be patient, and we'll be airborne soon. In the meantime, please remain in your seats. Turn off your cell phones and obey the no-smoking sign. Approximately 20 minutes after take-off, the flight attendants will begin serving drinks. In order to keep you waiting no longer than necessary, they will be coming around the cabin now to take your order. Thank you for your patience.

Questions 92 through 94 refer to the following recorded announcement.

Hello. You have reached the Center for the Performing Arts. Tonight in the small Concert Hall is the Young Musicians Recital at 8 P.M. In the large Concert Hall is the New Company Orchestra at 7:30. For ticket information, please press 1. For directions to the Center, press 2. To leave a message for any of the Center staff, press 3. To get on our mailing list to receive our monthly schedules, wait until you hear the beep at the end of this message. Then speak your name and address slowly and clearly. Press the pound sign when you are finished.

Questions 95 through 97 refer to the following weather report.

Welcome to the Wednesday evening weather report. Tonight will be clear and cold, followed by sunny skies tomorrow. Skies will remain clear through Thursday night and into Friday. Unfortunately, this spell of pleasant weather will end soon. Heavy snows are expected this weekend, with snow beginning to fall late Friday evening before midnight. Snow will continue through Saturday morning. Accumulations of 10 to 12 inches are expected before the snow ends late Saturday afternoon. Listeners are advised not to travel unless absolutely necessary. Make sure you have plenty of water and food on hand, as well as candles and flashlights in case of power outages. Relax, stay home, and enjoy the snow! Stay tuned to this station for periodic updates on weather conditions.

Questions 98 through 100 refer to the following announcement.

Welcome to our annual conference. Before we get started with this morning's program, we need to go over some changes to the schedule. Our first group speaker will begin her presentation thirty minutes later than the original time. She will now speak at nine-fifteen, instead of at eight forty-five, in our main meeting room. At twelve o'clock, lunch will be served in the Red River Room, while the Blue Mountain Room will be used for dinner. This evening, as listed in your pre-printed schedules, you may choose to attend another presentation or see a play. We have also just added another activity for your entertainment, dancing at Club Central. Music will be performed by the popular local band Little Joe and the Wildcats.Tickets may be purchased from the registration table during lunch.

Solutions

Solutions Test n° 1

Partie 1 (pages 3–8)

Remarque : la bonne réponse est signalée en premier.

Exemple :

(A) They're leaving the room.
(B) They're turning on the machine.
(C) They're standing near the table.
(D) They're reading the newspaper.

1. (A) Le camion de ravitaillement se trouve près de l'avion. La réponse (B) est incorrecte car le réservoir à kérosène est peut-être bas (*low*), mais l'avion ne vole pas bas. La réponse joue également sur la confusion entre les sons proches *crane* et *plane*. La réponse (C) joue sur la confusion entre les sons proches plan et plane et associe le mot fuel. La réponse (D) joue sur la confusion entre les sons proches *playing* et *plane* et entre *jet* et *wet*.

2. (C) Le technicien vérifie les tableaux et appuie sur des touches pour s'assurer que les systèmes fonctionnent. Les réponses (A), (B) et (D) indiquent des occupations et des lieux erronés.

3. (B) Le narrateur s'adresse au groupe. La réponse (A) est incorrecte car l'auditoire écoute le narrateur et pas un concert. La réponse (C) indique un contexte différent : l'auditoire est bien constitué d'employés, mais ils sont assis et ne retournent pas au travail. La réponse (D) est hors contexte : il n'y a pas de musiciens formant un orchestre, ni de chef d'orchestre.

4. (D) Les personnes se serrent la main. La réponse (A) joue sur la confusion entre *rubbing their fingers* et *shaking hands*. La réponse (B) ne décrit pas la bonne action et n'évoque pas la bonne partie du corps. La réponse (C) joue sur la confusion entre les sons proches *band* et *hand*.

5. (D) Le formateur est en face du groupe. La réponse (A) joue sur la confusion entre les sons proches *conductor* et *instructor* et les mots proches *train* et *trainer*. La réponse (B) joue sur la confusion entre le mot *course*, qui désigne l'itinéraire d'un bateau (associé au mot *captain*), et le mot *course* qui désigne une formation. La réponse (C) associe *teacher* et *trainer* et est incorrecte parce que la femme se tient près d'un tableau et non derrière un bureau.

6. (C) Les coffres à bagages du bus sont ouverts. Les réponses (A) et (B) sont hors contexte. La réponse (D) est incorrecte parce que ce sont des coffres (*bins*) qui sont vides, pas des boîtes (*boxes*).

7. (B) De la fumée sort de la cheminée. La réponse (A) joue sur la confusion entre les mots *fireplace* et *chimney*, qui désignent deux choses distinctes. La réponse (C) est incorrecte parce que c'est de la fumée qui sort de la cheminée et non du feu qui sort d'un gratte-ciel. La réponse (D) joue sur la confusion entre les mots proches *fired* (être mis à la porte) et *fire* (du feu) en associant *fire* et *smoke*.

8. (B) Les personnes sont en train de discuter. La réponse (A) est incorrecte parce qu'il y a effectivement des tasses à café mais que personne n'est en train de faire du café. La réponse (C) reprend le mot *cups*, qui désigne les tasses qui sont sur la table. La réponse (D) est incorrecte parce qu'ils ne sont pas en train d'utiliser une calculatrice.

9. (B) Le serveur est en train de nettoyer la table. La réponse (A) joue sur la confusion entre les locutions proches *buying an umbrella* et *by an umbrella*. La réponse (C) désigne une activité possible pour un serveur, mais qui n'est pas celle du serveur sur la photo. La réponse (D) joue sur la confusion entre les mots proches *waiting* et *waiter*, et *restroom* et *restaurant*.

10. (D) Un voyageur est assis sur une valise sur un quai de gare en attendant son train. La réponse (A) joue sur la confusion entre les sons proches *train* et *trainer* et reprend le mot *watch* qui correspond à ce que l'homme est en train de regarder. La réponse (B) associe les mots *tourist* et *bag*, mais l'homme regarde sa montre et non son sac. La réponse (C) joue sur la confusion entre les mots *washing* et *watching*, et l'homme soulève sa main (*hand*) pour regarder l'heure. Il n'est probablement pas pilote d'avion.

PARTIE 2 (PAGE 9)

Remarque : la bonne réponse est signalée en premier.

Exemple :

Where is the meeting room?
(A) To meet the new director.
(B) It's the first room on the right.
(C) Yes, at two o'clock.

11. (A) *How about the front row* suggère un emplacement où s'asseoir. La réponse (B) correspond à la question *when*, non à la question *where*. La réponse (C) joue sur la confusion entre les mots proches *sit* et *it*.

12. (A) *It is. I eat here often.* La seconde personne qui parle est d'accord pour dire que c'est un bon restaurant. La réponse (B) joue sur la confusion entre *rest* et *restaurant*. La réponse (C) joue sur la confusion entre les sons proches *late* et *great*.

13. (A) *It costs a hundred thirty dollars* répond à la question *how much*. Les réponses (B) et (C) reprennent le mot *suit* mais ne correspondent pas à la question *how much*.

14. (C) *My secretary took the message* répond à la question de savoir *who took it*. Les réponses (A) et (B) reprennent les mots *phone* et *telephone* mais ne renvoient pas à la question.

15. (A) *I'll have dinner about 6 P.M.* répond à la question *what time* en employant le sens futur du présent progressif *are eating*. La réponse (B) associe *dined* et *dinner*. La réponse (C) reprend le mot *dinner* mais ne correspond pas à la question.

16. (C) *Yes, it came an hour ago* répond à la question *has the mail arrived* en indiquant quand l'action a eu lieu. La réponse (A) joue sur la confusion entre les sons similaires *jet* et *yet*. La réponse (B) joue sur la confusion entre les sons similaires *failed* et *mail*.

17. (C) *It'll probably rain soon.* La deuxième personne qui parle conclut que, le ciel étant chargé de nuages, il va pleuvoir. La réponse (A) confond *crowded* avec le mot à consonance proche *cloudy*. La réponse (B) joue sur la confusion entre *guy* et le mot à consonance proche *sky*.

18. (B) *I hoped my aunt would come* répond à la question *who did you expect*. La réponse (A) joue sur la confusion entre les sons proches *accept* et *expect*. La réponse (C) joue sur la confusion entre les sons proches *suspect* et *expect*, et entre *came* et *come*.

19. (A) *It's at the end of the hall* répond à la question *where*. Les réponses (B) et (C) reprennent le mot *accountant* mais ne correspondent pas à la question.

20. (B) *There are about fifteen* répond à la question *how many*. La réponse (A) reprend le mot *class* mais ne correspond pas à la question. La réponse (C) reprend le mot *students* mais ne correspond pas à la question..

21. (C) *She only reads business magazines* répond à la question *which magazines does she read*. La réponse (A) contient le mot *magazine* mais ne correspond pas à une question de type *which*. La réponse (B) joue sur la confusion entre la prononciation de *read* au passé et celle de *read* au présent.

22. (A) *Then I'll call back another time.* Dans la mesure où M. Williams n'est pas dans son bureau maintenant, la personne qui parle décide de rappeler ultérieurement. La réponse (B) fait une association entre *works* et *office*. La réponse (C) reprend le mot *office*.

23. (B) *No, it won't* répond à la question *will it be finished by eight o'clock*. La réponse (A) reprend *o'clock*. La réponse (C) joue sur la confusion entre les sons proches *reporter* et *report*.

24. (A) *Because* indique généralement une raison après une question comprenant le mot *why*. La réponse (B) joue sur la confusion entre les sons proches *get* (recevoir) et *get up* (se lever). La réponse (C) reprend le mot *early*, mais le verbe est au passé et le sujet est *you*, pas *I*.

25. (C) *No, I'd prefer a salad* est une réponse polie à la question posée. La réponse (A) joue sur la confusion entre les sons proches *thinner* et *dinner*. La réponse (B) renvoie à la question *when did you have dinner*.

26. (A) *I learned when I was young* répond à la question *when*. La réponse (B) reprend le mot *swim* mais est au présent. La réponse (C) joue sur la confusion entre les sons proches *learned* et *learn* mais ne correspond pas à la question.

27. (B) *About three thousand dollars* répond à la question *how much*. La réponse (A) contient *because*, qui sert généralement à répondre à une question de type *why*. La réponse (C) reprend le mot *car* mais ne correspond pas à la question.

28. (C) *Because* sert généralement à répondre à une question de type *why*. La réponse (A) contient le mot *shirt* mais ne correspond pas à une question de type *why*. La réponse (B) joue sur la confusion entre les mots *change* (pièces de monnaie) et *change* (changer).

29. (C) *Western film* désigne un genre de film. La réponse (A) joue sur la confusion entre les mots *about* (environ, pour une notion de temps) et *about* (à propos de). La réponse (B) joue sur la confusion entre les sons proches *moved* et *movie*.

30. (A) *I'm so happy to hear that*. La seconde personne qui parle est heureuse d'apprendre que la première a trouvé une bonne situation. La réponse (B) utilise le mot *love* dans un contexte différent. La réponse (C) joue sur la confusion entre les mots à consonance proche *above* et *love*.

31. (A) *She left at noon* répond à la question de savoir quand (*when)* le médecin est parti. La réponse (B) joue sur la confusion entre les sons proches *docked* et *doctor*. La réponse (C) joue sur la confusion entre les mots proches *left* (reste) et *leave* (partir).

32. (B) *We didn't have time to type it* répond à la question de savoir pourquoi (*why)* la lettre n'a pas été tapée. La réponse (A) joue sur la confusion entre les mots *type* (genre) et *typed* (tapé à la machine ou à l'ordinateur). La réponse (C) joue sur la confusion entre les sons proches *little* et *letter*.

33. (A) *Here, you can use my pen* répond à une question de type : *Who has a black ink pen?* Les réponses (B) et (C) contiennent les mots *black* et *blacken* mais ne correspondent pas à la demande.

34. (A) *No, . . . in a hospital* répond à une question de type oui/non. La réponse (B) joue sur la confusion entre les sons proches *barn* et *born*. La réponse (C) contient les mots à consonances proches *bored* et *born at*.

35. (B) *Cold cereal and fruit* répond à une question de type *what*. La réponse (A) correspond à la question *when is breakfast*. La réponse (C) correspond à une question de type *why*.

36. (C) *About three hundred pages* répond à une question de type *how many*. La réponse (A) joue sur la confusion entre les sons proches *age* et *page*. La réponse (B) correspond à la question *what color are the pages*.

37. (C) *I'll pick some up* indique que la seconde personne qui parle a l'intention d'acheter plus d'enveloppes dans l'après-midi, parce que les gens sont *almost out of envelopes* (il n'y en a presque plus). La réponse (A) associe les mots *address* et *envelope*. La réponse (B) utilise le mot *out* dans un contexte différent.

38. (B) *The manager earned the most* répond à une question de type *who*. La réponse (A) utilise les mots associés *money* et *earning* mais ne correspond pas à la question. La réponse (C) joue sur la confusion entre les sons proches *earned* et *learned*.

39. (C) *At 7 :30* répond à la question *when will dinner be served*. La réponse (A) reprend le mot *served* mais ne renvoie pas à la question *when*. La réponse (B) associe les mots *diner* et *dinner*.

40. (A) *Take the number 14 bus* donne un conseil clair et précis à celui qui pose la question. La réponse (B) est au passé. La réponse (C) joue sur la confusion entre les sons proches *talk* et *take*.

PARTIE 3 (PAGES 10–12)

Remarque : la bonne réponse est signalée en premier.

41. (A) L'homme voudrait que la femme tape une lettre. La réponse (B) joue sur la confusion entre *sweater* et le mot à consonance proche *letter*. La réponse (C) reprend le mot *lunch*. La réponse (D) correspond au moment où la femme doit poster la lettre.

42. (C) La femme dit qu'elle est en train de photocopier un rapport. La réponse (A) indique ce qu'elle fera ensuite. La réponse (B) utilise le mot *course* dans un contexte différent. La réponse (D) joue sur la confusion entre le fait d'envoyer un e-mail (*sending e-mail*) et celui de poster une lettre (*mailing a letter*).

43. (B) L'homme dit *I'll be in my office*. La réponse (A) associe les mots *restaurant* et *lunch*. La réponse (C) confond *post office* et *office*. La réponse (D) joue sur la confusion avec le fait que la femme fasse la photocopie d'un rapport.

44. (C) L'homme dit *Wednesday before noon*. La réponse (B), *Monday afternoon*, correspond à ce qui avait été promis. La réponse (A) joue sur la confusion avec la réponse (B), et la réponse (D) joue sur la confusion avec la bonne réponse qui est très proche.

45. (D) Les techniciens se sont trompés de modèle de téléphone. La réponse (A) utilise le mot *order* hors contexte. La réponse (B) joue sur la confusion entre les mots à consonances proches *appointment* et *disappointment*. La réponse (C) est incorrecte : il y a bien eu une erreur dans la commande mais elle n'a pas été passée trop tard.

46. (D) La femme dit qu'ils attendent les téléphones depuis plus d'un mois (*over a month*). Les réponses (A) et (B) reprennent le mot *week*. La réponse (C) reprend le mot *month*.

47. (D) *Twelve dozen* correspond au nombre total de stylos souhaité par l'homme. La réponse (A) correspond au nombre de stylos à encre rouge foncé commandés. La réponse (B) correspond au nombre de stylos noirs commandés. La réponse (C) correspond au nombre de stylos rouges commandés.

48. (D) L'homme commande des stylos à encre rouge, noire et rouge foncé. Les réponses (A) et (B) jouent sur la confusion entre les mots proches *green* et *see*. La réponse (C) joue sur la confusion entre les mots proches *blue* et *two*.

49. (B) L'homme donne un billet de 100 dollars à la femme. La réponse (A) utilise le mot *check* hors contexte. La réponse (C) utilise le mot *bill* hors contexte. La réponse (D) n'est pas mentionnée.

50. (A) La discussion des personnes a lieu à la fin d'un repas. La réponse (B) associe *grocery store* avec la discussion qui porte sur ce que les personnes ont mangé. La réponse (C) joue sur la confusion entre les mots proches *book* et *cook*. La réponse (D) associe *bakery* et *cake*.

51. (C) L'homme dit *Have some more dessert*. La réponse (A) correspond à ce que l'homme a déjà fait. La réponse (B) joue sur la confusion entre les mots proches *coughing* et *coffee*. La réponse (D) joue sur la confusion entre les mots proches *sing* et *thing*.

52. (C) La femme dit *I'd love a cup of coffee*. La réponse (A) joue sur la confusion entre les mots proches *book* et *cook*. La réponse (B) reprend le mot *cake*. La réponse (D) joue sur la confusion entre les mots proches *mail* et *meal*.

53. (B) Les personnes parlent de la santé de la femme, et la femme appelle l'homme *doctor*, donc il doit être médecin (*physician*). La réponse (A) associe *travel agent* et *vacation*. La réponse (C) n'est pas mentionnée. La réponse (D) associe *golfer* et *play some golf*.

54. (B)La femme met sa santé en danger en travaillant trop et en ne se relaxant jamais. La réponse (A) associe *job* et *work*. La réponse (C) joue sur la confusion entre *walk* et *work*. La réponse (D) reprend le mot *vacation*.

55. (D) La femme dit qu'elle *may take on an assistant*. La réponse (A) associe *health club* et *ruining your health*. La réponse (B) reprend le mot *golf*. La réponse (C) reprend le mot *vacation*.

56. (B) Les personnes sont d'accord pour dire qu'elles n'aiment pas la chaleur et l'humidité des mois d'été. Les réponses (A) et (C) correspondent à des éléments qu'elles apprécient. La réponse (D) emploie le mot *stand* dans un contexte différent.

57. (A) La femme dit que la journée est ensoleillée. La réponse (B) décrit la pluie au printemps. La réponse (C) décrit le climat en été. La réponse (D) joue sur la confusion entre les mots proches *icy* et *nice*.

58. (B) La femme dit *a sunny September day like today*. La réponse (A) joue sur la confusion entre les sons proches *May* et *day*. Les réponses (C) et (D) ressemblent à la bonne réponse.

59. (B) La femme demande à l'homme de l'aider à trouver ses *boots and umbrella*. La réponse (A) correspond à ce que l'homme porte. La réponse (C) associe *bus ticket* et *bus*. La réponse (D) associe *watch* et *time*.

60. (C) L'homme porte un imperméable et la femme cherche ses bottes et son parapluie, donc il doit pleuvoir. La réponse (A) joue sur la confusion entre les sons proches *hot* et *got*. La réponse (B) joue sur la confusion entre les sons proches *cold* et *coat*. La réponse (D) joue sur la confusion entre les sons proches *mist* et *miss*.

61. (A) La femme dit que le bus partira dans quinze minutes. Les réponses (B) et (C) jouent sur la confusion entre les sons proches *twenty* et *plenty*. La réponse (D) ressemble à la bonne réponse.

62. (A) L'homme dit qu'il vit près de l'école. La réponse (B) correspond à l'endroit où il vivait autrefois. La réponse (C) joue sur la confusion avec *Mountain View*, le nom de la rue où il habite. La réponse (D) joue sur la confusion entre les sons proches *pool* et *school*.

63. (C) La femme dit qu'elle se rend à son travail en voiture. La réponse (A) correspond à la manière dont l'homme se rend à son travail. La réponse (B) joue sur la confusion entre les sons proches *train* et *rain*. La réponse (D) correspond à ce que pensait avoir compris la femme à propos du moyen de transport utilisé par l'homme pour se rendre à son travail.

64. (B) La femme dit qu'elle passera prendre l'homme à 7 h 30. Les réponses (A), (C) et (D) ressemblent à la bonne réponse.

65. (B) Elle n'a pas eu le temps d'acheter le journal. La réponse (A) associe *money* et *buy*. La réponse (C) joue sur la confusion entre le fait d'être livré à temps (*delivered on time)* et la suggestion de l'homme de se faire livrer (*have it delivered)*. La réponse (D) joue sur la confusion entre *yesterday's instead* et *yesterday's, either*.

66. (D) L'homme dit *You should have it delivered*. La réponse (A) correspond à ce que la femme dit n'avoir pas le temps de faire. La réponse (B) correspond à ce que l'homme a fait. La réponse (C) n'est pas mentionnée.

67. (B) L'homme dit *let me tell you about the story I read on today's front page*. La réponse (A) utilise le mot *story* dans un contexte différent. La réponse (C) reprend le mot *buy*. La réponse (D) reprend le mot *page*.

68. (D) La femme dit qu'elle est allée se coucher après 11 heures. Les réponses (A), (B) et (C) ressemblent à la bonne réponse.

69. (C) La femme dort en moyenne huit heures par nuit. La réponse (A) fait référence à l'heure à laquelle elle s'est levée ce matin. La réponse (B) correspond au nombre d'heures de sommeil qu'elle a eues la nuit précédente. La réponse (D) joue sur la confusion entre les sons proches *ten* et *than*.

70. (A) La femme dit *I had some extra work to finish*. La réponse (B) utilise le mot *work* dans un contexte différent. La réponse (C) joue sur la confusion entre les sons proches *reading* et *ready*. La réponse (D) correspond à ce que l'homme devine.

PARTIE 4 (PAGES 13–15)

Remarque : la bonne réponse est signalée en premier.

71. (B) Le nom de la société est Office Supplies, Incorporated. La réponse (A) joue sur la confusion entre *office space* et *office supplies*. La réponse (C) associe *down pillows* et *reduce*, en employant le mot *down* hors contexte. La réponse (D) joue sur la confusion entre les sons proches *(sail)boats* et *sale*.

72. (B) La vente se déroule du mardi au samedi. Les réponses (A) et (C) ne sont pas mentionnées. La réponse (D) joue sur la confusion entre *eight days* et *8 A.M.*

73. (C) La vente s'achève samedi à 18 heures. La réponse (A) correspond au début de la vente. La réponse (B) correspond au milieu de la vente. La réponse (D) n'est pas mentionnée.

74. (A) Hier, le temps était pluvieux. La réponse (B) n'est pas mentionnée. Les réponses (C) et (D) correspondent aux prévisions du week-end.

75. (A) Il pourrait neiger ce soir. Les réponses (B) et (C) ne sont pas mentionnées. La réponse (D) correspond au moment où le temps sera ensoleillé.

76. (D) La personne dit que la température du week-end sera de 11 degrés environ. Les réponses (A) et (B) jouent sur la confusion avec la *freezing rain* qui tombera ce soir. La réponse (C) joue sur la confusion entre les sons proches *seven* et *eleven*.

77. (D) Cette annonce est un avertissement et indique que la demande en électricité excédera la capacité d'offre. Les réponses (A), (B) et (C) sont incorrectes car la seconde phrase contient le verbe *warn*, et on n'y trouve pas d'éléments allant dans le sens d'une analyse (*analysis*), d'une révision (*review*), ou d'une correction (*correction*).

78. (B) L'été est la saison au cours de laquelle cette annonce est passée dans la mesure où elle est énoncée au présent et qu'il est question de *hot summer*, *d'air conditioners*, ainsi que de *fans*. Les réponses (A), (C) et (D) sont incorrectes car le temps est au présent.

79. (A) Lorsque la demande est plus forte que l'offre, alors une panne d'électricité survient. Les réponses (B) et (C) reprennent les mots *demand* et *supply* mais indiquent le

contraire de ce qui est à l'origine d'une panne. La réponse (D) utilise le mot *fans*, mais l'idée de *poor quality* n'est pas mentionnée comme une raison possible de panne d'électricité.

80. (D) Les personnes à qui s'adresse cette annonce sont des voyageurs. Les réponses (A) et (C) désignent les personnes qui sont occupées. La réponse (B) associe *telephone line technicians* avec *callers* et *on the line*.

81. (A) *All the agents are busy* correspond à une question de type *why*. La réponse (B) associe *late* et *delay*. La réponse (C) utilise *fares* mais exprime l'inverse de ce qui est dit. La réponse (D) associe *strike* (*picket line*) et *on the line*.

82. (B) Le message dit *International travelers should arrive three hours ahead of time*. La réponse (A) correspond au moment où les voyageurs nationaux doivent arriver. La réponse (C) joue sur la confusion entre les sons proches *four* et *before*. La réponse (D) joue sur la confusion entre les sons proches *five* et *arrive*.

83. (B) Les personnes qui assistent au repas d'affaires sont des *managers*. La réponse (A) associe *teachers* au fait que *Mr. Margalis was a trainer*. La réponse (C) joue sur la confusion entre le fait que *they are at a luncheon* et *waiters*. La réponse (D) joue sur la confusion entre le travail de M. Margalis *in his garden* et *gardeners*.

84. (B) M. Margalis est un formateur en retraite (*retired*). La réponse (A) exprime l'inverse de ce qu'il est. La réponse (C) joue sur la confusion entre *speechless* et le fait qu'il fasse un discours (*a speech*). La réponse (D) est incorrecte car il a travaillé au cours des vingt dernières années, ce qui signifie qu'il n'est pas jeune.

85. (C) Il s'agit d'un repas, donc *a dining hall* est la réponse la plus logique. La réponse (A) associe *his gardening* et *a garden*. La réponse (B) associe *office* et *management*. La réponse (D) joue sur la confusion entre les sons proches *train* (train) et *trainer* (formateur).

86. (A) Il faut un passe spécial pour entrer. La réponse (B) contient le mot *authorized*, mais *pass* n'est pas mentionné. La réponse (C) joue sur la confusion entre *secure* et *security*. La réponse (D) joue sur la confusion entre *hunting license* et *driver's license*.

87. (C) Les passes peuvent être obtenus auprès du *Security Office*. La réponse (A) joue sur la confusion entre les sons proches *secure* et *security*. La réponse (B) correspond à *who may enter* mais n'indique pas qui peut délivrer des passes. La réponse (D) utilise le mot *license*, mais il n'y a aucune allusion à *bureau*.

88. (C) Les visiteurs doivent rendre leur passe avant de sortir. La réponse (A) utilise le mot *sign* dans un contexte différent. La réponse (B) reprend le mot *exit* et joue sur la confusion entre les mots proches *fee* et *three*. La réponse (D) joue sur la confusion avec *You must keep your pass with you at all times during your visit*.

89. (B) Le travail à temps partiel est mentionné dans la troisième phrase. Les réponses (A), (C) et (D) ne sont pas mentionnées.

90. (D) Des compétences en bureautique sont exigées. La réponse (A) joue sur la confusion entre *law degree* et *law firm*. La réponse (B) associe *medical diploma* et *doctor's office*. La réponse (C) joue sur la confusion entre *advertising experience* et *advertising agency*.

91. (A) L'annonce précise *All job applicants must visit our office to take a skills test*. La réponse (B) joue sur la confusion avec *The results will be available immediately*. La réponse (C) associe *application form* et *applicants*. La réponse (D) joue sur la confusion entre *employment* et le mot associé *unemployed* et reprend le mot *law* dans un contexte différent.

92. (A) Il est 8 heures du matin. Les réponses (B), (C) et (D) ne sont pas mentionnées.

93. (D) *Don't forget to take your umbrella* correspond au conseil qui est donné. Les réponses (A), (B) et (C) ne sont pas mentionnées.

94. (B) *The skies are clear* correspond à la situation actuelle décrite par la personne qui fait les prévisions météo. Les réponses (A) et (C) correspondent aux prévisions pour l'après-midi. La réponse (D) correspond à un surnom que l'on donne à Chicago, la *Windy City*.

95. (C) Le message dit que cette société *takes care of all your insurance needs*, et parle également de *policy* et d'un *agent*, les deux ayant un lien avec les compagnies d'assurances. La réponse (A) joue sur la confusion entre les sons proches *police* et *policy*. La réponse (B) associe *travel agency* et *agent*. La réponse (D) associe *alarm* et *security*.

96. (A) Dans le message, il est demandé aux personnes qui appellent d'appuyer sur *one* en cas d'urgence. La réponse (B) correspond au numéro sur lequel appuyer pour obtenir des renseignements sur une police en cours. La réponse (C) correspond au numéro sur lequel appuyer pour obtenir des renseignements sur une nouvelle police. La réponse (D) correspond au numéro sur lequel appuyer pour signaler un changement d'adresse.

97. (B) Pour signaler un changement d'adresse, on peut utiliser le site Web de la compagnie. La réponse (A) correspond au numéro permettant d'obtenir des renseignements sur une police en cours. La réponse (C) est incorrecte car les seules options possibles pour cette action sont de se rendre sur le site Web ou d'utiliser un système automatique. La réponse (D) reprend le mot *mail*.

98. (D) Cette annonce a pour but d'inciter les clients d'un centre commercial à prendre leur repas au restaurant du centre. La réponse (A) associe *school* et *children*. La réponse (B) correspond à un lieu où il y a des restaurants, mais dans les aéroports, les gens n'entendent pas d'annonces destinées à des *shoppers*. La réponse (C) associe *grocery store* aux différents types de nourriture mentionnés.

99. (A) La personne dit que le plat du jour est du *chicken à la king*. Les réponses (B), (C) et (D) correspondent à des choix de plats qui sont effectivement mentionnés, mais pas en tant que plats du jour.

100. (A) Les enfants ont droit à un jouet gratuit avec leur repas. La réponse (B) reprend le mot *dessert*. La réponse (C) reprend le mot *vegetables*. La réponse (D) reprend le mot *entrance*.

PARTIE 5 (PAGES 16–19)

Remarque : la bonne réponse est signalée en premier.

101. (A) *In* est la bonne préposition et signifie *involved* ou *sharing*. La réponse (B) est impossible car *with* signifie *in the company of* et cela ne va pas dans la phrase. La réponse (C) signifie *originating from a source*. La réponse (D) signifie *going in one side and coming out the other*.

102. (C) *Because* est une conjonction de subordination qui exprime un lien de cause à effet et le résultat attendu de quelque chose. La réponse (A) est une conjonction de subordination qu'on emploie au conditionnel. Les réponses (B) et (D) sont des pronoms relatifs.

103. (D) *Had been* est conjugué au *past perfect* et exprime une condition irréelle dans le passé. On l'utilise dans la proposition introduite par *if*. La réponse (A) est au passé. La réponse (B) est au présent simple. La réponse (C) est au *present perfect*.

104. (B) *Payable* est le substitut le plus court à la proposition relative *which are paid*. La réponse (A) contient un participe passé et ne peut pas se mettre derrière le verbe causatif *make*. La réponse (C) contient un participe présent et ne peut pas se mettre derrière le verbe causatif *make*. La réponse (D) est au présent simple.

105. (C) Les conjonction et adverbe *both … and* fonctionnent ensemble et constituent la bonne réponse. Les réponses (A), (B) et (D) ne peuvent pas se construire avec *both*.

106. (B) *Although* est la conjonction de subordination qu'il convient d'utiliser pour exprimer un résultat inattendu. La réponse (A) exprime un résultat attendu. La réponse (C) est utilisée pour poursuivre une idée. La réponse (D) exprime un résultat attendu.

107. (C) *At* est la préposition à utiliser pour exprimer un moment précis. La réponse (A) signifie *during (or at the end of) a period of time*. La réponse (B) ne peut pas servir à exprimer un moment spécifique. La réponse (D) est un article.

108. (A) *Therefore* est l'adverbe transitionnel qui convient pour exprimer un résultat attendu. Les réponses (B), (C) et (D) expriment toutes un résultat inattendu.

109. (C) *Deliver* est la forme verbale qu'il faut utiliser après le verbe causatif *had*. La réponse (A) est un participe présent. La réponse (B) est un infinitif. La réponse (D) est un participe passé.

110. (B) *Start* est le temps qui permet d'exprimer quelque chose d'habituel avec l'adverbe *usually*. La réponse (A) suggère une action commencée dans le passé. La réponse (C) suggère une action qui est en train de se passer au moment où l'on parle. La réponse (D) suggère une action ayant commencé dans le passé et continuant dans le présent.

111. (D) *Turned down* est un verbe à préposition exprimant le rejet de quelque chose. La réponse (A) signifie *discovered*. La réponse (B) signifie *started a flow*. La réponse (C) signifie *sent to another place*.

112. (C) *Had to buy* exprime une nécessité passée. Les réponses (A) et (D) sont au présent et ne sont pas logiques avec le verbe *was* de la proposition qui précède. La réponse (B) exprime une certitude passée.

113. (D) *Since* est une conjonction de subordination exprimant un rapport de cause à effet. La réponse (A) formule un tel rapport mais la proposition principale devrait être au passé pour que la construction de la phrase soit parallèle. La réponse (B) est incorrecte à cause de l'utilisation du *present perfect have become* dans la proposition principale. La réponse (C) signifie *although* ou *during*.

114. (B) *Step down* est la réponse la plus logique pour exprimer l'idée de prendre sa retraite (*retire*). La réponse (A) signifie *leave a room or building*. La réponse (C) signifie *go down from a higher place*. La réponse (D) signifie *go in one side and come out another*.

115. (C) *After* est la conjonction de subordination qu'il faut utiliser pour exprimer un lien temporel logique. La réponse (A) exprime un rapport de cause à effet. La réponse (B) exprime une opposition. La réponse (D) signifie *till that time and no longer*.

116. (B) *Interest* est le nom approprié pour modifier le mot *rates*. La réponse (A) est un participe présent. La réponse (C) est un participe passé. La réponse (D) est un présent simple à la troisième personne.

117. (A) *Put off* est la réponse la plus logique car ce verbe signifie *postpone*. La réponse (B) signifie *set with*. La réponse (C) signifie *clothe*. La réponse (D) signifie *cause to do* ou *connect on a phone*.

118. (C) *See* est au présent, et c'est la forme qui convient dans une proposition au futur. La réponse (A) est au futur, mais on ne peut pas mettre de futur dans une subordonnée temporelle. La réponse (B) est au présent progressif, et le verbe *see* est un verbe qui se met rarement à la forme progressive. La réponse (D) est au *present perfect* progressif, et le verbe *see* est un verbe qui se met rarement à la forme progressive.

119. (A) L'ordre correct des mots dans la phrase impose de mettre *ever* avant le verbe à la forme impérative négative en utilisant l'auxiliaire *do*. Les réponses (B) et (C) utilisent *never* avec l'auxiliaire *do*, mais la syntaxe n'est pas correcte. La réponse (D) place *ever* après *accept*, ce qui est incorrect ici.

120. (B) *When* est la conjonction de subordination qui convient pour dire *at the same time*. Les réponses (A) et (C) expriment une opposition. La réponse (D) est une préposition.

121. (A) *With* est une préposition exprimant une association. La réponse (B) n'est pas possible dans ce contexte. Les réponses (C) et (D) sont toutes les deux impossibles avec le verbe *collaborate*.

122. (B) *Limited* est le temps correct à utiliser dans cette proposition introduite par *if*. La réponse (A) est un participe présent. La réponse (C) est un conditionnel passé. La réponse (D) est au présent progressif.

123. (A) *Raise* est l'infinitif qui convient ici. La réponse (B) suggère une action ayant commencé dans le passé. Les réponses (C) et (D) suggèrent une certaine progression.

124. (A) *Checked* est la réponse correcte avec le verbe causatif *want*. La réponse (B) ajoute le verbe *be*, inutile ici. La réponse (C) est un participe présent. La réponse (D) n'est pas correcte avec le verbe causatif *want*.

125. (D) *Therefore* exprime un rapport de cause à effet avec un résultat attendu. Les réponses (A) et (B) expriment une opposition. La réponse (C) n'est pas logique car il faudrait un exemple précis de ce qu'elle a fait.

126. (C) *Representing*, qui est l'abréviation d'une proposition ayant pour fonction de modifier ce qui est dit, est le participe qui convient ici. La réponse (A) est un nom. La réponse (B) est un nom faisant référence à une personne. La réponse (D) est un nom accompagné d'une préposition, et cette réponse aurait été correcte s'il y avait eu l'article *the* avant *representative* ainsi que des virgules autour de *Mr. James*, afin de rendre la proposition non restrictive.

127. (C) Les adverbes exprimant une fréquence définie peuvent se placer à la fin de la proposition. Dans les réponses (A), (B) et (D), l'adverbe est placé au mauvais endroit de la phrase.

128. (D) *And* est la conjonction de coordination qui convient ici et qui signifie *in addition to*. Les réponses (A) et (B) ne sont pas des conjonctions de coordination et ne peuvent pas être suivies d'une proposition. La réponse (C) exprime une opposition.

129. (A) *While* signifie *pendant que*. Les réponses (B), (C) et (D) expriment toutes un rapport de cause à effet.

130. (B) *In* est la préposition qu'il faut utiliser pour accompagner un nom de ville. Les réponses (A), (C) et (D) sont toutes des prépositions exprimant une situation géographique, mais elles ne sont pas logiques dans ce contexte.

131. (A) *Competitors* est l'objet pluriel de la préposition faisant référence à des personnes. La réponse (B) est au singulier. Les réponses (C) et (D) sont toutes les deux des adjectifs.

132. (C) *Decision* est le nom et le sujet de la phrase. La réponse (A) est un adjectif. Les réponses (B) et (D) sont des verbes.

133. (A) *In* est la préposition à utiliser pour accompagner le nom d'une ville. Les réponses (B), (C) et (D) sont toutes des prépositions exprimant une situation géographique, mais elles ne sont pas logiques dans ce contexte.

134. (C) *Findings* signifie *results*. La réponse (A) est un terme qui signifie *abandoned infants that have been found*. La réponse (B) est le pluriel d'un mot signifiant "objet trouvé". La réponse (D) est le passé du verbe *find*.

135. (D) *Suspected* est un verbe au passé, la forme qui convient pour s'accorder avec *staff*. Les réponses (A) et (B) sont toutes deux des noms. La réponse (C) est un adjectif.

136. (C) *Look up* signifie *to search for in a reference source*. La réponse (A) signifie *to overlook*. La réponse (B) signifie *to be careful*. La réponse (D) signifie *to rely upon*.

137. (B) *Considered* est la forme passive attendue ici. Les réponses (A) et (C) sont toutes deux des adjectifs. La réponse (D) est la forme active du présent simple du verbe.

138. (D) Le passé à la forme simple du verbe est nécessaire parce qu'il y a le marqueur temporel passé *a year ago* dans la phrase. La réponse (A) est au présent simple. La réponse (B) est au présent progressif. La réponse (C) est au *present perfect*.

139. (C) *Awarded* est le passé à la forme simple exprimant un moment précis du passé, et c'est la forme qui convient dans cette phrase. La réponse (A) est au participe présent. La réponse (B) est au *past perfect* et suggère un moment antérieur à un moment du passé. La réponse (D) est au présent simple et suggère quelque chose d'habituel.

140. (A) *Spend* est la forme correcte qu'il faut utiliser après le verbe causatif *had*. La réponse (B) est l'infinitif. La réponse (C) est au passé à la forme simple. La réponse (D) est un participe présent.

PARTIE 6 (PAGES 20–24)

Remarque : la bonne réponse est signalée en premier.

141. (B) Une *candy company makes*, ou *manufactures* de bonbons. La réponse (A) signifie *eat* ou *use*. La réponse (C) signifie *buy*. La réponse (D) signifie *want*.

142. (C) Lorsque des employés sont blessés lors d'un accident, ils ne vont pas travailler pendant quelques jours. La réponse (A) signifie *stay away from* mais ne va pas dans le contexte. La réponse (B) signifie *add*. La réponse (D) signifie *keep*.

143. (A) Il s'agit d'un adjectif comparatif dont la fonction est de décrire les personnes qui travaillent avec des *cobots*. La réponse (B) est un adverbe comparatif. Les réponses (C) et (D) sont des noms.

144. (D) *It* fait référence au nom singulier *a message*. La réponse (A) est un nom pluriel. Les réponses (B) et (C) sont utilisées pour faire référence à des personnes et non à des choses.

145. (C) Après avoir utilisé quelque chose, vous devez *sign out*. Les réponses (A) et (B) formeraient les verbes *sign in* et *sign up*, qui expriment ce que vous devez faire avant d'utiliser quelque chose. La réponse (D) ne peut pas être utilisée dans ce contexte.

146. (A) Le coordinateur de programmes souhaite que les gens fassent un nombre limité de photocopies car ces dernières coûtent cher (*costly*). Les réponses (B), (C) et (D) n'expriment pas des raisons suffisamment plausibles qui justifieraient cette limitation.

147. (A) L'adverbe *quickly* explique de quelle manière l'auteur du message désire que les articles soient expédiés. Les réponses (B) et (C) sont des adjectifs. La réponse (D) est un nom.

148. (C) L'auteur souhaite que les chaises soient de la même couleur que les bureaux, en d'autres termes, il souhaite que les articles *match*. Les réponses (A) et (B) signifient l'inverse. La réponse (D) n'a pas de sens dans ce contexte.

149. (A) Il s'agit d'une forme impérative qui dit au lecteur ce qu'il doit faire. La réponse (B) est un verbe au passé. La réponse (C) est un infinitif. La réponse (D) est un futur.

150. (C) La personne à laquelle il est fait référence est un client (*customer*) qui avait commandé un repas dans un restaurant du nom de *Little Tea Room*. La réponse (A) joue sur la confusion avec la personne à qui la lettre est adressée. La réponse (B) est associée à l'hôpital. La réponse (D) joue sur la confusion avec la serveuse qui a servi le repas.

151. (C) La forme modale *will* permet de mettre le verbe au futur. La réponse (A) exprime une obligation. La réponse (B) exprime une possibilité. La réponse (D) ne peut pas précéder une base verbale.

152. (A) L'expression *so that* signifie *in order to* ou *for the purpose of*. Les réponses (B), (C) et (D) ne peuvent pas servir à compléter une expression ayant ce sens.

Partie 7 (pages 25–41)

Remarque : la bonne réponse est signalée en premier.

153. (D) L'employé d'un magasin de vêtements est la personne la plus susceptible de postuler parce qu'une expérience de deux ans dans l'industrie du vêtement est exigée. La réponse (A) associe *engineer* et *professional*. La réponse (B) associe *real estate agent* et *sales*. La réponse (C) associe *professor* et *college degree*.

154. (C) Un diplôme d'études supérieures est exigé, mais pas le niveau master. Les réponses (A) et (B) sont toutes deux mentionnées dans l'annonce. La réponse (D) est l'équivalent de *excellent communication skills.*

155. (D) Cet article parle des désagréments de l'excès d'emballages. La réponse (A) joue sur la confusion avec la référence aux matières recyclables, la réponse (B) fait une confusion avec la référence aux logiciels informatiques, et la réponse (C) fait une confusion avec la référence aux décharges, mais il s'agit là de détails et non de l'idée principale.

156. (B) Les produits sont emballés afin de les rendre plus attrayants. La réponse (A) est en contradiction avec *it does not really protect the goods*. La réponse (C) joue sur la confusion entre les mots proches *consumption* et *consumer*. La réponse (D) associe *environmental* et *environmentalists.*

157. (B) L'excès d'emballages aboutit dans les poubelles, lesquelles finissent dans les décharges du pays. La réponse (A) correspond à ce que les écologistes aimeraient voir arriver pour les emballages. Les réponses (C) et (D) sont en contradiction avec *end up in the garbage dumps.*

158. (C) Ce tableau compare le nombre de salariés qui empruntent le bus pour se rendre à leur travail à celui des étudiants qui empruntent le même mode de transport. La réponse (A) n'est pas mentionnée. La réponse (B) joue sur la confusion entre *means of transportation* et *bus*. La réponse (D) joue sur la confusion entre les mots proches *drivers* et *riders.*

159. (B) Le mois de juillet est celui au cours duquel le nombre de salariés ayant emprunté le bus pour se rendre à leur travail a été le plus élevé. La réponse (A) indique le mois au cours duquel la fréquentation des étudiants a été la plus forte. Les réponses (C) et (D) indiquent les mois au cours desquels la fréquentation a été la plus faible

160. (D) Le mois au cours duquel les bus ont été le moins fréquentés est le mois de décembre. Les réponses (A), (B) et (C) indiquent les mois au cours desquels la fréquentation a été la plus forte.

161. (A) L'augmentation des tarifs postaux mènera certaines entreprises à la faillite. Les réponses (B) et (C) jouent sur la confusion avec un autre sens du mot *drive* – manœuvrer un véhicule. La réponse (D) ne va pas dans le contexte.

162. (A) Les sociétés de marketing direct indiquent que l'augmentation des tarifs postaux telle qu'elle est proposée frappera leur secteur de plein fouet et que certaines d'entre elles devront fermer leurs portes. La réponse (B) n'est pas mentionnée. La réponse (C) associe *postal employees* et *postal rates* ; les employés de la Poste devraient être peu affectés par les plaintes des clients. La réponse (D) n'est pas mentionnée.

163. (C) La plupart des entreprises de marketing direct utilisent le tarif économique. La réponse (A) joue sur la confusion entre *book rate* et *catalog*. La réponse (B) joue sur la confusion entre *first class* et *the rise in first-class postage rates*. La réponse (D) correspond à la hausse éventuelle du tarif économique.

164. (B) Une *catalog house* est une entreprise de marketing direct, qui commercialise des produits directement auprès du consommateur en utilisant la Poste plutôt que de faire de la publicité *via* un intermédiaire. La réponse (A) joue sur la confusion entre *postal clients* et *postal rate*. La réponse (C) associe *financially stable company* et *bankruptcy*. La réponse (D) est incorrecte car les *catalog houses* utilisent le tarif économique.

165. (A) La sécurité est le sujet principal de ce passage. Les réponses (B), (C) et (D) sont toutes mentionnées mais elles correspondent à des détails de ce message dont l'objet principal est la sécurité.

166. (D) One-Call est le service auprès duquel les particuliers peuvent se renseigner, avant de creuser le sol, pour savoir où sont situés les tuyaux de gaz. La réponse (A) associe *call* et *telecommunications*. La réponse (B) associe *excavating* et *digging*. La réponse (C) indique quelles sont les personnes qui doivent appeler One-Call avant de creuser.

167. (C) Ils coordonnent les forces de sécurité en cas de fuite ou d'incendie. La réponse (A) indique les risques que les entreprises chargées des infrastructures de ce type souhaitent prévenir. La réponse (B) associe *drilling* et *pipelines*. La réponse (D) indique les moyens qui permettent de contrôler et de surveiller les tuyauteries.

168. (C) S'il y a un problème dans un tuyau, des équipes proches peuvent être envoyées sur place pour effectuer les réparations nécessaires. Les réponses (A) et (D) indiquent ce qui peut arriver à une équipe d'intervention, mais elles ne correspondent pas au contexte. La réponse (B) indique ce que l'équipe d'intervention fera aux tuyauteries.

169. (A) Ce tableau est utilisé pour identifier et résoudre un problème au cas où un réseau de télévision ne fonctionnerait pas. La réponse (B) joue sur la confusion entre *TV program* et *TV*. Les réponses (C) et (D) ne sont pas mentionnées.

170. (B) En cas d'écran sans image, *WHAT TO DO* suggère de faire la chose suivante : *adjust brightness control*. La réponse (A) associe *turn down the volume* et *sound heard*. La réponse (C) correspond à ce que l'on doit faire en cas d'absence d'image. La réponse (D) correspond au conseil donné au cas où il y aurait une image mais pas de son.

171. (D) S'il n'y a ni image ni son, *WHAT TO DO* suggère de faire la chose suivante : *adjust tuning*. La réponse (A) n'est pas mentionnée. La réponse (B) nécessite de monter le volume ou de débrancher les écouteurs. La réponse (C) nécessite l'ajustement de la luminosité.

172. (A) Personne ne doit de l'argent étant donné que Mme Tomkins a déjà payé le livre. La réponse (B) désigne la personne qui a déjà payé. La réponse (C) désigne la personne qui envoie sans cesse des lettres de relance pour non-paiement. La réponse (D) associe *author* et *book*.

173. (C) Le chèque a été fait le 13 octobre. La réponse (A) correspond à la date à laquelle la lettre a été rédigée. La réponse (B) n'est pas mentionnée. La réponse (D) correspond au moment où China Books a déposé le chèque.

174. (A) Mme Tomkins a reçu deux relances et a envoyé deux lettres mais n'a payé qu'une seule fois. Les réponses (B) et (C) sont mentionnées. La réponse (D) est également vraie : en effet, même si l'entreprise continue d'envoyer des lettres de relance, elle a reçu le paiement car la banque a fait le nécessaire concernant le chèque.

175. (C) Ce rapport a pour objet le "*paperless office*", à savoir un bureau sans papiers. La réponse (A) joue sur la confusion entre *selling computers* et *using computers*. La réponse (B) associe *desktop publishing* et *computers*. La réponse (D) est mentionnée mais il ne s'agit pas du sujet principal.

176. (A) L'idée du "*paperless office*" était de réduire l'utilisation des papiers, et l'objectif de préserver l'environnement et d'améliorer le problème des déchets solides. La réponse (B) aurait pu être vraie à première vue, mais cela ne correspond pas à l'intention de départ. Les réponses (C) et (D) ne sont pas mentionnées.

177. (A) L'université souhaite recruter un professeur de médecine. Les réponses (B), (C) et (D) correspondent à des activités possibles de l'université, mais elles ne conviennent pas dans le contexte.

178. (B) La supervision des recherches relève de la responsabilité d'un chef de clinique. Les réponses (A) et (D) sont trop générales pour un professeur de médecine. La réponse (C) n'est pas mentionnée.

179. (B) *Medical board certification* exigé. La réponse (A) n'est pas mentionnée. La réponse (C) joue sur la confusion entre *clinical nutrition training experience* et *expected to develop … clinical nutrition programs*. La réponse (D) n'est pas mentionnée.

180. (D) *Abstracts of published articles* n'est pas mentionné. Les réponses (A), (B) et (C) sont toutes citées comme des critères à remplir.

181. (B) Joey Farina est le directeur du *Fish Market Restaurant*. La réponse (A) joue sur la confusion avec le nom du restaurant. La réponse (C) joue sur la confusion avec le type de restaurant. La réponse (D) correspond au lieu où Sandra James travaille.

182. (D) Il s'agit de la date de livraison demandée par Joey Farina et qui figure sur l'ordre d'achat. La réponse (A) correspond à la date à laquelle il a préparé la commande. La réponse (B) correspond à la date à laquelle la commande a été envoyée. La réponse (C) correspond à la date de la lettre de Sandra James.

183. (A) Dans sa lettre datée du 11 avril, Sandra James dit *I received your purchase order yesterday*, ce qui veut dire qu'elle l'a reçu le 10 avril, le lendemain du jour où la lettre a été postée, le 9 avril. Les réponses (B), (C) et (D) ne sont pas correctes si l'on en croit les informations fournies.

184. (C) Sandra James dit que Joey Farina doit payer le tarif du service express pour recevoir sa commande avant la date spécifiée, mais ce tarif ne figure pas sur l'ordre d'achat. Les réponses (A), (B) et (D) correspondent à des articles qui figurent sur la commande.

185. (D) Les frais de transport et de manutention sont habituellement de 10 %. Joey Farina n'a compté que 5 %, mais Sandra James dit que ces frais sont deux fois plus élevés que ce que M. Farina pensait. Les réponses (A), (B) et (C) correspondent à des montants erronés.

186. (B) Jarek Cichy a envoyé un fax avec un formulaire indiquant que l'un de ses employés est nominé pour recevoir une récompense. La réponse (A) correspond à l'objet de la note, pas à celui du fax. La réponse (C) est mentionnée dans le fax mais elle ne correspond pas à la raison pour laquelle il l'a envoyé. La réponse (D) est mentionnée dans la note.

187. (A) Jarek Cichy dit dans le fax qu'il sera de retour à son bureau le 13 décembre, ce qui correspond à la veille de la fête. La réponse (B) est en contradiction avec la bonne réponse. La réponse (C) correspond à la date à laquelle il partira en voyage. La réponse (D) correspond à la date à laquelle il a envoyé le fax.

188. (A) La note explique que les membres du conseil d'administration organisent cette fête chaque année *to show their appreciation of the hard work you have all done*. La réponse (B) correspond à ce qui se passera lors de la fête, mais n'exprime pas l'objectif affiché pour l'occasion. La réponse (C) joue sur la confusion avec le cadeau que les personnes du service remettront au lauréat. La réponse (D) n'est pas mentionnée.

189. (C) C'est Anezka Novotna, la personne du service marketing nominée, qui recevra la récompense. La réponse (A) désigne la personne à laquelle les membres du personnel doivent donner leur participation pour le cadeau. La réponse (B) désigne l'auteur du fax et de la note. La réponse (D) désigne l'une des personnes qui remettent la récompense.

190. (C) Basia est l'assistante de Jarek Cichy, du service marketing. La réponse (A) correspond au lieu où Jarek Cichy doit partir en voyage. La réponse (B) désigne le groupe qui remettra la récompense. La réponse (D) est associée au fait de collecter l'argent.

191. (D) L'annonce dit que BTC est *one of the world's top 5 electronics companies*. Les réponses (A) et (B) sont associées aux services de l'entreprise mentionnée dans l'annonce. La réponse (C) est associée à l'électronique.

192. (D) L'assurance vie est un avantage auquel il n'est pas fait allusion dans l'annonce. La réponse (A) fait référence à *educational assistance*. La réponse (B) renvoie à *health coverage*. La réponse (C) fait référence à *paid vacation*.

193. (A) L'annonce dit … *go to our website and fill out the "Request for Information" form*. La réponse (B) fait référence à une personne qui a témoigné dans l'annonce. Les réponses (C) et (D) sont liées à ce qui est écrit dans les textes, mais ne sont pas mentionnées.

194. (D) Bert Roberts a travaillé pendant cinq ans pour une société et deux ans pour une autre, ce qui lui donne une expérience de sept ans au total. La réponse (A) correspond au nombre d'années durant lesquelles il a travaillé chez R & J. La réponse (B) n'est pas mentionnée. La réponse (C) correspond au nombre d'années pendant lesquelles il a travaillé chez Servitrix, Ltd.

195. (C) Bert Roberts vit en Nouvelle-Zélande, et BTC est situé en Inde, il est donc probable qu'il devra partir vivre en Inde pour pouvoir travailler chez BTC. La réponse (A) n'est pas correcte car il a déjà un master. La réponse (B) fait une association avec les témoignages donnés dans l'annonce, mais il n'est mentionné nulle part qu'il s'agit d'une exigence qui s'applique aux nouveaux employés. La réponse (D) fait une association avec l'un des avantages proposés, mais cela ne correspond pas à une exigence.

196. (B) B. J. Technology a reçu une récompense, et J. S. Choi l'a acceptée au nom de l'entreprise. La réponse (A) fait référence à l'organisation qui a délivré la récompense. La réponse (C) correspond à l'endroit où a eu lieu la cérémonie de remise de la récompense. La réponse (D) fait une confusion avec Victoria Williams, l'auteur de l'e-mail.

197. (C) La récompense a été remise par Kazadi Koite car Jakob Skolnik n'a pas pu assister à la cérémonie pour raisons de santé. Les réponses (A) et (D) correspondent à d'autres noms qui figurent sur le programme. La réponse (B) correspond à l'auteur de l'e-mail.

198. (A) La réception s'est tenue dans la salle 1. Les réponses (B), (C) et (D) correspondent à d'autres salles mentionnées par Victoria Williams dans son e-mail.

199. (D) La cérémonie a débuté à 7 heures, la salle avait été réservée pour une durée de trois heures, et les invités sont restés jusqu'à la fin, ce qui fait que l'événement a pris fin à 10 heures. La réponse (A) joue sur la confusion avec le nombre d'heures pendant lequel la salle a été réservée. La réponse (B) n'est pas mentionnée. La réponse (C) correspond à l'heure à laquelle la cérémonie a commencé.

200. (D) Victoria Williams suggère de réserver une autre salle, plus grande, car il y a eu beaucoup de monde à la cérémonie. La réponse (A) correspond à ce qui a été fait cette année. La réponse (B) n'est pas correcte car elle parle d'autres salles dans le même hôtel. La réponse (C) joue sur la confusion avec *More guests attended than we expected*.

Solutions Test n° 2

PARTIE 1 (PAGES 43–48)

Remarque : la bonne réponse est signalée en premier.

Exemple :

(A) They're leaving the room.
(B) They're turning on the machine.
(C) They're standing near the table.
(D) They're reading the newspaper.

1. (A) L'homme avec une valise est debout derrière une voiture ; il s'apprête à ouvrir le coffre pour y mettre sa valise. La réponse (B) joue sur la confusion entre les sons proches *cabinet* et *taxi (cab)*. La réponse (C) joue sur la confusion entre les mots *trunk* (une grosse boîte) et *trunk* (le coffre d'une voiture). La réponse (D) reprend le mot *car*.
2. (A) Les personnes sont en train de regarder des tableaux dans un musée. La réponse (B) contient les mots associés *painting* et *picture*, mais ce que dit la phrase n'est pas conforme à l'action de la photo. Les réponses (C) et (D) contiennent le mot associé *picture* mais dans le contexte de la photographie.
3. (B) Le technicien est en train d'ajuster des fils. La réponse (A) joue sur la proximité des sons *crew* et *(screw)driver*. La réponse (C) emploie le mot associé *fixes* mais ne fait pas référence à la bonne occupation. La réponse (D) joue sur la confusion entre les sons proches *mail* et *male*.
4. (A) L'homme fait une présentation. La réponse (B) joue sur la confusion entre les mots proches *presents* et *presentation*. La réponse (C) utilise le mot associé *jacket*, mais l'homme n'en porte pas sur la photo. La réponse (D) joue sur la confusion entre *training horses* et *conducting a training session*.
5. (D) Deux personnes se serrent la main sur un escalier de briques. La réponse (A) ne fait pas référence à la bonne action. La réponse (B) joue sur la confusion entre les mots proches *taking fans* et *shaking hands*. La réponse (C) joue sur la confusion entre les sons proches *sanding* et *standing*.
6. (A) L'ouvrier gravit un escalier. La réponse (B) joue sur la confusion entre *a gas tank in a car* et *a storage tank*. La réponse (C) joue sur la confusion entre les sons proches *sank* et *tank*. La réponse (D) joue sur la confusion entre les locutions proches *ascending the ladder* et *sending a letter*.
7. (C) Les ouvriers sont en train de vérifier l'équipement. Les réponses (A), (B) et (D) décrivent une autre occupation que celle des personnes qui sont sur la photo.
8. (C) Les pilotes préparent le décollage. La réponse (A) joue sur la confusion entre *flight attendants* et *pilots* et entre *get off* et *take off*. La réponse (B) joue sur la confusion entre les sons proches *pie ought* et *pilot* et entre *take out* et *take off*. La réponse (D) joue sur la confusion entre *musical instruments* et le *instrument panel* de l'avion.
9. (B) Deux hommes effectuent des réparations. La réponse (A) joue sur la confusion entre *gas used to operate an oven* et *the flammable gas sign*. La réponse (C) n'est pas correcte car l'un des hommes est à genou tandis que l'autre est debout. La réponse (D) n'est pas correcte car leurs outils sont disposés autour d'eux mais ne sont pas rangés.
10. (D) L'ouvrier est entouré de bidons. La réponse (A) associe *in the middle of* et *surrounded by*. La réponse (B) suggère qu'il regarde son ordre de mission mais il ne le tape pas. La réponse (C) utilise le mot associé *oil*.

PARTIE 2 (PAGE 49)

Remarque : la bonne réponse est signalée en premier.

Exemple :

Where is the meeting room?
(A) To meet the new director.
(B) It's the first room on the right.
(C) Yes, at two o'clock.

11. (B) *In the top drawer* répond à la question *where*. La réponse (A) associe *post office* et *stamps*. La réponse (C) joue sur la confusion entre les sons proches *stamped* et *stamps*.

12. (C) *To go to the doctor* répond à la question *why did you leave early*. La réponse (A) utilise le mot *because*, souvent utilisé pour répondre à une question de type *why*, mais joue sur la confusion entre les contraires *late* et *early*. La réponse (B) joue sur la confusion entre *arriving early* et *leaving early*.

13. (B) *First, I'll open the mail* répond à la question *what is your first chore*. La réponse (A) joue sur la confusion entre les sons proches *thirsty* et *first*. La réponse (C) joue sur la confusion entre les sons proches *short* et *chore* et entre *workday* et *today*.

14. (C) *Twice a year* répond à la question *how often*. La réponse (A) est au passé, ce qui ne convient pas. La réponse (B) n'est pas réaliste.

15. (A) *That cup is his* répond à la question *whose coffee cup is this*. La réponse (B) reprend le mot *this* mais ne correspond pas à la question. La réponse (C) renvoie à la question *do you like coffee*.

16. (A) *Yes, actually we're early* répond à la question *will we be on time*. La réponse (B) associe *watch* et *time*. La réponse (C) joue sur la confusion entre les sons proches *he* et *we* et associe *4:30* avec *time*.

17. (B) *I only know a few words* répond à la question *how well do you speak Chinese*. La réponse (A) correspond à la question *how does she feel*. La réponse (C) joue sur la confusion entre *Chinese food* et *the Chinese language*.

18. (C) *I was too tired* répond à la question *why didn't you study*. La réponse (A) joue sur la confusion entre les sons proches *students* et *study*. La réponse (B) reprend le mot *test* mais ne correspond pas à la question.

19. (B) *They plan to stay home* répond à la question *what are they going to do tomorrow*. La réponse (A) correspond à la question *what are they doing now*. La réponse (C) joue sur la confusion entre *the day after* et *tomorrow*.

20. (C) *On the ground floor* répond à la question *where*. La réponse (A) reprend le mot *ticket* et joue sur la confusion entre les sons proches *counted* et *counter*. La réponse (B) renvoie à la question *where is your ticket*.

21. (C) *Beef and noodles* répond à la question *what's for lunch*. La réponse (A) correspond à la question *where*. La réponse (B) correspond à la question *when*.

22. (A) Les personnes qui parlent n'iront pas à la plage parce qu'il va pleuvoir. La réponse (B) joue sur la confusion entre *trains* et le mot proche *rain*. La réponse (C) utilise le mot *report* dans un contexte différent.

23. (C) *About four* répond à la question *how many*. La réponse (A) correspond à la question *when will you see that movie*. La réponse (B) joue sur la confusion entre les sons proches *moved* et *movies* et entre *(over)seas* et *see*.

24. (B) *The brown chair* répond à la question *which chair*. La réponse (A) joue sur la confusion entre les sons proches *table* et *comfortable*. La réponse (C) joue sur la confusion entre les sons proches *care* et *chair*.

25. (B) La première personne doit poster un paquet, et la seconde propose d'emporter le paquet à la poste. La réponse (A) associe *letters* et *mail*. La réponse (C) joue sur la confusion entre les mots proches *packed* et *package*.

26. (C) *A young couple* répond à la question *who rented the apartment*. La réponse (A) joue sur la confusion entre les mots proches *renters* et *rented*. La réponse (B) joue sur la confusion entre les mots proches *stairs* et *upstairs*.

27. (B) *He said no rooms were available* répond à la question *what did the hotel clerk say*. La réponse (A) joue sur la confusion entre les sons proches *stayed* et *say*. La réponse (C) emploie le mot *clerk* dans un contexte différent.

28. (A) *I advertised for one in the paper* répond à la question *how did you find a computer programmer*. La réponse (B) associe *computer* et *computer program* et correspond à la question *where is the computer*. La réponse (C) joue sur la confusion entre *program* et *programmer*.

29. (C) La seconde personne admire le nouveau costume de la première. La réponse (A) joue sur la confusion entre les sons proches *fruit* et *suit*. La réponse (B) reprend *New York*.

30. (B) *Last week* répond à la question *when was the package mailed*. La réponse (A) joue sur la confusion entre les mots proches *packed* et *package*. La réponse (C) correspond à la question *when does the mail come*.

31. (B) La seconde personne est d'accord sur le fait que la première n'a pas suffisamment de vacances. La réponse (A) associe *travel agency* et *vacation*. La réponse (C) reprend *new job*.

32. (A) *Three hundred thousand dollars* répond à la question *how much money*. La réponse (B) reprend plusieurs mots utilisés dans la question sans correspondre à celle-ci. La réponse (C) joue sur la confusion entre les contraires *spent* et *earned*.

33. (A) *Whenever we want* répond à la question *when*. La réponse (B) joue sur la confusion entre les sons proches *bread* et *break*. La réponse (C) joue sur la confusion entre les sons proches *broke* (cassé) et *break* (pause).

34. (B) *I turned it off* répond à la question *who turned off the photocopier*. La réponse (A) joue sur la confusion entre les mots proches *copied the photos* et *photocopier*. La réponse (C) joue sur la confusion entre les mots proches *photographer* et *photocopier* et entre les verbes *turned in* et *turned off*.

35. (A) *Smoking is not allowed anywhere* est une autre façon de dire *all rooms are for nonsmokers*, ce qui répond à la question *which room*. La réponse (B) joue sur la confusion entre les mots proches *smoke* et *nonsmokers*. La réponse (C) joue sur la confusion entre les sons proches *no one* et *nonsmokers*.

36. (A) *It can seat 500 people* répond à la question *how large is the auditorium*. La réponse (B) emploie le mot proche *larger* dans un contexte différent. La réponse (C) joue sur la confusion entre les questions *how often* et *how large*.

37. (C) *Only one* répond à la question *how many*. La réponse (A) renvoie à la question *which bag can I take*. La réponse (B) renvoie à la question *how many planes are there*.

38. (A) La première personne n'a pas assez dormi, et la seconde lui conseille de se coucher plus tôt. La réponse (B) joue sur la confusion entre les sons proches *keep* et *sleep*. La réponse (C) reprend *last night*.

39. (A) *Health insurance* répond à la question *what kind of insurance do you have*. La réponse (B) associe *insurance agent* et *health insurance*. La réponse (C) correspond à la question *why do you have insurance*.

40. (C) *Fourteen hours by plane* répond à la question *how long does it take*. La réponse (A) correspond à la question *do you like to travel*. La réponse (B) associe *big cities* avec *New York* et *Tokyo*, et *the subway* avec *travel*.

Partie 3 (pages 50–52)

Remarque : la bonne réponse est signalée en premier.

41. (A) La femme partira à 4 heures. La réponse (B) indique le début de l'heure de pointe. La réponse (C) correspond au premier horaire mentionné par la femme ; ensuite, elle change d'avis. La réponse (D) correspond à l'heure de décollage de son avion.

42. (B) La femme ira à l'aéroport pour prendre l'avion. La réponse (A) joue sur la confusion entre les sons proches *train* et *plane*. La réponse (C) correspond au lieu où elle se trouve actuellement. La réponse (D) joue sur la confusion entre les sons proches *bus* et *rush*.

43. (C) L'homme donne à la femme quelques journaux à lire dans l'avion. La réponse (A) joue sur la confusion entre les mots proches *brush* et *rush*. La réponse (B) joue sur la confusion entre les mots proches *book* et *look*. La réponse (D) joue sur la confusion entre les mots proches *paper* et *newspapers*.

44. (B) L'homme demande quinze (*fifteen*) dollars à la femme. La réponse (A) joue sur la confusion entre les sons proches *fourteen* et *forty*. La réponse (C) correspond à la somme en liquide dont dispose la femme. La réponse (D) joue sur la confusion entre les sons proches *fifty* et *fifteen*.

45. (C) L'homme a besoin d'argent pour prendre le taxi pour se rendre à une réunion. La réponse (A) joue sur la confusion entre les mots proches *lunch* et *rush*. La réponse (B) joue sur la confusion entre les mots proches *tax* et *taxi*. La réponse (D) joue sur la confusion entre les sons proches *reading* et *meeting*.

46. (B) L'homme dit qu'il a besoin de l'argent jusqu'à demain. La réponse (A) correspond au moment où la femme est allée à la banque. La réponse (C) reprend le mot *tomorrow*. La réponse (D) reprend l'expression *next week* ; la femme dit qu'elle a besoin de son argent avant.

47. (A) Les deux personnes aiment les comédies. Les réponses (B), (C) et (D) correspondent à des films que la femme n'aime pas à cause de la violence.

48. (C) L'homme dit que le prochain film commence à 7 h 30. La réponse (A) joue sur la confusion entre les mots proches *four* et

more. La réponse (B) ressemble à la bonne réponse. La réponse (D) joue sur la confusion entre les mots proches *ten* et *then*.

49. (D) L'homme souhaite sortir dîner. La réponse (A) correspond à ce que la femme ne veut pas faire. Les réponses (B) et (C) correspondent à ce que la femme suggère de faire.

50. (D) La réunion aura lieu vendredi. La réponse (A) joue sur la confusion entre *Tuesday* et *two days*. La réponse (B) correspond à la date initialement prévue pour la réunion. La réponse (C) n'est pas mentionnée.

51. (A) Mme Schmidt, la comptable, est malade. La réponse (B) joue sur la confusion avec ce que la femme dit : *I'll make sure the conference room will be ready*. La réponse (C) reprend *Ms. Schmidt* et *conference* mais ne renvoie pas à la question. La réponse (D) joue sur la confusion entre les mots proches *reading* et *meeting* et reprend le mot *budget*, qui est mentionné comme l'objet de la réunion.

52. (A) La femme dit qu'elle appellera les gens à propos du changement concernant la réunion. La réponse (B) correspond à la méthode qu'elle ne veut pas utiliser. La réponse (C) associe *letter* et *mail*. La réponse (D) n'est pas mentionnée.

53. (D) La femme dit qu'elle a manqué d'essence. Les réponses (A) et (B) jouent sur la confusion entre *slept late* et *walked slowly* et la suggestion de l'homme de se lever plus tôt et de marcher. La réponse (C) correspond à ce qu'elle a fait hier.

54. (C) L'homme va à son travail à pied. La réponse (A) indique de quelle manière la femme s'est rendue à son travail hier. La réponse (B) indique de quelle manière elle s'y est rendue aujourd'hui. La réponse (D) emploie le mot *train* dans un contexte différent.

55. (D) L'homme dit qu'il met quarante-cinq minutes pour se rendre au travail. Les réponses (A), (B) et (C) ressemblent à la bonne réponse.

56. (B) L'homme a laissé ses lunettes sur le bureau de la femme dans la pièce où elle travaille. La réponse (A) n'est pas correcte parce que l'homme n'a pas laissé ses lunettes sur son bureau mais sur celui de la femme. La réponse (C) indique ce que l'homme tend à la femme. La réponse (D) correspond au lieu où ils se rencontreront après qu'il sera retourné au bureau récupérer ses lunettes.

57. (B) La femme donne ses clés à l'homme pour qu'il puisse ouvrir son bureau. La réponse (A) joue sur la confusion entre les mots proches *kiss* et *keys*. La réponse (C) correspond à ce que l'homme tend à la femme. La réponse (D) joue sur la confusion entre les mots proches *locket* et *locked*.

58. (D) La femme dit que sa voiture est garée en face de la poste. La réponse (A) associe *parking lot* et *parked*. La réponse (B) joue sur la confusion entre *her office* et *post office*. La réponse (A) reprend l'expression *across the street*.

59. (C) Les personnes parlent de la chaleur. La réponse (A) associe *eating* avec *egg* et *ice cream*. La réponse (B) reprend le mot *business*. La réponse (D) reprend le mot *sidewalk*.

60. (C) L'homme dit qu'il vend des glaces. La réponse (A) reprend le mot *egg*. La réponse (B) emploie le mot *cooler* dans un contexte différent. La réponse (D) reprend le mot *air conditioner*.

61. (B) La femme dit qu'elle travaille dans un bureau. Les réponses (A) et (C) jouent sur la confusion entre *pool* et *school* et le mot proche *cool*. La réponse (D) associe *restaurant* avec *egg* et *ice cream*.

62. (C) Les personnes parlent d'un costume que l'homme a acheté. Les réponses (A), (B) et (D) sont citées comme des choses que l'homme avait déjà.

63. (A) L'homme a apporté le costume qu'il a acheté lorsqu'il était à Hong Kong. La réponse (B) joue sur la confusion entre les mots proches *mall* et *all*. La réponse (C) joue sur la confusion entre les expressions proches *downtown* et *out of town*. La réponse (D) correspond à l'endroit où l'homme dit ne jamais acheter de costumes.

64. (C) La femme dit *What a handsome suit*. Les réponses (A) et (B) correspondent à l'opinion de l'homme sur les costumes vendus au grand magasin du secteur. La réponse (D) correspond à ce que la femme dit de la cravate de l'homme.

65. (A) L'homme part faire de la marche en montagne pendant ses vacances. Les réponses (B), (C) et (D) correspondent à ce que la femme pense qu'il fera.

66. (D) L'homme dit qu'il attend avec impatience son séjour de trois semaines en montagne. La réponse (A) joue sur la confusion avec le moment où commenceront les vacances de l'homme. La réponse (B) joue sur la confusion entre les mots proches *eight* et *wait*. La réponse (C) reprend les mots *two* et *weeks*.

67. (B) L'homme dit que ses vacances commenceront dimanche. La réponse (A) joue sur la confusion entre les mots proches *afternoon* et *soon*. La réponse (C) joue sur la confusion entre *Tuesday* et l'expression *two days*. La réponse (D) joue sur la confusion entre les mots proches *few* et *two*.

68. (D) La femme dit qu'ils ont quatre bus. La réponse (A) reprend le mot *one* de la locution *one bus leave every*... La réponse (B) joue sur la confusion entre les mots proches *two* et *to*. La réponse (C) n'est pas mentionnée.

69. (A) Les bus viendront chercher les gens à l'hôtel pour les emmener au centre de conférences. La réponse (B) correspond à la destination des bus. La réponse (C) associe *bus station* et *bus*. La réponse (D) associe *loading dock* avec l'allusion au chargement des bus (*loading the buses*).

70. (C) Il y a un bus tous les quarts d'heure. La réponse (A) indique le temps nécessaire pour charger le bus. La réponse (B) correspond au délai pour aller d'un lieu à un autre. La réponse (D) correspond à la durée de l'aller-retour.

PARTIE 4 (PAGES 53–55)

Remarque : la bonne réponse est signalée en premier.

71. (A) Le centre des impôts (*Revenue Office*) de la mairie sera ouvert samedi de 8 heures à midi. Les réponses (B), (C) et (D) sont contradictoires avec les informations fournies.

72. (B) Il faut remplir des formulaires d'imposition. Les réponses (A), (C) et (D) ne correspondent pas au type de document susceptible d'être traité par le centre des impôts.

73. (C) Il devrait y avoir beaucoup de monde, il est donc conseillé aux gens de venir en avance pour éviter de devoir faire la queue. La réponse (A) joue sur la confusion entre *refund* et *revenue*. La réponse (B) joue sur la confusion entre *become citizens* et *citizens who are filing*. La réponse (D) joue sur la confusion entre les mots proches *files* (documents) et *file* (s'inscrire).

74. (D) La référence à un parking d'aéroport indique que cette annonce est passée dans un aéroport. Les réponses (A) et (B) sont mentionnées comme des destinations. La réponse (C) associe *airplane* et *airport*.

75. (A) Les passagers doivent suivre les pancartes bleues pour trouver des voitures à louer. La réponse (B) indique les transports publics. La réponse (C) indique des navettes spécifiques desservant des parkings. La réponse (D) joue sur la confusion entre les mots proches *yellow* et *follow*.

76. (B) Les passagers qui ont laissé leur véhicule dans un parking d'aéroport doivent suivre les pancartes vertes ou orange pour trouver une navette. Les réponses (A) et (C) renvoient à des moyens de transports publics. La réponse (D) n'est pas mentionnée.

77. (B) La personne qui parle espère que tout le monde a apprécié le déjeuner, puis elle présente l'invité, ce qui indique que le discours aura lieu après le repas. La réponse (A) est en contradiction avec *I hope you all enjoyed your lunch*. La réponse (C) joue sur la confusion entre *next month* et *monthly luncheons*. La réponse (D) joue sur la confusion entre *next Friday* et *on this beautiful Friday*.

78. (B) Les déjeuners ont lieu tous les mois. La réponse (A) joue sur la confusion entre *every Friday* et *this beautiful Friday*. Les réponses (C) et (D) sont en contradiction avec *monthly*.

79. (D) Mme Chang est l'auteur d'un best-seller. Les réponses (A) et (B) jouent sur la confusion entre *politician* et *criminal* et le titre de son livre. La réponse (C) associe *saleswoman* et *best-selling*.

80. (B) L'annonceur dit que les badges perdus doivent être déclarés auprès d'un responsable. La réponse (A) n'est pas correcte car c'est le responsable, non l'employé, qui doit faire la demande pour remplacer le badge. La réponse (C) reprend le mot *visitor*. La réponse (D) correspond à ce que l'on est susceptible de demander aux visiteurs et non aux employés.

81. (A) Les visiteurs doivent être accompagnés par des employés portant un badge d'identification. La réponse (B) joue sur la confusion entre *permission from security personnel* et *asked by security personnel to leave*. La réponse (C) indique la manière dont les employés doivent se présenter, et ce, quelles que soient les circonstances. La réponse (D) n'est pas mentionnée.

82. (A) Tous les employés sont priés de porter un badge d'identification. La réponse (B) est improbable. Les réponses (C) et (D) correspondent aux personnes qui ne doivent pas porter un badge mais qui doivent être accompagnées d'un employé portant un badge.

83. (B) Le *Spartan Golf Club* annonce l'ouverture de son tout nouveau parcours de golf. La réponse (A) joue sur la confusion entre les expressions proches *Civic Center* et *city center*. La réponse (C) indique l'endroit où les golfeurs peuvent faire leur demande d'adhésion. La réponse (D) joue sur la confusion entre les sons proches *residential* et *professional*.

84. (D) Des cartes d'adhésion sont offertes. La réponse (A) est mentionnée, mais les cours de golf ne sont pas l'élément essentiel de l'annonce. Les réponses (B) et (C) ne sont pas citées.

85. (D) Le tarif pour une année d'inscription est de mille cent dollars. La réponse (A) se rapproche du coût d'une inscription pour six mois. La réponse (B) correspond au coût d'une inscription pour six mois. La réponse (C) ressemble à la bonne réponse.

86. (A) *It's perfect beach weather*. Les réponses (B), (C) et (D) ne sont pas mentionnées.

87. (C) *The sun is shining*. Les réponses (A), (B) et (D) ne sont pas mentionnées.

88. (D) *It will rain on Saturday*. Les réponses (A) et (B) correspondent au temps d'aujourd'hui. La réponse (C) correspond au temps de vendredi.

89. (D) Les biens immobiliers de l'homme valaient plus de deux millions de dollars. La réponse (A) est en contradiction avec *two million dollars*. La réponse (B) joue sur la confusion entre les contraires *under* et *over*. La réponse (C) joue sur la confusion entre *a million* et *two million*.

90. (C) L'homme a légué tous ses biens immobiliers à son chien. Les réponses (A) et (B) sont en contradiction avec *left his entire estate to his dog*. La réponse (D) joue sur la confusion entre *his best friend* et *man's best friend*.

91. (A) L'enterrement aura lieu dimanche. La réponse (B) ressemble à la bonne réponse. La réponse (C) n'est pas mentionnée. La réponse (D) joue sur la confusion entre les sons proches *Thursday* et *third*.

92. (D) Le bureau est ouvert du lundi au vendredi. Les réponses (A), (B) et (C) sont en contradiction avec *Monday through Friday*.

93. (A) Le renouvellement des permis de conduire peut être obtenu l'après-midi de 12 heures à 16 heures. Les réponses (B) et (C) indiquent des services qui peuvent être obtenus de 8 heures à 16 heures. La réponse (D) ne correspond pas à un service qui relève du *Office of Motor Vehicles*.

94. (B) Le bureau ferme à 16 heures. La réponse (A) correspond à l'horaire auquel ils commencent à recevoir les personnes qui souhaitent renouveler leur permis de conduire. Les réponses (C) et (D) ne sont pas possibles dans la mesure où le bureau ferme à 16 heures.

95. (C) La personne appelle pour se plaindre du fait que sa commande ne soit toujours pas arrivée. Les réponses (A) et (B) ne sont pas correctes puisqu'elle n'a pas reçu sa commande. À la réponse (D), la personne fait allusion au fait que sa carte de crédit a été débitée, mais elle ne dit pas qu'elle l'a été d'un montant supérieur à ce qui était prévu.

96. (D) La personne qui appelle a passé sa commande il y a quatre semaines. La réponse (A) reprend *one*, qui correspond au nombre d'écrans d'ordinateur qu'elle a commandés. La réponse (B) correspond à la date à laquelle elle aurait dû être livrée. La réponse (C) reprend *three*, qui correspond au nombre de cartouches d'encre qu'elle a commandées.

97. (A) La personne qui appelle dit *Please check on this and call me today*. La réponse (B) emploie le mot *check* dans un contexte différent. La réponse (C) joue sur la confusion entre *right away* et le mot proche *today*. La réponse (D) correspond à quelque chose qui a déjà été fait.

98. (D) CompCo a célébré son ouverture aujourd'hui. La réponse (A) correspond à quelque chose qui a déjà été fait et qui se passera de nouveau à l'avenir, mais qui ne date pas d'aujourd'hui. La réponse (B) associe *training workshop* et *the banquet in the training center*. La réponse (C) correspond à ce que les autorités de la ville font avec d'autres entreprises.

99. (B) CompCo a déjà embauché cent personnes. La réponse (A) correspond au nombre d'employés que l'entreprise embauchera d'ici la fin de l'année. La réponse (C) correspond au nombre total d'employés que comptera CompCo d'ici la fin de l'année. La réponse (D) correspond au nombre de personnes qui ont perdu leur emploi lorsque PC omputer Systems a fermé.

100. (A) Deux cents personnes ont perdu leur emploi lorsque PC Computer Systems a fermé. La réponse (B) fait allusion à une entreprise susceptible de s'installer bientôt dans le secteur. La réponse (C) joue sur la confusion entre les mots proches *contract* et *attract*. La réponse (D) joue sur la confusion avec *The city leaders are working to attract more technology businesses to the area.*

PARTIE 5 (PAGES 56–59)

Remarque : la bonne réponse est signalée en premier.

101. (A) Les adverbes de fréquence indéfinis peuvent se placer avant le verbe principal. Les réponses (B), (C) et (D) ne correspondent pas à des emplacements possibles pour ces adverbes.

102. (C) *Depend on* est un verbe à préposition. Les réponses (A), (B) et (D) ne correspondent pas à ce que l'on trouve après *depend.*

103. (B) *Nonetheless* est une conjonction qui indique un résultat inattendu. La réponse (A) indique une substitution. La réponse (C) indique une séquence. La réponse (D) indique un résultat inattendu mais elle doit être suivie d'une proposition nominale.

104. (D) *Operating* fait partie du titre de *chief operating officer*. La réponse (A) est un nom qui fait référence à *people*. La réponse (B) est un adjectif mais il n'est pas utilisé dans ce titre. La réponse (C) est un nom qui fait référence à *things*.

105. (C) *And* est une conjonction de coordination qui relie deux éléments. La réponse (A) sert à exclure les deux éléments. La réponse (B) est généralement couplée avec *neither*. La réponse (D) indique un choix entre plusieurs éléments.

106. (B) To *run out of* signifie *not to have any more*. La réponse (A) signifie *to meet nexpectedly*. La réponse (C) joue sur la confusion avec *run out of*. La réponse (D) correspond à *to go beyond a limit.*

107. (C) *While* est une conjonction de subordination qui indique une simultanéité d'actions. Les réponses (A) et (B) indiquent un rapport de cause à effet. La réponse (D) exprime un but.

108. (C) *Of all* indique qu'un élément est singularisé par rapport à l'ensemble d'un groupe. La réponse (A) exprime un éloignement. La réponse (B) exprime une similarité. La réponse (D) indique une exception.

109. (A) *During* est une préposition qui exprime une période. La réponse (B) indique une association. La réponse (C) indique un lieu. La réponse (D) indique une direction.

110. (B) *For example* indique qu'un élément est un exemple. Les réponses (A) et (D) correspondent à des résultats inattendus. La réponse (C) indique une alternative.

111. (C) La facture sera signée par quelqu'un d'autre, c'est donc le participe passé qui est utilisé. La réponse (A) est un nom qui signifie "signature". Les réponses (B) et (D) correspondent à des formes incorrectes du verbe.

112. (C) On peut trouver des adverbes de fréquence indéfinie après diverses formes du verbe *be*. Les réponses (A), (B) et (D) ne sont pas des emplacements possibles pour ces adverbes.

113. (B) Le participe passé *based* complète le verbe *will be based on*. La réponse (A) est un adjectif. La réponse (C) est un gérondif. La réponse (D) est au présent.

114. (A) *Were* est la forme de *be* que l'on doit utiliser dans une phrase conditionnelle pour exprimer une condition irréelle. Les réponses (B), (C) et (D) ne correspondent pas aux formes qu'il convient d'utiliser dans de telles phrases.

115. (D) *To stand up to* signifie *to support a point of view against others*. La réponse (A) signifie *to substitute*. La réponse (B) indique une position ou une attitude. La réponse (C) signifie *to associate with others for a cause.*

116. (B) Le futur antérieur indique une action future qui aura lieu avant une autre action au futur. La réponse (A) est la forme passive du futur. La réponse (C) est au présent. La réponse (D) est au passé.

117. (D) *Housing market* est un terme d'affaires. La réponse (A) signifie "pigeon voyageur". La réponse (B) est un participe passé. La réponse (C) est un nom qui fait référence à une chose.

118. (C) *Besides* sert à ajouter un point supplémentaire. La réponse (A) indique une association. La réponse (B) indique un rapport de cause à effet. La réponse (D) indique un résultat.

119. (A) *Because* indique un rapport de cause à effet. La réponse (B) indique un résultat inattendu. La réponse (C) est un terme conditionnel. La réponse (D) indique une séquence temporelle.

120. (C) Les adverbes de fréquence définie peuvent se placer à la fin d'une proposition. Les réponses (A), (B) et (D) sont des adverbes de fréquence indéfinie.

121. (B) *Successor* signifie *a person who follows another in a job or role*. La réponse (A) est un adjectif. La réponse (C) est un nom qui fait référence à une chose. La réponse (D) est un adjectif qui indique une séquence.

122. (D) Les adverbes de fréquence indéfinie peuvent se placer entre l'auxiliaire et le verbe principal. Les réponses (A), (B) et (C) ne correspondent pas à des emplacements valables pour ces adverbes.

123. (D) *Have been satisfied* est la forme passive du *present perfect*, lequel indique une action qui a commencé dans le passé et continue dans le présent. La réponse (A) est au présent. La réponse (B) est au *present perfect* (forme active). La réponse (C) est au *present perfect* progressif.

124. (C) *Either . . . or* sont les deux termes que l'on associe pour exprimer un choix ou une alternative. Les réponses (A), (B) et (D) ne s'utilisent pas avec *either.*

125. (B) *Composed of* est un verbe à préposition qui indique une composition. Les réponses (A), (C) et (D) n'ont pas de sens lorsqu'elles sont associées au verbe *compose*.

126. (D) *Take on* signifie *to accept a challenge*. La réponse (A) correspond à *to leave*. La réponse (B) signifie *to remove*. La réponse (C) signifie *to remove from someone's possession.*

127. (C) *Employees* est un nom qui fait référence aux personnes travaillant dans une entreprise. La réponse (A) est un nom qui fait référence à une chose. Les réponses (B) et (D) sont des verbes.

128. (A) *Despite* indique un résultat inattendu. La réponse (B) exprime un rapport de cause à effet. La réponse (C) renvoie à une association. La réponse (D) exprime une similarité.

129. (C) *Financial* est un adjectif qui modifie *affairs*. La réponse (A) est un verbe. La réponse (B) est un gérondif. La réponse (D) est un participe passé.

130. (D) *Already* est un adverbe de fréquence indéfinie qui indique une action déjà accomplie et qui se place entre l'auxiliaire et le verbe principal. La réponse (A) signale une situation qui dure encore. La réponse (B) est un adverbe de fréquence définie. La réponse (C) indique une action qui n'a pas eu lieu à l'heure indiquée.

131. (C) *And* est une conjonction qui relie deux éléments. La réponse (A) indique un contraste entre deux éléments. La réponse (B) s'utilise généralement avec *neither*. La réponse (D) exprime un rapport de cause à effet.

132. (B) *Take over* signifie *to obtain control of*. La réponse (A) signifie *to leave*. La réponse (C) signifie *to bring something to a person or place*. La réponse (D) signifie *to remove.*

133. (A) *But* est une conjonction qui exprime un contraste entre deux éléments. La réponse (B) sert à relier deux éléments. La réponse (C) indique une association. La réponse (D) indique un contraste mais sert à relier deux propositions et non deux locutions.

134. (B) *If* peut servir dans le cas d'une situation possible. La réponse (A) indique une simultanéité d'actions. La réponse (C) correspond à un résultat inattendu. La réponse (D) sert à ajouter une idée.

135. (C) *On* s'emploie pour préciser une date. La réponse (A) indique un lieu ou un moment. La réponse (B) est un article. La réponse (D) est employée avec des dates uniquement pour indiquer une période bornée, comme *from April 28 to May 1.*

136. (A) *Advertising costs* décrit le coût de la production d'annonces publicitaires. La réponse (B) est un nom qui fait référence à des choses au pluriel. La réponse (C) représente les coûts qui ont été portés à la connaissance du public. La réponse (D) est un verbe.

137. (C) *A drop in (quarterly) profits* est une expression d'affaires. La réponse (A) peut être employée pour indiquer le niveau de la baisse. La réponse (B) spécifie le niveau auquel la baisse a commencé : *dropped from two million to one million.* La réponse (D) indique une association.

138. (D) *Founded* signifie *established* ou *started.* La réponse (A) *found* signifie *located.* La réponse (B) est un adjectif. La réponse (C) est la base verbale de *find.*

139. (B) *Nevertheless* indique un résultat inattendu. La réponse (A) ajoute des informations supplémentaires. La réponse (C) indique un exemple. La réponse (D) indique une simultanéité d'actions.

140. (D) Mme Alva va rédiger un communiqué de presse, c'est donc la base verbale *write* qui est employée. La réponse (A) est au présent. La réponse (B) est à l'infinitif. La réponse (C) est un participe présent.

Partie 6 (pages 60–64)

Remarque : la bonne réponse est signalée en premier.

141. (A) Une *addition* est un élément ou une section ajoutée à quelque chose. Les autres réponses ont un sens proche mais sont valables pour des utilisations plus spécifiques. La réponse (B) fait généralement référence à des produits chimiques. La réponse (C) est un terme utilisé en arithmétique. La réponse (D) est un *addenda*, c'est-à-dire un élément que l'on ajoute à un document.

142. (C) Le verbe *consider* est suivi d'un gérondif. La réponse (A) est la base verbale. La réponse (B) est à l'infinitif. La réponse (D) est au futur.

143. (C) L'adjectif possessif à la deuxième personne *your* fait référence à la personne à qui la lettre est adressée ; les *facilities and services* correspondent à ceux de l'hôtel dans lequel cette personne travaille. Les réponses (A) et (B) sont des adjectifs à la première personne. La réponse (D) est à la troisième personne.

144. (B) La forme correcte de l'expression est *in addition to.* Les réponses (A), (C) et (D) sont des prépositions qui ne sont pas valables avec cette expression.

145. (A) Lorsque des passagers ont *too much,* ou *excess baggage,* ils doivent payer un supplément. Les réponses (B), (C) et (D) ressemblent à la bonne réponse mais ont des sens très différents.

146. (A) Il s'agit d'une phrase à l'impératif, indiquant au lecteur ce qu'il doit faire au cas où il aurait des questions à poser. Ce type de phrase ne nécessite pas de sujet. Les autres réponses sont des formes verbales qui nécessitent un sujet. La réponse (B) est un verbe au présent. La réponse (C) est un infinitif. La réponse (D) est une forme modale accompagnée d'un verbe.

147. (D) Une forme modale comme *can* doit être suivie de la base verbale. La réponse (A) est une forme future. La réponse (B) est un participe passé. La réponse (C) est un infinitif.

148. (C) Le verbe *focus* est suivi de la préposition *on.* Les réponses (A), (B) et (D) sont des prépositions qui ne peuvent pas suivre le verbe *focus.*

149. (A) Cette phrase décrit ce que les dentistes font normalement ou habituellement, c'est donc le temps présent à la forme simple qui est employé. La réponse (B) est au *preterit* simple. La réponse (C) est au *past perfect.* La réponse (D) est au conditionnel.

150. (A) *We* fait référence à l'auteur de la lettre et à ses collègues. Les réponses (B) et (C) n'ont aucun sens dans ce contexte. La réponse (D) est un adjectif possessif, il ne peut donc être employé comme sujet de la phrase.

151. (C) *Various* est un adjectif qui se rapporte à *manufacturing companies.* La réponse (A) est un verbe au temps présent. La réponse (B) est un nom. La réponse (D) est un adjectif mais dont le sens ne convient pas dans le contexte.

152. (C) *Would like* est suivi d'un verbe à l'infinitif. La réponse (A) est un verbe au présent. La réponse (B) est un participe présent. La réponse (D) est un nom.

PARTIE 7 (PAGES 65–83)

Remarque : la bonne réponse est signalée en premier.

153. (C) C'est une *superior double room* qui a été réservée. La réponse (A) joue sur la confusion entre *single* et *superior double room*. La réponse (B) joue sur la confusion entre *twin* et *double*. La réponse (D) n'est pas mentionnée.

154. (D) Le dîner n'est pas inclus dans le prix de la chambre. Les réponses (A), (B) et (C) correspondent toutes à des éléments inclus dans le prix de la chambre.

155. (A) M. Peterman a envoyé sa réservation par fax. Les réponses (B), (C) et (D) sont en contradiction avec *thank you for your confirmation fax*.

156. (D) C'est un grand cabinet d'avocats qui cherche à embaucher un comptable. La réponse (A) joue sur la confusion entre *a computer company* et *computer skills*. La réponse (B) associe *accounting office* et *accountant*. La réponse (C) joue sur la confusion entre *advertising agency* et *job advertisement*.

157. (C) Un diplôme de droit n'est pas mentionné comme critère de sélection. Les réponses (A), (B) et (D) sont mentionnées.

158. (B) Un comptable est la personne la plus susceptible d'être intéressée par un poste dans le domaine de la comptabilité. La réponse (A) associe *lawyer* et *law firm*. La réponse (C) associe *a computer science major* et *computer skills*. La réponse (D) associe *director of human resources* et *supervisory experience*.

159. (D) Un système automatique utilise des machines, donc *mechanical* est la bonne réponse. Les réponses (A), (B) et (C) ne conviennent pas dans le contexte.

160. (A) On trouverait ce type de lettre dans le manuel d'utilisation d'un four à micro-ondes. Les réponses (B) et (C) sont en contradiction avec *in this manual*. La réponse (D) joue sur la confusion entre *design store* et *product has been designed to give you many years of trouble-free operation*.

161. (B) *Sophisticated* signifie *advanced*. Les réponses (A), (C) et (D) pourraient également être utilisées pour décrire un four à micro-ondes, mais elles ont des sens différents.

162. (B) L'utilisateur doit suivre les instructions du manuel. Les réponses (A) et (C) ne sont pas mentionnées. La réponse (D) joue sur la confusion entre *redesign the kitchen* et *this product has been designed*.

163. (D) Le communiqué de presse concerne le *Summer Consumer Electronics Show*. La réponse (A) correspond au lieu où la manifestation se déroulera. La réponse (B) joue sur la confusion entre *Chicago's convention centers* et *the McCormick Convention Center in Chicago*. La réponse (C) désigne les personnes qui seront présentes lors de la manifestation.

164. (A) *Thirteen hundred manufacturers* exposeront. La réponse (B) n'est pas mentionnée. La réponse (C) joue sur la confusion entre *13 000* et *1 300*. La réponse (D) correspond au nombre de distributeurs de produits électroniques attendus lors de la manifestation.

165. (A) Les fabricants exposeront des équipements récents faisant appel à de la technologie de pointe. La réponse (B) associe *distribution of networks* et *distributors*. La réponse (C) associe *retail outlets* et *retailers*. La réponse (D) joue sur la confusion entre *shelving samples* et *products won't appear on retailers' shelves*.

166. (B) Ces listes de programmes télé concernent des émissions à thématique commerciale. Les réponses (A) et (D) ne sont pas mentionnées. La réponse (C) associe *Travelogues* et *World View*.

167. (A) *Business Today* commence à 14 heures. L'émission de la réponse (B) commence à 13 heures. L'émission de la réponse (C) commence à 16 heures. L'émission de la réponse (D) commence à 11 h 30.

168. (D) Une personne qui souhaite investir regarderait sans doute *Making Money*. Les réponses (A), (B) et (C) désignent des chaînes qui diffusent des émissions qui ne seraient pas aussi utiles que *Making Money*.

169. (B) Il s'agit d'une annonce pour un emploi. La réponse (A) associe *government* et *national*. La réponse (C) joue sur la confusion entre *television listing* et *providing TV service*. La réponse (D) joue sur la confusion entre *publicity for the opening of a National Career Center* et *job opportunities*.

170. (D) Un professionnel de l'informatique serait sans doute la personne la plus à même de s'intéresser à des postes de programmation et de développement informatique. Les réponses (A), (B) et (C) désignent des personnes susceptibles d'être intéressées par le fait de travailler pour des entreprises qui fournissent des services télé, radio et marketing, et non des services informatiques.

171. (A) Mme Makestos est à la recherche d'un emploi. La réponse (B) n'est pas correcte car elle est actuellement sans emploi. La réponse (C) est improbable dans la mesure où elle postule à un emploi basé en Grèce. La réponse (D) joue sur la confusion entre *applying to school* et *working during her summer vacations.*

172. (C) *Competent* signifie *skilled*. La réponse (A) signifie *reliable*, déjà mentionné dans la même phrase. La réponse (B) correspond à une qualité appréciable chez un employé mais n'est généralement pas mentionnée dans une lettre de recommandation. La réponse (D) est un mot qui n'est généralement pas utilisé pour décrire les qualités d'un employé.

173. (B) Mme Makestos a travaillé chez International Films pendant ses vacances d'été au cours des trois années passées. Les réponses (A) et (C) sont en contradiction avec *during her summer vacations for the past three years*. La réponse (D) n'est pas correcte parce qu'elle n'a travaillé que pendant l'été.

174. (C) Il s'agit d'une lettre de recommandation. La réponse (A) est en contradiction avec les compliments adressés à Mme Makestos. La réponse (B) joue sur la confusion entre *a job inquiry* et la lettre de recommandation pour la candidature de Mme Makestos. La réponse (D) joue sur la confusion entre *a request for information* et *contact me if you need further information.*

175. (A) Ce type de formulaire est susceptible d'être lu sur un écran d'ordinateur. La réponse (B) joue sur la confusion entre *movie screen* et *computer screen*. La réponse (C) associe *phone book* et *e-mail address*. La réponse (D) est en contradiction avec *"Moscow Daily" web home page*, que l'on trouve sur Internet.

176. (D) Tous les abonnements sont assortis d'une clause de garantie de remboursement. La réponse (A) est vraie, que l'abonné soit satisfait ou non. La réponse (B) n'est pas correcte car cela signifie que, même si l'abonné n'était pas satisfait, il souhaiterait continuer à recevoir la publication. La réponse (C) n'est pas mentionnée.

177. (C) Le journal soutient des ONG qui s'occupent de questions d'environnement. Les réponses (A), (B) et (D) ne sont pas mentionnées.

178. (C) La formation en interne est la forme la plus courante de formation. La réponse (A) correspond à de la formation en externe. La réponse (B) joue sur la confusion entre *ineffective* et *efficiency*. La réponse (D) n'est pas mentionnée.

179. (A) La formation en interne peut être assimilée à de l'apprentissage. La réponse (B) est le contraire de la formation en interne. La réponse (C) joue sur la confusion entre *a supervisory position* et *an employee learning from his or her supervisor*. La réponse (D) joue sur la confusion entre *a company benefit* et le fait que la formation soit bénéfique (*a benefit*) pour l'employé comme pour l'entreprise.

180. (A) L'objectif de la formation est d'améliorer l'efficacité des employés. Les réponses (B) et (C) ne sont pas mentionnées. La réponse (D) est la conséquence d'une formation accordée à un employé.

181. (A) Marjorie travaille sans doute au département audiovisuel, au même étage que le bureau des objets trouvés, ce qui signifie qu'elle exerce au niveau 1. Les réponses (B), (C) et (D) ne sont pas correctes.

182. (D) Les livres en arabe se trouvent au niveau 2, or la science politique est le seul département qui soit indiqué à ce niveau dans le tableau. Les réponses (A), (B) et (C) ne sont pas correctes.

183. (C) Olga va mettre une pancarte indiquant *"Today's workshop is canceled"* parce que Hussein ne sera pas là pour l'animer. La réponse (A) joue sur la confusion avec le rendez-vous d'Hussein avec les enfants pour faire la lecture. Un atelier est mentionné dans la réponse (B), mais il n'y a pas d'allusion à un changement de lieu dans les textes. La réponse (D) correspond à quelque chose qu'Olga fera en personne, et qu'elle ne signalera donc pas par une pancarte.

184. (A) Hussein a joint un exemplaire de l'annuaire du service à Olga parce qu'elle est nouvelle dans l'entreprise. Les réponses (B), (C) et (D) expriment des raisons possibles pour lesquelles une personne aurait du mal à se repérer dans les différents rayons de la bibliothèque, mais elles ne constituent pas des réponses correctes.

185. (C) Hussein espère reprendre le travail demain. La réponse (A) correspond à ce qu'il fait aujourd'hui. La réponse (B) est associée à l'annuaire de la bibliothèque. La réponse (D) correspond à ce qu'Hussein aurait dû faire aujourd'hui.

186. (B) Christina est intéressée par une commande d'ordinateurs auprès de l'entreprise de Heinz. La réponse (A) emploie le mot *train* dans un contexte différent. La réponse (C) emploie le mot *package* dans un contexte différent. La réponse (D) correspond à quelque chose qui se passe au sein de l'entreprise de Christina, mais il ne s'agit pas de ce dont elle souhaite discuter avec Heinz.

187. (B) Ils se rencontreront au bureau de la société de Heinz à Potsdam. La réponse (A) correspond à l'endroit où Christina se trouvera mercredi. Les réponses (C) et (D) sont deux villes dans lesquelles l'entreprise de Christina possède des bureaux.

188. (C) Christina suggère qu'ils se rencontrent jeudi et Heinz est d'accord. La réponse (A) correspond au premier jour du séjour de Heinz à Berlin. La réponse (B) correspond au premier jour du séjour de Christina à Berlin. La réponse (D) correspond au dernier jour du séjour de Heinz à Berlin.

189. (D) Heinz sera en réunion avec le P.-D.G. de son entreprise toute la matinée. La réponse (A) est associée à d'autres villes citées dans les e-mails. La réponse (B) signale le fait que M. Eckert arrivera d'une autre ville. La réponse (C) joue sur la confusion avec le poste de responsable de formation de M. Eckert.

190. (B) Christina demande à Heinz d'apporter un guide de formation, et il est d'accord. La réponse (A) correspond au produit vendu par l'entreprise de Heinz. Les réponses (C) et (D) correspondent à ce que Christina doit apporter à la réunion à la demande de Heinz.

191. (A) Il s'agit de la personne à qui la lettre est adressée. La réponse (B) désigne la personne qui travaille pour la Green Construction Company. La réponse (C) correspond à la personne qui travaille au service des achats de la banque. La réponse (D) indique la personne qui travaille au service comptabilité.

192. (B) La Green Construction Company fabrique des produits écologiques. La réponse (A) est incorrecte car les produits sont plus chers. La réponse (C) est fausse car les produits consomment moins d'électricité. La réponse (D) est vraie, mais il n'y a là rien de spécial : la plupart des produits peuvent être commandés par fax.

193. (B) La société prend 7 %, ce qui correspond à 3 % de moins que les frais habituellement facturés pour le transport. La réponse (A) correspond au montant qui a été déduit des frais de transport habituels. La réponse (C) correspond aux frais de transport habituels. La réponse (D) joue sur la confusion avec le coût de transport de 220 dollars qui figure sur l'ordre d'achat.

194. (B) Le tarif est de 200 dollars de moins que les 500 dollars demandés par la Green Construction Company. La réponse (A) correspond à la différence de prix entre les deux types de tapis. La réponse (C) correspond au prix d'un tapis écologique. Le tarif de la réponse (D) est 200 dollars plus cher que celui d'un tapis écologique.

195. (B) Le prix est deux fois plus bas que les 100 dollars de l'éclairage écologique. La réponse (A) n'est pas mentionnée. La réponse (C) correspond au prix d'un éclairage écologique. La réponse (D) correspond au prix des quatre éclairages écologiques qui figurent sur l'ordre d'achat.

196. (B) La réunion a commencé trente minutes après l'horaire prévu. La réponse (A) correspond à l'heure à laquelle elle était censée commencer. La réponse (C) correspond à l'heure à laquelle Jorgen Spelman est arrivé. La réponse (D) correspond à l'heure à laquelle la réunion était censée terminer.

197. (B) Narelle Dundee, l'auteur du fax, a parlé en premier de son sujet, les changements de la gestion, car Jorgen Spelman est arrivé en retard. La réponse (A) désigne le sujet qui aurait dû être abordé en premier. Les réponses (C) et (D) correspondent aux sujets qui ont été présentés plus tard.

198. (C) Tout le monde a été content d'entendre le rapport de Madeira Jones sur les finances. Les réponses (A) et (B) portent sur l'impression que l'auditoire a eue après avoir écouté le rapport sur la technologie. La réponse (D) porte sur le sentiment des gens après avoir écouté le rapport sur les défis du recrutement.

199. (C) Le troisième intervenant a également présenté un rapport sur les avancées technologiques. La réponse (A) désigne la personne initialement prévue pour présenter ce rapport. La réponse (B) désigne l'auteur du fax. La réponse (D) désigne la personne qui a parlé des défis du recrutement.

200. (C) La réunion a commencé tard et s'est terminée tard, mais elle a duré les trois heures initialement prévues. La réponse (A) correspond au temps supplémentaire qu'ils prévoient pour la prochaine réunion. La réponse (B) indique une durée plus courte d'une demi-heure que celle initialement prévue. La réponse (D) correspond à la durée prévue pour la prochaine réunion.

Solutions Test n° 3

Partie 1 (pages 85–90)

Remarque : la bonne réponse est signalée en premier.

Exemple :

(A) They're leaving the room.
(B) They're turning on the machine.
(C) They're standing near the table.
(D) They're reading the newspaper.

1. (C) Il y a du poisson à vendre. La réponse (A) n'est pas correcte car l'homme est en train de mettre de la glace sur le poisson, mais il n'est pas en train de pêcher. La réponse (B) joue sur la confusion entre les mots proches *salty* et *sale*. La réponse (D) joue sur la confusion entre *turning to ice* et *putting ice on the fish*.
2. (A) Deux hôtesses de l'air sont en train de servir des boissons aux passagers d'un avion. La réponse (B) utilise le mot associé *seats*. La réponse (C) indique le lieu de la scène, mais pas l'activité qui s'y déroule. La réponse (D) n'indique pas la bonne activité *(selling)* des hôtesses mais décrit ce qu'elles portent *(uniforms)*.
3. (B) Trois personnes sont en train de descendre du train. La réponse (A) joue sur la confusion entre les mots proches *plane* et *train*. La réponse (C) joue sur la confusion entre les mots proches *workers* et *walkers*, et entre *stationery* et *station*. La réponse (D) n'est pas correcte parce qu'elles portent toutes des chapeaux.
4. (B) L'homme est en train de manœuvrer un élévateur de palettes qui est un engin lourd. La réponse (A) joue sur la confusion entre les sons proches *fork* et *forklift*. La réponse (C) indique ce que l'homme est en train de soulever. La réponse (D) utilise les mots associés *driving* et *work*.
5. (A) Les tables sont dressées à l'extérieur. La réponse (B) est incorrecte car personne n'est assis à une table. La réponse (C) associe *picnic* et *outdoors*. La réponse (D) est fausse car les chaises sont autour des tables et non contre le mur.
6. (A) Deux voyageurs sont en train d'enregistrer leurs bagages au comptoir d'une compagnie aérienne. La réponse (B) utilise les mots associés aux déplacements en avion *passengers* et *security*. La réponse (C) utilise également les mots associés aux voyages *baggage handlers* et *bags*. La réponse (D) joue sur la confusion entre les mots proches *train* et *plane*, et n'indique pas la bonne action.
7. (A) Les voitures sont garées sur un parking en longues rangées courbées. La réponse (B) joue sur la confusion entre les mots *park* (un parc) et *park* (garer ou se garer). La réponse (C) joue sur la confusion entre les sons proches *barking* et *parking*. La réponse (D) utilise le mot associé *motorist*.
8. (A) Il s'agit d'une voiture en cours de fabrication. Les réponses (B) et (C) correspondent à des actions qui ont lieu plus tard, mais qui ne sont pas représentées sur la photo. La réponse (D) joue sur la confusion entre les mots *line* et *(assembly) line*.
9. (B) Le groupe est en train de participer à une réunion et de regarder un écran de télé. La réponse (A) n'indique pas la bonne action. La réponse (C) joue sur la confusion entre *buying a television* et *watching the monitor*. La réponse (D) utilise le mot associé *looking*.
10. (B) L'équipement, les uniformes et l'environnement suggèrent qu'il s'agit de scientifiques dans un laboratoire. La réponse (A) joue sur la confusion entre *telescopes* et *microscopes*. La réponse (C) utilise le mot associé *physicians* ; les personnes pourraient être des médecins en uniforme, mais ils ne sont pas en train d'opérer quelqu'un. La réponse (D) utilise le mot associé *uniforms*.

PARTIE 2 (PAGE 91)

Remarque : la bonne réponse est signalée en premier.

Exemple :
Where is the meeting room?
(A) To meet the new director.
(B) It's the first room on the right.
(C) Yes, at two o'clock.

11. (B) *She'll be here any minute* répond à la question *what time is she coming*. La réponse (A) renvoie à la question *what time is it*. La réponse (C) joue sur la confusion entre les sons proches *combing* et *coming*.

12. (B) *Next to the post office* répond à la question *where*. La réponse (A) associe *check* et *bank*. La réponse (C) joue sur la confusion entre les sons proches *banquet* et *bank*.

13. (A) *After breakfast* répond à la question *when*. La réponse (B) correspond à la question *when will you retire*. La réponse (C) correspond à la question *how long have you been working*.

14. (A) *Maria* répond à la question *who*. La réponse (B) joue sur la confusion entre *who's* et *whose*. La réponse (C) joue sur la confusion entre les sons proches *everyone* et *who is one*.

15. (B) *It's cheaper* répond à la question *why* en donnant une explication. La réponse (A) joue sur la confusion entre les sons proches *us* et *bus*. La réponse (C) joue sur la confusion entre les sons proches *much* et *bus*.

16. (C) *Classical* répond à la question *what kind of music is this*. La réponse (A) joue sur la confusion entre les sons proches *mistake* et *music*. La réponse (B) joue sur la confusion entre les mots *type* (verbe) et *type* (genre).

17. (B) *Half a dozen* répond à la question *how many*. La réponse (A) convient à la question *how many ordered wine*. La réponse (C) joue sur la confusion entre les sons proches *arrangements* et *oranges*.

18. (B) *I was home all day* répond à la question *where were you*. La réponse (A) reprend les mots *you*, *were* et *yesterday* mais ne cadre pas avec la question. La réponse (C) correspond à la question *when are you going*.

19. (A) *The ones in French* répond à la question *which of these books haven't you read*. La réponse (B) renvoie à la question *when do you read*. La réponse (C) correspond à la question *which books should I read*.

20. (B) *Yesterday* correspond à la question *what day did the guest arrive*. La réponse (A) correspond à la question *when will the guest arrive*. La réponse (C) joue sur la confusion entre les sons proches *guess* et *guest*.

21. (C) *It always begins a few minutes late* répond à la question *when will the performance begin*. La réponse (A) joue sur la confusion entre les sons proches *foreman* et *performance*. La réponse (B) reprend le mot *performance* mais ne correspond pas à la question.

22. (A) *Every three months or 3 000 miles* répond à la question *when*. La réponse (B) renvoie à la question *when did you change it*. La réponse (C) joue sur la confusion entre *change the color of the car* et *change the oil in the car*.

23. (C) *The package was for me* répond à la question *who received the package*. La réponse (A) joue sur la confusion entre les sons proches *age* et *package*. La réponse (B) correspond à la question *who opened the mail*.

24. (C) *He's too busy* est une réponse polie à la requête. La réponse (A) correspond à la question *which type of letters do you prefer*. La réponse (B) joue sur la confusion entre *send a letter* et *type a letter*.

25. (B) *There are only two chairs* répond à la question *how many*. La réponse (A) associe *sit down* et *chairs*. La réponse (C) joue sur la confusion entre les sons proches *round* et *around*.

26. (A) La première personne a froid et la seconde lui suggère de mettre un pull. La réponse (B) joue sur la confusion entre les mots proches *old* et *cold*. La réponse (C) reprend la locution *in here*.

27. (B) La première personne n'a pas assez d'argent pour prendre le bus, alors la seconde lui propose de lui prêter de l'argent. La réponse (A) joue sur la confusion entre les mots *fair* et *fare*. La réponse (C) associe *ride* et *bus*.

28. (C) *In room 300* répond à la question *where*. La réponse (A) joue sur la confusion entre les sons proches *eating* et *meeting*. La réponse (B) joue sur la confusion entre les sons proches *glass* et *class*.

29. (C) Étant donné que l'appartement de la première personne qui parle se trouve à un étage élevé, la seconde personne devine qu'il doit y avoir une jolie vue. La réponse (A) joue sur la confusion entre les mots proches *department* et *apartment*. La réponse (B) joue sur la confusion entre les mots proches *door* et *floor*.

30. (B) *We want to hear the news* répond à la question *why* et donne une explication. La réponse (A) correspond à la question *where is the radio*. La réponse (C) joue sur la confusion entre les mots proches *ready* et *radio*.

31. (C) *About a dozen* répond à la question *how many*. La réponse (A) correspond à la question *where*. La réponse (B) joue sur la confusion entre les sons proches *drawing* et *drawer*, et *pen* et *pencil*.

32. (B) *Two miles from here* répond à la question *where*. La réponse (A) correspond à la question *when do you play golf*. La réponse (C) joue sur la confusion entre les sons proches *because* et *course*, et *Gulf* et *golf*.

33. (A) *On time* renvoie à la question *when did the plane take off*. La réponse (B) joue sur la confusion entre *the plane's takeoff* et *take off the shirt*. La réponse (C) associe *leave* et *take off*.

34. (C) *The subway* renvoie à la question *what is the fastest way to get downtown*. La réponse (A) joue sur la confusion entre les contraires *slow* et *fast*. La réponse (B) joue sur la confusion entre les sons proches *tallest* et *fastest*.

35. (B) *About two blocks* répond à la question *how far*. La réponse (A) associe *hungry* et *restaurant*. La réponse (C) associe *serves good food* et *restaurant*.

36. (A) *I didn't sleep last night* répond à la question *why are you so tired*. La réponse (B) joue sur les sons proches *tire* et *tired*, et *air* et *are*. La réponse (C) joue sur la confusion entre les sons proches *required* et *tired*, *wear* et *why are*, et *ties* et *tired*.

37. (A) Étant donné que l'ascenseur est hors service, la seconde personne suggère d'emprunter les escaliers. La réponse (B) joue sur la confusion avec le mot *broken*. La réponse (C) joue sur la confusion entre les sons proches *eleven* et *elevator*.

38. (B) Les personnes parlent du repas dans un restaurant ; la seconde personne estime que le repas est délicieux. La réponse (A) joue sur la confusion entre les mots proches *expense* et *expensive*. La réponse (C) associe *waitress* et *restaurant*.

39. (B) *Bob's desk* répond à la question *whose desk*. La réponse (A) correspond à la question *where is your desk*. La réponse (C) reprend le mot *window* mais ne correspond pas à la question.

40. (C) *Let's clean up the office first* répond à la question *what shall we do first*. La réponse (A) joue sur la confusion entre les contraires *last* et *first*. La réponse (B) joue sur la confusion entre les sons proches *towel* et *shall*.

PARTIE 3 (PAGES 92–94)

Remarque : la bonne réponse est signalée en premier.

41. (B) La femme s'est garée dans le garage. La réponse (A) joue sur la confusion avec *across the street*. Les réponses (C) et (D) jouent sur la confusion avec la question de l'homme, *Did you park in the lot next door?*

42. (C) Le garage coûte cinq dollars de l'heure à la femme pour parquer sa voiture. La réponse (A) joue sur la confusion avec *two minutes*, ce qui correspond au temps qu'il reste avant le début du concert. La réponse (B) joue sur la confusion entre *four* et *for*. La réponse (D) joue sur la confusion entre les mots proches *eight* et *late*.

43. (C) Ils vont à un concert. La réponse (A) joue sur la confusion entre les mots proches *class* et *fast*. La réponse (B) joue sur la confusion entre les mots proches *movie* et *moving*. La réponse (D) emploie *play* dans un contexte différent en associant le mot à *soccer game*.

44. (D) L'homme dit *It must have just slipped my mind*, ce qui signifie qu'il a oublié. La réponse (A) reprend la locution *last week*. La réponse (B) correspond à ce que la femme devine. La réponse (C) associe *phone number* et *phone call*.

45. (A) La femme a fêté son anniversaire. La réponse (B) joue sur la confusion entre les mots proches *trip* et *slipped*. La réponse (C) est associée à la question de la femme *Were you sick?* La réponse (D) joue sur la confusion avec le fait que la femme attend que l'homme l'appelle.

46. (B) L'homme propose à la femme de l'inviter à dîner. Les réponses (A) et (C) sont associées à *birthday* mais ne correspondent pas à ce que l'homme va faire. La réponse (D) emploie le mot *sweet* dans un contexte différent.

47. (C) Les personnes parlent d'un programme qui passait hier soir et qui passe tous les mercredis, on doit être jeudi. Les réponses (A) et (D) sont impossibles. La réponse (B) correspond au soir où le programme est diffusé.

48. (A) L'homme a sans doute regardé l'émission de télévision dont il est en train de parler. Les réponses (B) et (C) correspondent à ce que la femme a fait. La réponse (D) emploie le mot *watch* dans un contexte différent.

49. (D) La femme rentre chez elle à 7 heures. La réponse (A) emploie le mot *one* dans un contexte différent. La réponse (B) joue sur la confusion entre *four* et *for*. La réponse (C) correspond à l'heure à laquelle l'émission de télévision est diffusée.

50. (A) L'homme fait pousser des légumes, donc il a une ferme. Les réponses (B) et (D) sont associées à *vegetables*. La réponse (C) est associée à *flowers*.

51. (B) L'homme est agriculteur depuis treize ans. Les réponses (A) et (C) jouent sur la confusion entre *four*, *fourteen* et *for*. La réponse (D) ressemble à la bonne réponse.

52. (B) L'homme dit qu'autrefois il prenait sa voiture tous les jours pour aller au travail. La réponse (A) joue sur la confusion entre les mots proches *hotel* et *tell*. La réponse (C) associe *hospital* et *sick*. La réponse (D) associe *car dealership* et *car*.

53. (A) L'homme dit que la pièce est ennuyeuse. La réponse (B) est incorrecte car la femme dit, *We don't have to stay to the end*. La réponse (C) correspond à ce que l'homme dit qu'il pourrait se passer. La réponse (D) joue sur la confusion avec *Who told us to see it?*

54. (D) La femme dit que les billets ont coûté 75 dollars. Les réponses (A) et (B) ressemblent à la bonne réponse. La réponse (C) joue sur la confusion avec la locution proche *for two-fifty*.

55. (D) L'homme suggère de louer un film et de rester à la maison. La réponse (A) n'est pas correcte car l'homme veut dépenser moins d'argent, pas plus. La réponse (B) joue sur la confusion avec *rent a movie*. La réponse (C) joue sur la confusion entre les mots proches *guest* et *just*.

56. (C) Les personnes jouent au golf, donc elles doivent se trouver sur un parcours de golf. La réponse (A) joue sur la confusion entre *tea* et *tee*. La réponse (B) emploie le mot *club* dans un contexte différent. La réponse (D) associe *bowling* et *ball*.

57. (B) La femme dit à l'homme de ne pas s'énerver. La réponse (A) est incorrecte : la femme dit à l'homme de *take a practice swing*, mais elle ne dit pas comment il devrait s'y prendre. La réponse (C) emploie le mot *club* dans un contexte différent. La réponse (D) correspond à ce que l'homme dit qu'il va faire.

58. (B) L'homme demande à la femme de se taire. La réponse (A) correspond à ce que la femme veut faire. La réponse (C) joue sur la confusion entre les mots proches *call* et *ball*. La réponse (D) joue sur la confusion entre les locutions proches *all night* et *all right*.

59. (D) L'homme dit que son avion part à 3 h 30. La réponse (A) joue sur la confusion entre les mots proches *noon* et *soon*. La réponse (B) correspond à l'heure approximative à laquelle la conversation a lieu. La réponse (C) ressemble à la bonne réponse.

60. (C) L'homme dit qu'il prendra le taxi pour aller à l'aéroport. La réponse (A) correspond à ce que la femme devine. La réponse (B) joue sur la confusion entre les mots proches *car* et *far*. La réponse (D) n'est pas mentionnée.

61. (A) La femme rappelle à l'homme qu'il rentrera dimanche matin. La réponse (B) joue sur la confusion entre les mots proches *night* et *right*. Les réponses (C) et (D) jouent sur la confusion entre les mots proches *Monday* et *Sunday*.

62. (B) La femme demande : *Is this elevator going up or down?* La réponse (A) joue sur la confusion entre les mots proches *door* et *floor*. La réponse (C) joue sur la confusion entre les mots proches *apartment* et *department*. La réponse (D) correspond au lieu où la femme veut aller.

63. (B) La femme dit qu'elle va au septième étage. La réponse (A) joue sur la confusion entre les mots proches *four* et *floor*. La réponse (C) joue sur la confusion entre les sons proches *eight* et *great*. La réponse (D) ressemble à la bonne réponse.

64. (D) L'homme dit que la vente s'achève vendredi. La réponse (A) joue sur la confusion entre les mots proches *Sunday* et *Monday*. La réponse (B) correspond au moment où la vente a commencé. La réponse (C) joue sur la confusion entre les mots proches *Tuesday* et *today*.

65. (A) Les personnes mentionnent *get wet*, *swim*, *water* et *pool*, elles sont donc à la piscine. La réponse (B) associe *beach* et *swim*. La réponse (C) joue sur la confusion entre les mots proches *school* et *pool*. La réponse (D) associe *racetrack* et *race*.

66. (C) La femme dit *I'll race you across the pool*. La réponse (A) associe *sweater* et *cold*. La réponse (B) joue sur la confusion entre les mots proches *sun* et *fun*. La réponse (D) joue sur la confusion entre les mots proches *toss* et *across*.

67. (C) L'homme dit qu'il a froid. La réponse (A) joue sur la confusion entre les mots proches *old* et *cold*. La réponse (B) correspond à ce que l'homme ne souhaite pas être, c'est-à-dire mouillé. La réponse (D) joue sur la confusion entre les sons proches *tired* et *try it*.

68. (D) La femme fait allusion à un restaurant. La réponse (A) emploie le mot *park* dans un contexte différent. La réponse (B) correspond au lieu où l'homme veut se garer. La réponse (C) correspond à l'endroit où la femme suggère de se garer.

69. (A) L'homme dit qu'ils doivent être là-bas dans quinze minutes. Les réponses (B), (C) et (D) ressemblent à la bonne réponse.

70. (A) L'homme craint de ne pas arriver à suivre la femme et de se perdre. La réponse (B) joue sur la confusion entre les locutions proches *being followed* et *following the woman*. La réponse (C) joue sur la confusion avec le fait que la femme conduise doucement afin de ne pas distancer l'homme. La réponse (D) n'est pas mentionnée.

Partie 4 (pages 95–97)

Remarque : la bonne réponse est signalée en premier.

71. (B) C'est l'été. Les réponses (A), (C) et (D) sont en contradiction avec *it's another hot and humid summer day*.

72. (A) Il y aura des averses en début d'après-midi. Les réponses (B), (C) et (D) ne sont pas mentionnées.

73. (B) La personne dit que le ciel s'éclaircira en début de soirée. La réponse (A) correspond au moment où la pluie commencera à tomber. La réponse (C) reprend le mot*tomorrow*. La réponse (D) n'est pas mentionnée.

74. (D) Le cabinet du Dr Miller est fermé le vendredi. Les réponses (A), (B) et (C) correspondent aux jours d'ouverture du cabinet.

75. (A) Les personnes susceptibles d'appeler le 800-555-3212 sont celles qui présentent une urgence médicale liée aux dents. Les réponses (B), (C) et (D) ne sont pas mentionnées.

76. (C) Sur le répondeur, il est précisé qu'il faut laisser un message afin que le médecin puisse rappeler. La réponse (A) correspond à la manière de procéder pour prendre rendez-vous. La réponse (B) correspond à ce qu'il convient de faire en cas d'urgence. La réponse (D) mentionne un jour où le cabinet est ouvert.

77. (B) La société Stonebark va ouvrir sa première filiale à l'étranger le 1er mars à Melbourne. La réponse (A) a déjà été annoncée. La réponse (C) se déroulera après le début du concours du mois d'avril. La réponse (D) se déroulera avant la fin de l'année.

78. (A) Les clients peuvent se rendre sur le site Web de la société et voter pour leur café préféré. Les réponses (B) et (C) jouent sur la confusion avec les nouveaux cafés qui vont ouvrir. La réponse (D) n'est pas mentionnée.

79. (D) La personne dit que *Stonebark is well posed to become an international favorite in the near future*. La réponse (A) est incorrecte car la personne qui parle dit que Stonebark est la chaîne du pays qui se développe le plus. La réponse (B) joue sur la confusion entre *special* et *specialty*. La réponse (C) joue sur la confusion entre *favorable* et *favorite*.

80. (C) Le magasin loue des ordinateurs et vend des ordinateurs d'occasion réparés. La réponse (A) est en contradiction avec la bonne réponse. La réponse (B) joue sur la confusion entre les mots proches *furniture* et *refurbished*. La réponse (D) joue sur la confusion entre le mot *repair* et son synomyme *refurbish*.

81. (B) La période minimale de location est la journée. La réponse (A) correspond à une période de temps plus courte. Les réponses (C) et (D) correspondent à des périodes de temps plus longues.

82. (B) Le magasin est ouvert de 10 h 30 à 20 h 30. Les réponses (A), (C) et (D) sont proches de *10:30*.

83. (D) L'annonce concerne un tremblement de terre au Japon. La réponse (A) associe *riot* et *damage to*. Les réponses (B) et (C) sont des catastrophes naturelles qui ne sont pas mentionnées.

84. (B) Le dernier tremblement de terre a eu lieu il y a deux mois. La réponse (A) joue sur la confusion entre le chiffre *one* et le pronom *one*, comme dans *The last one occurred…* La réponse (C) joue sur la confusion entre *three* et *the third*. La réponse (D) reprend le mot *year.*

85. (B) Il y a eu très peu de dégâts matériels. Les réponses (A), (C) et (D) sont en contradiction avec *little damage.*

86. (A) Les annonces de vols proviennent d'un aéroport. La réponse (B) associe *plane* et *airport*. La réponse (C) associe *consulate* et *passport*. La réponse (D) associe *bus station* et *gate 16.*

87. (B) L'avion part de la porte 16. La réponse (A) joue sur la confusion entre les sons proches *fifteen* et *sixteen*. La réponse (C) correspond au numéro du vol. La réponse (D) joue sur la confusion entre les sons proches *sixty* et *sixteen.*

88. (D) L'annonce dit que les gens accompagnés d'enfants en bas âge peuvent passer en priorité. La réponse (A) joue sur la confusion avec les passagers qui passent la douane. La réponse (B) joue sur la confusion avec les gens qui montrent leur billet à l'hôtesse d'embarquement. La réponse (C) joue sur la confusion avec l'allusion avec les bagages à main autorisés.

89. (B) Les deuxième et troisième niveaux sont réservés au parking du personnel. La réponse (A) est en contradiction avec les deux niveaux mentionnés. La réponse (C) joue sur la confusion entre *three levels* et *the third level*. La réponse (D) joue sur la confusion entre les mots *four* et *for.*

90. (A) Les espaces rouges sont réservés aux véhicules de maintenance. Les voitures correspondant aux réponses (B) et (C) doivent être garées dans les espaces bleus. La réponse (D) n'est pas mentionnée.

91. (A) Les espaces jaunes sont réservés à la direction. La place de la réponse (B) est réservée aux employés. La réponse (C) n'est pas mentionnée. La réponse (D) est en contradiction avec *reserved spaces.*

92. (D) Les touristes sont en train d'écouter un guide. La réponse (A) associe *politicians* et *United Nations*. La réponse (B) correspond à la personne qui parle. La réponse (C) associe *diplomats* et *the United Nations.*

93. (C) Le groupe voyage en car. Les réponses (A), (B) et (D) sont en contradiction avec *be back on the bus by two o'clock.*

94. (B) La personne qui parle dit que le groupe restera à la *City Hall* pendant trois heures. La réponse (A) correspond à une confusion avec *2:00*, l'heure à laquelle le car partira pour la *City Hall*. La réponse (C) joue sur la confusion entre *four* et *for*. La réponse (D) correspond à une confusion avec *5:30*, l'heure à laquelle le car partira pour conduire le groupe au lieu du dîner.

95. (D) La librairie *Barry* cesse ses activités. La réponse (A) joue sur la confusion avec *holiday hours*. La réponse (B) joue sur la confusion avec *our final month*. La réponse (C) joue sur la confusion avec *school texts.*

96. (D) Les livres de poche sont à moitié prix. Les réponses (A), (B) et (C) correspondent à d'autres articles vendus dans le magasin, mais aucune réduction de prix n'est mentionnée les concernant.

97. (B) La librairie est fermée le dimanche. Les réponses (A), (C) et (D) correspondent à d'autres jours notés dans les horaires de la librairie.

98. (D) Le soleil se lèvera à 8 h 30. Les réponses (A) et (B) jouent sur la confusion avec l'heure à laquelle le soleil se lèvera demain. La réponse (C) ressemble à la bonne réponse.

99. (A) Une alerte au brouillard plus tard dans la soirée est lancée à destination des petits bateaux. La réponse (B) joue sur la confusion avec le vent demain matin. La réponse (C) reprend le mot *shore*, mais sans allusion à la question de savoir s'il est *rocky* ou non. La réponse (D) reprend le mot *sunset*, mais sans que l'on sache si l'heure du coucher de soleil est considérée comme tôt ou non.

100. (C) Il y aura du soleil demain après-midi. La réponse (A) joue sur la confusion avec le temps de la matinée. La réponse (B) joue sur la confusion entre les mots proches *snow* et *blow*. La réponse (D) correspond au temps qu'il fera plus tard dans la semaine.

PARTIE 5 (PAGES 98–101)

Remarque : la bonne réponse est signalée en premier.

101. (C) *Consulting firm* est un terme d'affaires. La réponse (A) est un nom qui fait référence à une chose. La réponse (B) est un nom qui fait référence à une personne. La réponse (D) est un verbe.

102. (A) *Count on* signifie *to depend on*. La réponse (B) signifie *to start counting at a particular point*. La réponse (C) signifie *to include*. La réponse (D) signifie *to total*.

103. (D) Une action passée qui se déroule après une action antérieure se met au *preterit* simple. La réponse (A) est au futur. La réponse (B) est au présent. La réponse (C) est au *present perfect*.

104. (D) Pour exprimer une condition irréelle dans le présent, on doit utiliser *could* dans la proposition introduite par *if*. Les réponses (A), (B) et (C) ne sont pas des formes modales possibles pour exprimer une condition irréelle.

105. (A) L'équipement sera livré par quelqu'un d'autre, c'est donc le participe passé qui est employé. La réponse (B) est un participe présent. Les réponses (C) et (D) ne peuvent pas suivre *want*.

106. (B) *Therefore* exprime un rapport de cause à effet. Les réponses (A) et (C) expriment un résultat inattendu. La réponse (D) exprime un but.

107. (B) *Because of* exprime un rapport de cause à effet et peut être suivi d'une proposition nominale. La réponse (A) doit être suivie d'un sujet et d'un verbe. La réponse (C) exprime un résultat inattendu et doit être suivie d'un sujet et d'un verbe. La réponse (D) doit être suivie d'un sujet et d'un verbe lorsqu'elle exprime un rapport de cause à effet.

108. (C) *In* est utilisé pour exprimer une durée de type "mois". La réponse (A) aurait pu être utilisée avec *month* mais indique un futur immédiat. La réponse (B) est utilisée avec des dates. La réponse (D), *the*, ne s'utilise pas avec des noms de mois.

109. (B) Les adverbes de fréquence définie peuvent se placer à la fin d'une phrase. Les réponses (A), (C) et (D) ne sont pas des emplacements valables pour ces adverbes.

110. (D) *And* sert à relier deux éléments. La réponse (A) exprime un contraste entre des éléments. La réponse (B) est généralement employée conjointement avec *neither*. La réponse (C) indique une séquence ou un rapport de cause à effet.

111. (C) *In* est utilisé pour indiquer un lieu à l'intérieur d'une ville. La réponse (A) est employée pour exprimer un moment précis. La réponse (B) est un article, pas une préposition. La réponse (D) indique une direction.

112. (C) *Consequently* indique un rapport de cause à effet. La réponse (A) résume les points précédents. La réponse (B) ajoute des informations supplémentaires. La réponse (D) indique un exemple.

113. (A) Ce sont les employés qui partent, c'est donc la base verbale du verbe qui est employée. La réponse (B) est au passé. La réponse (C) est au passé à la forme progressive. La réponse (D) est au passé à la forme passive.

114. (A) Les conditions possibles présentes ou futures s'expriment à l'aide du présent dans la proposition introduite par *if*. La réponse (B) s'utilise pour exprimer des conditions irréelles avec *be*. La réponse (C) est au *present perfect*. La réponse (D) est au futur.

115. (D) Ce sont les clients qui semblent être intéressés, c'est donc la base verbale qui est utilisée. Les réponses (A) et (C) sont des participes, qui sont rarement utilisés avec des verbes d'état. La réponse (B) est au futur.

116. (C) *Find out* est un verbe à préposition qui signifie *to uncover information*. Les réponses (A), (B) et (D) ne peuvent pas compléter le verbe.

117. (A) Une action qui commence dans le passé et qui continue dans le présent s'exprime à l'aide du *present perfect*. La réponse (B) est au passé. La réponse (C) est au présent. La réponse (D) est au futur.

118. (D) Pour exprimer une condition irréelle passée, on emploie le *past perfect* dans la proposition introduite par *if* et *could have* ou *would have* suivi du participe passé dans l'autre proposition. La réponse (A) est au passé. La réponse (B) est au futur. La réponse (C) est au conditionnel présent.

119. (D) Les factures seront faxées par quelqu'un d'autre, c'est donc le participe passé qui est employé. La réponse (A) est la base verbale. La réponse (B) est un participe présent. La réponse (C) est au passif.

120. (B) *Were* est la forme de *be* qui convient dans une proposition introduite par *if* pour exprimer une condition irréelle. La réponse (A) est au présent. La réponse (C) est au futur. La réponse (D) est au conditionnel.

121. (D) *And* sert à relier deux éléments. La réponse (A) indique un choix parmi différents éléments. Les éléments (B) et (C) ne sont pas des conjonctions de coordination.

122. (A) Il faut mettre le passé à la forme simple. La réponse (B) est au passé mais ne s'accorde pas avec le sujet singulier *shortage*. La réponse (C) est au *present perfect*. La réponse (D) est au *present perfect* et ne s'accorde pas avec *shortage.*

123. (C) *Should be given* exprime une intention ou une recommandation. La réponse (A) est au passé et au passif, et ne s'accorde pas avec *funds*. La réponse (B) nécessite un sujet actif. La réponse (D) *is given* est au présent et au passif, mais ne s'accorde pas avec *funds.*

124. (A) Les payes seront déposées par quelqu'un d'autre, c'est donc le participe passé qui est utilisé. La réponse (B) est un participe présent. La réponse (C) est au présent et au passif. La réponse (D) est la base verbale.

125. (B) *Therefore* exprime un rapport de cause à effet ou un résultat. La réponse (A) indique un résultat inattendu. La réponse (C) indique une occurrence simultanée. La réponse (D) exprime un contraste.

126. (D) *Throughout* est employé pour exprimer différents lieux dans une ville ou dans une autre zone ou région. Les réponses (A) et (B) peuvent s'employer avec des noms de rues mais pas de villes. La réponse (C) signifie *concerning.*

127. (A) *Retirement plan* est un terme d'affaires. La réponse (B) est un participe présent. La réponse (C) est la base verbale. La réponse (D) est le participe passé.

128. (D) *After* indique une séquence temporelle d'événements. La réponse (A) indique une simultanéité d'actions. La réponse (B) indique un rapport de cause à effet et n'est pas suivie d'un sujet et d'un verbe. La réponse (C) indique une simultanéité d'actions mais n'est pas suivie d'un sujet d'un verbe.

129. (C) *Already* est un adverbe concernant une action qui a eu lieu plus tôt que prévu. La réponse (A) indique la fin d'une échéance. La réponse (B) signifie *at any point in time.* La réponse (D) est un adjectif.

130. (C) *When* indique une séquence temporelle, en particulier lorsqu'une action est influencée par une autre. La réponse (A) n'est pas logique. La réponse (B) n'est pas la forme correcte *as soon as*. La réponse (D) ne peut pas être suivie d'un verbe et d'un sujet.

131. (D) *Of* est employé pour relier des portions de temps à un tout. La réponse (A) indique une direction. La réponse (B) est employée avec des heures précises de la journée. La réponse (C) indique une source ou une origine.

132. (A) *For example* désigne un exemple précis à partir d'une affirmation plus générale. La réponse (B) indique une séquence temporelle. Les réponses (C) et (D) expriment des résultats inattendus.

133. (D) Les employés sont les personnes qui ont le sentiment de former une famille, c'est donc la base verbale du verbe qui est utilisée. La réponse (A) est un participe présent. La réponse (B) est au présent et au singulier. La réponse (C) est au passé.

134. (C) Les conditions réelles dans le présent peuvent s'exprimer à l'aide du présent au passif dans la proposition introduite par *if.* La réponse (A) est au passé et au passif. La réponse (B) est au futur et au passif. La réponse (D) est au présent mais à la forme active.

135. (B) *Will be opening* exprime un futur en cohérence avec *within the next year*. La réponse (A) est au passé. La réponse (C) est au *present perfect*. La réponse (D) est au conditionnel.

136. (D) *Stop by* est un verbe composé qui signifie *to visit someone briefly*. La réponse (A) signifie *to interrupt a trip briefly*. La réponse (B) signifie *to stop for a specific purpose* (suivi d'un nom, comme dans *stop for gas*). La réponse (C) signifie *stop in order to complete an action.*

137. (A) *Dispute* signifie *an argument* ou *a disagreement*. La réponse (B) est un gérondif. La réponse (C) est un adjectif. La réponse (D) est un nom qui fait référence à une personne dans un conflit.

138. (C) *Authorized* est un adjectif qui signifie *a dealer who is authorized (to deal with a particular product or service)*. La réponse (A) est un nom qui fait référence à une personne. La réponse (B) est un nom qui fait référence à une chose. La réponse (D) est un adjectif qui signifie *requiring dependence upon authority.*

139. (B) *Leave out* est un verbe à préposition qui signifie *to omit*. La réponse (A) signifie *leaving with a destination in mind*. La réponse (C) signifie *to bequeath a possession*. La réponse (D) signifie *leaving a location.*

140. (B) Le futur à la forme simple est nécessaire. Les réponses (A) et (D) sont au présent progressif. La réponse (C) est au futur antérieur.

Partie 6 (pages 102–106)

Remarque : la bonne réponse est signalée en premier.

141. (A) Il est plus prudent de débrancher (*unplug*) les appareils électriques avant de partir en voyage. La réponse (B) signifie *connect*. La réponse (C) signifie *turn on*. La réponse (D) signifie *repair.*

142. (A) *Between . . . and . . .* est utilisé pour décrire la longueur ou la durée de quelque chose. Les réponses (B), (C) et (D) pourraient être utilisées pour décrire la longueur de quelque chose mais ne s'emploient pas avec le mot *and.*

143. (D) Il s'agit d'une forme impérative exprimant un ordre ou un conseil au lecteur. La réponse (A) est un nom. La réponse (B) est un adjectif. La réponse (C) est un verbe au présent.

144. (D) *Bargain* signifie *a low price*. Les réponses (A), (B) et (C) n'ont rien à voir avec un prix bas ou une réduction.

145. (B) Le participe passé du verbe est utilisé pour compléter le verbe à la voix passive. La réponse (A) est la base verbale. La réponse (C) est au participe présent. La réponse (D) est un nom.

146. (B) Dans la mesure où cette publicité concerne une agence de location de voitures, logiquement c'est pour réserver une voiture ou un véhicule qu'un client appellerait. Les réponses (A), (C) et (D) correspondent à des choses qui peuvent être réservées mais pas dans une agence de location de voitures.

147. (A) La note donne la liste des conditions nécessaires pour être éligible au programme de départ en retraite anticipée. Les réponses (B), (C) et (D) correspondent à des éléments qu'une personne peut être amenée à gérer ou à rencontrer (*meet*), mais elles ne conviennent pas dans le contexte.

148. (C) *Interested* est un adjectif qui décrit la manière dont les employés se sentent. Les réponses (A) et (B) pourraient être utilisées en tant que noms ou verbes, mais pas en tant qu'adjectifs. La réponse (D) décrit quelque chose qui provoque l'intérêt chez une personne.

149. (B) Les employés doivent déposer leur candidature avant le 1er décembre s'ils souhaitent profiter d'un programme qui doit débuter (*will begin*) en janvier prochain. La réponse (A) est un verbe au passé. La réponse (C) est au *past perfect*. La réponse (D) est au *present perfect*.

150. (B) Le gérondif est employé comme sujet de la phrase. La réponse (A) est un verbe au présent. La réponse (C) est un verbe à l'infinitif. La réponse (D) est un sujet plus un verbe.

151. (A) *Guides* signifie *leads* ou *teaches*, ce qui correspond à l'objectif de la brochure. Les réponses (B), (C) et (D) ne conviennent pas dans le contexte.

152. (C) Il s'agit d'une question indirecte, la syntaxe est donc celle d'une phrase affirmative. La réponse (A) comprend un sujet mais pas le mot *is*, qui est nécessaire pour compléter la forme du futur avec *going to*. Dans les réponses (B) et (D), la syntaxe est celle d'une question.

Partie 7 (pages 107–125)

Remarque : la bonne réponse est signalée en premier.

153. (C) En 1950, la population mondiale était de 2,5 milliards d'individus. La réponse (A) joue sur la confusion entre *half a billion* et *2.5 billion*. La réponse (B) correspond à la population de 1925. La réponse (D) joue sur la confusion entre *5 billion* et *2.5 billion.*

154. (D) En 1975, la population a atteint 4 milliards de personnes. La réponse (A) correspond au moment où la population a atteint 1 milliard. La réponse (B) correspond à celui où elle a atteint 2 milliards. La réponse (C) correspond au moment où elle a atteint 2,5 milliards.

155. (A) En 1900, la population était de 1 milliard, soit la moitié de 2 milliards. Les réponses (B), (C) et (D) indiquent des populations de 2 milliards et plus.

156. (B) L'article parle de l'embauche d'employés. La réponse (A) joue sur la confusion entre *reading a newspaper* et *placing job ads in newspapers*. La réponse (C) n'est pas mentionnée. La réponse (D) joue sur la confusion entre *going to high school* et *high schools as a source of new employees.*

157. (A) Les *high schools* sont mentionnées comme une source habituelle de nouveaux employés. La réponse (B) correspond à une source interne. La réponse (C) joue sur la confusion entre les sons proches *spies* et *high (school).* La réponse (D) n'est pas mentionnée.

158. (C) Les entreprises utilisent également les journaux pour trouver leurs futurs employés. Les réponses (A), (B) et (D) ne sont pas mentionnées.

159. (C) AeroSys est une entreprise basée à Berlin. Les réponses (A), (B) et (D) sont des grandes villes qui ne sont pas mentionnées.

160. (B) AeroSys a passé un accord pour fournir un système satellitaire. Les réponses (A) et (C) correspondent aux éléments qui pourront communiquer les uns avec les autres. La réponse (D) correspond aux services qui utiliseront les communications.

161. (D) Le *ticketing service* n'est pas mentionné. Les réponses (A), (B) et (C) sont toutes mentionnées.

162. (D) Les *textbooks* ne sont pas cités comme des parties du programme. Les réponses (A), (B) et (C) sont toutes mentionnées comme telles.

163. (D) Les étudiants peuvent travailler et jouer à loisir sur les ordinateurs. Les réponses (A), (B) et (C) sont en contradiction avec *whenever they like.*

164. (A) Les familles des étudiants sont encouragées à s'impliquer. La réponse (B) joue sur la confusion entre *actors* et l'expression *get into the act* (*get involved*). La réponse (C) joue sur la confusion entre les sons proches *away* et *play*. La réponse (D) n'est pas mentionnée.

165. (B) Ce paragraphe concerne l'implication des familles, et *siblings* désigne les membres de la famille. Les réponses (A), (C) et (D) correspondent aux personnes qui peuvent être importantes pour un étudiant, mais qui ne font pas partie de la famille.

166. (B) L'article traite de différents types de communication. La réponse (A) associe *marketing* et *communication*. La réponse (C) est un type de communication. La réponse (D) est mentionnée mais il ne s'agit pas du sujet principal.

167. (A) Les mots correspondent à la forme de communication la plus usitée. Les réponses (B), (C) et (D) ne sont pas utilisées autant que les mots.

168. (B) Ce paragraphe décrit l'action comme une forme de communication. Les réponses (A), (C) et (D) ne conviennent pas dans le contexte.

169. (C) La télévision n'est pas un exemple d'action. Les réponses (A), (B) et (D) sont toutes mentionnées.

170. (B) Les professionnels de la santé sont les personnes les plus susceptibles de lire cette annonce sur la santé des personnes âgées. La réponse (A) est peu probable. La réponse (C) associe *word processors* avec *computing* et *computerized products*. La réponse (D) est peu probable.

171. (C) Les *blood-pressure monitors* peuvent faire partie des produits informatisés servant à contrôler la santé des patients. Les réponses (A) et (B) ne sont pas liées à la santé. La réponse (D) ne correspond pas à un produit informatisé.

172. (B) L'usine a fermé car elle était à l'origine de rejets de mercure à des niveaux dangereux pour la santé. La réponse (A) joue sur la confusion entre *too much trash* et *trash incinerator, the largest in the nation*. La réponse (C) est incorrecte car la transformation des déchets en énergie était bien l'objectif de l'usine. La réponse (D) est en contradiction avec *the environmental officials shutting it down.*

173. (D) La fonction de l'usine était de transformer les déchets en énergie. La réponse (A) correspond à quelque chose que l'usine fait, mais ce n'est pas sa fonction première. La réponse (B) correspond à la fonction des agents environnementaux. La réponse (C) correspond à un résultat inattendu du processus de conversion.

174. (B) La Stummering Corporation a été confrontée à un problème d'absentéisme. La réponse (A) renvoie à la question de savoir qui a décidé que quelque chose devait être fait. La réponse (C) associe *low pay* et *the cash incentive offered*. La réponse (D) n'est pas mentionnée.

175. (A) Les employés arrivaient en retard trois fois par semaine en moyenne. La réponse (B) joue sur la confusion entre *fifteen times a week* et *fifteen minutes late.* La réponse (C) joue sur la confusion entre *three times between January and June* et *three times a week between January and June*. La réponse (D) joue sur la confusion entre *fifteen times* et *fifteen minutes.*

176. (B) Chaque salarié ponctuel pouvait se voir offrir une prime en nature. La réponse (A) est mentionnée, mais ne correspond pas à une mesure d'incitation. Les réponses (C) et (D) sont peut-être des mesures d'incitation, mais elles ne sont pas mentionnées.

177. (A) *Replicated* signifie *copied* ; d'autres sociétés ont pu copier le programme concluant mené à la Stummering Corporation. Les réponses (B), (C) et (D) pourraient convenir dans la phrase, mais elles n'ont pas le sens requis.

178. (B) L'objet de la lettre est le refus de la candidature d'une personne. La réponse (A) correspond à l'objet de la lettre de M. Porter. La réponse (C) correspond à quelque chose qui est généralement demandé avant qu'une entreprise ne cherche à recruter un candidat. La réponse (D) joue sur la confusion entre *to learn about the corporation* et *thank you for your interest in the corporation.*

179. (A) M. Porter joint son CV dans sa lettre. Les réponses (B) et (C) ne sont pas mentionnées. La réponse (D) correspond à ce à quoi la lettre de M. Porter renvoie.

180. (C) M. Porter est comptable. La réponse (A) correspond au poste occupé par M. Simons. La réponse (B) associe *detective* et *inquiry*. La réponse (D) n'est pas mentionnée.

181. (B) Marina est la personne qui a appelé et laissé le premier message qui contient la commande de fournitures. La réponse (A) désigne la personne qui a pris le message. La réponse (C) désigne la personne qui a pris le second message. La réponse (D) désigne la personne qui a appelé et laissé le second message.

182. (D) Dans le message, la personne qui appelle dit souhaiter un meuble vertical pour trier les dossiers en métal (*metal*). La réponse (A) décrit les téléphones qui ont été commandés. La réponse (B) décrit l'un des photocopieurs. La réponse (C) décrit les bureaux et les chaises.

183. (A) La plupart des articles commandés se trouvent actuellement à Moscou ; seules la grosse photocopieuse et la table se trouvent ailleurs. La réponse (B) correspond à la provenance de la table. Les réponses (C) et (D) correspondent à l'endroit où doit se rendre Alonya cette semaine.

184. (D) La table arrivera un jour après l'échéance qui, selon le premier message, est dans une semaine. La réponse (A) joue sur la confusion avec *one day after your deadline*. La réponse (B) n'est pas mentionnée. La réponse (C) correspond à l'échéance.

185. (C) Alonya se rendra à Berlin demain. La réponse (A) correspond à ce qu'elle a fait aujourd'hui. Il n'est pas précisé quand elle fera ce qui est indiqué dans les réponses (B) et (D.

186. (D) Dans son e-mail, M. Grimaldi dit : *We talked to 1 000 investors…* La réponse (A) correspond au nombre de personnes qui ont investi dans des fonds communs de placement l'année dernière. La réponse (B) correspond au nombre de personnes qui ont investi dans des fonds communs de placement cette année. La réponse (C) correspond au nombre de personnes qui ont investi dans des actions étrangères cette année.

187. (B) Selon le tableau, 625 personnes ayant participé à l'étude ont investi dans l'or cette année. La réponse (A) correspond au nombre de personnes ayant investi dans l'or l'année dernière. La réponse (C) correspond au nombre de personnes qui ont investi dans des actions étrangères l'année dernière. La réponse (D) correspond au nombre de personnes ayant investi dans l'indice IRA 900 cette année.

188. (C) L'e-mail explique qu'une catégorie a été divisée entre *buildings* et *property* cette année, mais que ce n'était pas le cas l'année dernière. En regardant le tableau, on peut voir que cette catégorie correspond à la rubrique *Real Estate*. Les réponses (A), (B) et (D) sont des réponses plausibles mais incorrectes.

189. (D) M. Grimaldi souhaite faire connaître les investissements qui vont avoir du succès. Les réponses (A), (B) et (C) incluent les investissements qui seront moins attrayants ou qui resteront stables.

190. (A) M. Grimaldi souhaite discuter des investissements qui vont devenir moins attrayants. Les réponses (B), (C) et (D) incluent les investissements qui deviendront plus attrayants ou qui resteront stables.

191. (C) Les robots feront des démonstrations de travaux ménagers : ils nettoieront le sol, feront la vaisselle et sortiront les ordures. Les réponses (A), (B) et (D) jouent sur la confusion avec les équipements électroniques qui seront exposés lors de la convention.

192. (B) Le film est prévu pour le 21 janvier. La réponse (A) correspond à la première journée de la convention. Les réponses (C) et (D) correspondent à des dates d'autres événements prévus.

193. (B) Mai dit que le billet pour Hank, sa fille Emma et elle-même, coûtera 25 dollars en tout. Cela correspond au prix pour deux adultes (Mai et Hank) et un enfant (Emma) âgé de cinq à douze ans. La réponse (A) n'est pas correcte car le salon est interdit aux enfants de moins de cinq ans. Les réponses (C) et (D) sont fausses car un ticket pour une personne de cet âge coûterait le même prix que celui d'un adulte.

194. (A) Mai dit que le président d'une société dans laquelle Hank détient des actions interviendra. Selon l'annonce, cette société est Automation, Inc. Les réponses (B), (C) et (D) correspondent à d'autres éléments mentionnés sur le calendrier des événements.

195. (B) La démonstration de sécurité est un événement spécial, et le tarif de ce type d'événement est de 3 dollars. La réponse (A) correspond au prix à payer pour commander des billets en ligne. La réponse (C) correspond au coût du billet pour un enfant. La réponse (D) correspond au coût du billet pour un adulte.

196. (C) L'objet mentionné dans l'e-mail de Ping spécifie *retirement party*. La réponse (A) correspond à la raison pour laquelle Gertrude est allée au restaurant le mois dernier. La réponse (B) joue sur la confusion avec la réunion à laquelle Gertrude assistera demain après-midi, avant la réception. La réponse (D) joue sur la confusion avec *last month*, qui correspond à la dernière fois où Gertrude est allée au restaurant.

197. (C) Gertrude, Rae et Alex veulent tous partir avec Ping. Les réponses (A), (B) et (D) sont en contradiction avec la bonne réponse.

198. (A) Ping veut partir à 6 h 15, et Gertrude veut partir trente minutes plus tôt. La réponse (B) correspond au moment où Ping veut partir. La réponse (C) correspond à trente minutes avant le début de la réception. La réponse (D) correspond à l'heure du début de la réception.

199. (D) L'appareil photo est un cadeau destiné à Samir pour sa retraite. Les réponses (A), (B) et (C) correspondent à d'autres personnes citées dans les messages e-mail.

200. (B) Gertrude achètera le cadeau ; Rae lui donnera l'argent qu'elle a collecté pour payer le cadeau. Les réponses (A), (C) et (D) correspondent à d'autres choses qu'elles feront, mais Rae ne paiera pas Gertrude pour cela.

Solutions Test n° 4

PARTIE 1 (PAGES 125–130)

Remarque : la bonne réponse est signalée en premier.

Exemple :

(A) They're leaving the room.
(B) They're turning on the machine.
(C) They're standing near the table.
(D) They're reading the newspaper.

1. (A) Un technicien de laboratoire ou un scientifique porte un vêtement et des lunettes de protection. La réponse (B) utilise le mot associé *hat*. La réponse (C) ne décrit pas la bonne action. La réponse (D) utilise un mot associé à *clothing : dressing*.

2. (C) Un home est en train de travailler près d'une piscine ; il est sans doute en train de la nettoyer. La réponse (A) utilise le mot associé *water* ainsi qu'une référence à la piscine vide. La réponse (B) utilise le mot associé *swimmers*. La réponse (D) mentionne *the pool*.

3. (A) Un homme est en train de soulever sa valise et de la mettre dans le coffre de sa voiture. La réponse (B) n'est pas correcte car la femme se tient debout à côté de l'homme mais ne marche pas derrière lui. La réponse (C) ne décrit pas la bonne action. La réponse (D) reprend le mot *suitcases* mais ne décrit pas la bonne action.

4. (B) Une femme est assise à une table en train de remplir un formulaire. La réponse (A) utilise le mot associé *notebook*. La réponse (C) ne décrit pas la bonne action. La réponse (D) mentionne le mot *table*.

5. (C) Une femme est en train de parler au téléphone et il y a un plan derrière elle. La réponse (A) utilise le mot associé *cord*. La réponse (B) utilise le mot associé *telephone booth*. La réponse (D) reprend le mot *map*.

6. (B) On voit des avions stationnés devant le terminal d'un aéroport. La réponse (A) joue sur la confusion entre les mots proches *panes* et *planes*. La réponse (C) joue sur la confusion entre les mots proches *trains* et *planes*. La réponse (D) joue sur la confusion entre les mots proches *cranes* et *planes*.

7. (D) Un homme est en train de travailler sur un ordinateur ; il a la main droite sur la souris. La réponse (A) joue sur la confusion entre *mouse* (le rongeur) et *mouse* (accessoire informatique). La réponse (B) reprend la locution *pad of paper* qui se trouve à côté de l'homme. La réponse (C) utilise le mot associé au fait de travailler en étant très concentré : *examining*.

8. (A) Un ferry est en train de faire une traversée. La réponse (B) utilise les mots associés au mot *ferry* : *passengers, boarding, pier*. Les réponses (C) et (D) ne décrivent pas le bon type de bateau ni le lieu qui correspond à celui de la photo.

9 (B) Des clients sont assis dans un restaurant en train de lire le journal. La réponse (A) utilise les mots associés à un restaurant : *customers, waiting for a table*. La réponse (C) ne décrit pas le bon endroit. La réponse (D) utilise le mot associé *menus*.

10. (A) L'homme est en train de se verser une tasse de café. La réponse (B) utilise le mot associé *emptying* au lieu de *emptying the pot*. La réponse (C) utilise le mot associé *liquid*. La réponse (D) reprend les mots *pot of coffee*.

PARTIE 2 (PAGE 131)

Remarque : la bonne réponse est signalée en premier.

Exemple :

Where is the meeting room?
(A) To meet the new director.
(B) It's the first room on the right.
(C) Yes, at two o'clock.

11. (A) *At 8 A.M.* répond à la question *what time*. La réponse (B) reprend le mot *open*. La réponse (C) associe *clock* et *what time*.

12. (B) Tout comme la première personne qui parle, la seconde aime aller au parc ou sortir dehors. La réponse (A) joue sur la confusion entre les locutions proches *parking lot* et *park a lot*. La réponse (C) joue sur la confusion entre les mots proches *dark* et *park*.

13. (B) *I'm late for a meeting* répond à la question *why* en apportant une explication. La réponse (A) joue sur la confusion entre les mots proches *talks* et *walks*. La réponse (C) renvoie à la question *why are they walking*.

14. (A) *My name is Ralph Smith* répond à la question *who is calling*. La réponse (B) correspond à la question *who am I calling*. La réponse (C) reprend les mots *call* et *who*.

15. (B) *Any minute* répond à la question *when do you expect your visitor*. La réponse (A) correspond à la question *how long was her visit*. La réponse (C) joue sur la confusion entre les mots proches *visit* et *visitor*.

16. (C) *My car* répond à la question *whose car shall we take*. La réponse (A) joue sur la confusion entre les sons proches *shallow* et *shall*. La réponse (B) joue sur la confusion entre *bus* et *car*.

17. (A) *Not very* répond à la question *how hungry are you*. La réponse (B) joue sur la confusion entre les sons proches *Hungary* et *hungry*. La réponse (C) renvoie à la question *why are you hungry*.

18. (A) M. Sato a appelé, donc la seconde personne va le rappeler. La réponse (B) associe *phone* et *call*. La réponse (C) joue sur la confusion entre *file* et *while*.

19. (A) *Yes, your wife called* répond à la question de type *oui/non : do I have any messages*. La réponse (B) joue sur la confusion entre les sons proches *massage* et *message*. La réponse (C) joue sur la confusion entre les sons proches *ages* et *messages*.

20. (B) *It rained all morning* répond à la question *why is the ground wet*. La réponse (A) joue sur la confusion entre les sons proches *grown* et *ground*, et entre *yet* et *wet*. La réponse (C) joue sur la confusion entre les sons proches *round* et *ground*.

21. (A) *In the files* répond à la question *where*. La réponse (B) joue sur la confusion entre les sons proches *voice* et *invoices*. La réponse (C) reprend le mot *invoice* mais ne correspond pas à la question.

22. (B) *I'm too busy* répond à la question *why don't you take a vacation*. La réponse (A) correspond à la question *why don't you take them*. La réponse (C) joue sur la confusion entre les sons proches *transportation* et *vacation*.

23. (C) La seconde personne pense que demain ne sera pas un bon jour pour aller à la plage car il risque de pleuvoir. La réponse (A) joue sur la confusion entre les sons proches *train* et *rain*. La réponse (B) joue sur la confusion entre les sons proches *again* et *rain* et reprend le mot *tomorrow*.

24. (A) *Green is a good color* répond à la question *what color will you paint the walls*. La réponse (B) correspond à la question *why*. La réponse (C) joue sur la confusion entre *read* et *red*.

25. (B) *We all like sugar* répond à la question *do any of you like sugar in your coffee*. La réponse (A) joue sur la confusion entre les sons proches *cigars* et *sugar*. La réponse (C) reprend le mot *sugar* mais ne correspond pas à la question.

26. (A) *About three more months* répond à la question *how much time will it take*. La réponse (B) renvoie à la question *how high is the building*. La réponse (C) renvoie à la question *when will you be here*.

27. (C) *That newspaper belongs to me* répond à la question *whose newspaper is on the table*. La réponse (A) correspond à la question *where is the newspaper*. La réponse (B) joue sur la confusion entre les sons proches *new* et *newspaper*.

28. (B) *Yes, the mail is on your desk* répond à la question *did the mail come yet*. La réponse (A) correspond à la question *did you eat yet*. La réponse (C) correspond à la question *did anyone come*.

29. (A) Mme Green arrive à 15 heures, et la seconde personne ira la chercher à l'aéroport. La réponse (B) associe *ticket* et *plane*. La réponse (C) joue sur la confusion entre les mots proches *same* et *plane*.

30. (C) *I have to finish this report* répond à la question *why are you working late*. La réponse (A) associe *night* et *late*. La réponse (B) renvoie à la question *why are you leaving*.

31. (A) *In my office* répond à la question *where*. La réponse (B) correspond à la question *where did you apply*. La réponse (C) correspond à la question *how long did they wait*.

32. (C) *I like the new hotel by the river* est une recommandation. La réponse (A) joue sur la confusion entre les sons proches *reservation* et *recommendation*. La réponse (B) joue sur la confusion entre *good enough* et *good hotel*.

33. (B) *I prefer a pen* répond à la question *which do you prefer*. La réponse (A) reprend le mot *pencil* mais ne renvoie pas à la question. La réponse (C) reprend le mot *pen* mais ne renvoie pas à la question.

34. (B) La première personne se plaint du fait que la photocopieuse tombe tout le temps en panne, et la seconde suggère d'en acheter une neuve. La réponse (A) utilise le mot *break* dans un contexte différent. La réponse (C) joue sur la confusion etre les mots proches *town* et *down*.

35. (A) *Nine employees* répond à la question *how many employees do you have*. La réponse (B) joue sur la confusion entre les sons proches *hard* et *have*. La réponse (C) ne correspond pas à la question.

36. (A) *On the bus* répond à la question *where*. La réponse (B) correspond à la question *when did you buy your coat*. La réponse (C) correspond à la question *where can I leave my coat*.

37. (C) *Not until summer* répond à la question *when will the weather get warmer*. La réponse (A) joue sur la confusion entre les sons proches *warmer* et *her*. La réponse (B) joue sur la confusion entre les sons proches *whenever* et *weather*.

38. (B) *The clerk* répond à la question *who is copying the report*. La réponse (A) joue sur la confusion entre les mots proches *reporter* et *report*. La réponse (C) joue sur la confusion entre les sons proches *copyright* et *copying*.

39. (A) *No, it's very uncomfortable* répond à la question *is your chair comfortable*. La réponse (B) joue sur la confusion entre les sons proches *chairman* et *chair* et entre *available* et *comfortable*. La réponse (C) joue sur la confusion entre les sons proches *fair* et *chair* et entre *capable* et *comfortable*.

40. (B) *Only about a mile* répond à la question *how far*. La réponse (A) renvoie à la question *how do you feel*. La réponse (C) joue sur la confusion entre les mots *hear* et *here*.

Partie 3 (pages 132–134)

Remarque : la bonne réponse est signalée en premier.

41. (B) L'homme cherche une tasse de manière à pouvoir boire un thé. La réponse (A) joue sur la confusion entre *papers* et *paper cups*. La réponse (C) joue sur la confusion entre les mots proches *ink* et *sink*. La réponse (D) joue sur la confusion entre les mots proches *caps* et *cups*.

42. (D) La femme dit que les tasses pour les boissons chaudes se trouvent dans le placard. Les réponses (A), (B) et (C) jouent sur la confusion avec *the cabinet over the sink*, ce qui correspond à l'endroit où se trouvent les *water cups*.

43. (A) L'homme veut boire une tasse de thé. La réponse (B) joue sur la confusion entre *write* et *right*. La réponse (C) correspond à ce que l'homme pense qu'il fera s'il ne trouve pas de tasse. La réponse (D) reprend le mot *sugar*, ce qui correspond à quelque chose que la femme offre à l'homme.

44. (C) La femme fait allusion à une clé, à un numéro de chambre, à l'heure à laquelle il faut libérer la chambre et à un réveil téléphonique ; les personnes qui parlent doivent donc se trouver dans un hôtel. La réponse (A) correspond à un endroit d'où l'on doit partir tôt le matin. La réponse (B) associe *bank* et *check*, mais la locution complète est *check-out time* (l'heure à laquelle on doit libérer sa chambre d'hôtel). La réponse (D) correspond au lieu où l'homme se rendra demain matin.

45. (C) L'homme dit qu'il doit partir à 5 h 30 pour prendre l'avion. La réponse (A) joue sur la confusion entre les mots proches *two* et *to*. La réponse (B) ressemble à la bonne réponse. La réponse (D) joue sur la confusion entre les sons proches *ten* et *then*.

46. (A) L'homme dit qu'il va régler sa note maintenant. La réponse (B) correspond à l'heure à laquelle il faut libérer la chambre. La réponse (C) joue sur la confusion entre les mots proches *tonight* et *flight*. La réponse (D) correspond au moment où l'homme devra partir.

47. (B) L'homme fait allusion au retard de son bus. La réponse (A) joue sur la confusion entre les mots proches *walk* et *week*. La réponse (C) joue sur la confusion entre les mots proches *train* et *again*. La réponse (D) joue sur la confusion entre les mots proches *car* et *far*.

48. (B) La femme dit *That's the third time this month*. La réponse (A) joue sur la confusion entre les sons proches *two* et *too*. La réponse (C) joue sur la confusion entre les mots proches *four* et *far*. La réponse (D) joue sur la confusion entre les mots proches *eight* et *late*.

49. (B) L'homme promet d'être à l'heure le lendemain. La réponse (A) joue sur la confusion entre les mots proches *nine* et *time*. La réponse (C) joue sur la confusion entre les mots proches *boss* et *bus*. La réponse (D) emploie le mot *rest* dans un contexte différent.

50. (B) La femme veut emprunter un tournevis. La réponse (A) joue sur la confusion avec la question de savoir quand la femme rendra le tournevis. La réponse (C) emploie le mot *back* dans un contexte différent. La réponse (D) correspond à l'endroit où se trouve le tournevis.

51. (A) La femme promet de rendre le tournevis avant l'heure du déjeuner. La réponse (B) joue sur une confusion avec la bonne réponse. La réponse (C) joue sur la confusion entre les mots proches *afternoon* et *soon*. La réponse (D) correspond au moment où l'homme réparera la chaise.

52. (C) L'homme demande à la femme de poser le tournevis sur son bureau. La réponse (A) joue sur la confusion avec l'endroit où se trouve la boîte à outils. La réponse (B) correspond à ce que l'homme a l'intention de réparer. La réponse (D) emploie le mot *back* dans un contexte différent.

53. (D) L'homme dit qu'il prend un mois complet de vacances. La réponse (A) joue sur la confusion avec *the first week of August*. Les réponses (B) et (C) correspondent à des durées de vacances que la femme juge insuffisantes.

54. (A) L'homme dit qu'il prend toujours ses vacances en août. Les réponses (B), (C) et (D) jouent sur la confusion avec le mot proche *remember*.

55. (B) L'homme dit qu'il a hâte de se baigner. La réponse (A) joue sur la confusion avec *rent a house*. La réponse (C) correspond à la manière dont la femme passe ses vacances. La réponse (D) joue sur la confusion entre les mots proches *beach* et *each*.

56. (B) La femme achète des chemises pour son mari. La réponse (A) joue sur la confusion entre les mots proches *shoes* et *choose*. La réponse (C) ressemble à la bonne réponse. La réponse (D) joue sur la confusion entre les mots proches *hats* et *that's*.

57. (D) La femme achète deux chemises grises. La réponse (A) joue sur la confusion entre les mots proches *green* et *sixteen*. La réponse (B) joue sur la confusion entre les mots proches *white* et *right*. La réponse (C) joue sur la confusion entre les mots proches *blue* et *two*.

58. (D) Les chemises coûtent 25 dollars chacune et la femme en achète deux. La réponse (A) joue sur la confusion avec la taille de la chemise. La réponse (B) correspondrait au prix de deux chemises si le prix à l'unité était de 16 dollars. La réponse (C) correspond au prix d'une chemise.

59. (A) L'homme dit à la femme de tourner à gauche au croisement. La réponse (B) correspond à la seule direction que la femme peut prendre au croisement. Les réponses (C) et (D) jouent sur la confusion avec le mot proche *toward*.

60. (C) L'homme dit qu'il est à présent 6 h 45. La réponse (A) joue sur la confusion avec *ten minutes*, ce qui correspond au temps qu'il lui faudrait pour se rendre au concert à pied. La réponse (B) joue sur la confusion avec *the concert starts in 15 minutes*. La réponse (D) correspond à l'heure à laquelle le concert commence.

61. (C) Les personnes qui parlent font allusion à un concert. La réponse (A) joue sur la confusion entre les mots proches *ball* et *hall*. La réponse (B) n'est pas mentionnée. La réponse (D) emploie le mot *park* dans un contexte différent.

62. (B) L'homme dit que les brochures se trouvent dans des cartons blancs dans la salle de fournitures. La réponse (A) correspond au lieu où la femme enverra quelques-unes des brochures. La réponse (C) correspond au lieu où les brochures se trouveront prochainement. La réponse (D) correspond au lieu de provenance des brochures.

63. (B) La femme a besoin des brochures cet après-midi. La réponse (A) correspond au moment où les brochures sont arrivées. La réponse (C) joue sur la confusion entre les mots proches *tonight* et *white*. La réponse (D) joue sur la confusion avec *this morning*, c'est-à-dire le moment où les brochures sont arrivées.

64. (B) La femme dit qu'il faut qu'elle poste une centaine de brochures pour Singapour. La réponse (A) joue sur la confusion entre les mots proches *twenty* et *plenty*. La réponse (C) ressemble à la bonne réponse. La réponse (D) correspond au nombre de brochures commandées.

65. (A) L'homme dit que la réunion a eu lieu à 14 heures. La réponse (B) correspond à l'heure à laquelle la conversation a lieu. La réponse (C) joue sur la confusion avec le nombre de fois où l'homme a appelé la femme. La réponse (D) joue sur la confusion entre les mots proches *nine* et *line*.

66. (B) La femme a très mauvaise mémoire et l'homme n'a pas pu lui rappeler la réunion, on peut donc conclure qu'elle l'avait oubliée. La réponse (A) joue sur la confusion avec les tentatives faites par l'homme pour appeler la femme. La réponse (C) emploie le mot *busy* dans un contexte différent ; c'est la ligne téléphonique qui était occupée, pas la femme. La réponse (D) joue sur la confusion entre les mots proches *sick* et *six*.

67. (D) L'homme dit que la prochaine réunion aura lieu vendredi. La réponse (A) joue sur la confusion entre les mots proches *Tuesday* et *today*. La réponse (B) joue sur la confusion entre *Wednesday* et *Wendy*, le nom de la femme. La réponse (C) correspond au moment où la femme souhaite que l'homme l'appelle.

68. (C) L'homme dit qu'il est en train de prendre son petit déjeuner. La réponse (A) joue sur la confusion entre les mots proches *work* et *walk*. La réponse (B) joue sur la confusion avec la demande de la femme qu'on l'emmène jusqu'à l'école en voiture. La réponse (D) joue sur la confusion entre les mots proches *letter* et *later*.

69. (A) L'homme dit que la journée est chaude et ensoleillée. La réponse (B) correspond à ce que la femme dit qu'il pourrait se passer plus tard. La réponse (C) joue sur la confusion entre les mots proches *cool* et *school*. La réponse (D) joue sur la confusion entre les mots proches *icy* et *nice*.

70. (C) L'homme dit à la femme d'aller à l'école à pied. La réponse (A) correspond au ouhait de la femme concernant le moyen de transport qu'elle préférerait, mais l'homme ne veut pas l'emmener en voiture. La réponse (B) correspond à la manière dont elle pourrait rentrer chez elle s'il pleut. La réponse (D) joue sur la confusion entre les mots proches *train* et *rain*.

PARTIE 4 (PAGES 135–137)

Remarque : la bonne réponse est signalée en premier.

71. (B) L'aéroport est fermé en raison d'un épais brouillard. La réponse (A) joue sur la confusion entre *heavy traffic* et *heavy fog*. Les réponses (C) et (D) ne sont pas mentionnées.

72. (C) Le brouillard se lèvera en fin de journée et les avions seront alors autorisés à décoller et à atterrir. La réponse (A) correspond au moment où l'aéroport a fermé. La réponse (B) correspond au moment où le centre météorologique a relaté la fermeture de l'aéroport. La réponse (D) joue sur la confusion entre les contraires *late* et *early*.

73. (C) La personne qui parle dit que les passagers doivent appeler leur compagnie aérienne pour obtenir des informations sur les annulations de vols. Les réponses (A) et (B) jouent sur la confusion avec la suggestion d'appeler *before leaving for the airport*. La réponse (D) joue sur la confusion avec la source des informations.

74. (A) Le train arrive à Penn Station à New York à 9 h 30. La réponse (B) joue sur la confusion entre *2:40* et *2-hour 40-minute trip*. La réponse (C) joue sur la confusion entre 6 heures et 6 h 50, c'est-à-dire les horaires de départ du train depuis Washington. La réponse (D) joue sur la confusion entre les sons proches *6:15* et *6:50*.

75. (A) Le train express est sans arrêts. Les réponses (B), (C) et (D) sont en contradiction avec *nonstop trip*.

76. (C) Le train est *all-reserved* et n'est accessible qu'aux passagers munis d'une réservation. La réponse (A) joue sur la confusion entre les mots proches *late* et *gate*. La réponse (B) joue sur la confusion avec les instructions selon lesquelles *Passengers may check their excess luggage at the gate*. La réponse (D) emploie le mot *check* dans un contexte différent.

77. (B) Le message dit que tous les hôtels sont pleins. La réponse (A) pourrait être la raison pour laquelle les hôtels sont pleins, mais elle n'est pas mentionnée. La réponse (C) joue sur la confusion entre *hotels are closed* et *hotels are full*. La réponse (D) associe *long lines* et *waiting list*.

78. (D) Les hôtels sont pleins pour la période allant du 15 au 30 août. Les réponses (A), (B) et (C) sont en contradiction avec la période mentionnée.

79. (D) Les gens peuvent laisser leur nom et leur numéro de téléphone afin d'être mis sur liste d'attente. La réponse (A) joue sur la confusion entre *mailing list* et *waiting list*. La réponse (B) correspond aux conditions préalables avant que le centre n'appelle les personnes placées sur liste d'attente. La réponse (C) joue sur la confusion entre *applying for any job available* et *applying for any available rooms*.

80. (C) Cette annonce est passée dans une salle d'attente. La réponse (A) associe *restaurant* et *coffee break*. La réponse (B) associe *school* avec *report* et *question-and-answer period*. La réponse (D) associe *train station* et *board* en jouant sur la confusion entre *board the train* et *board meeting*.

81. (C) Comme il est à présent 10 h 30 et que la réunion reprendra dans quinze minutes, cela signifie qu'elle reprendra à 10 h 45. La réponse (A) joue sur la confusion entre *10:15* et *fifteen-minute break*. La réponse (B) correspond à l'heure actuelle. La réponse (D) n'est pas possible s'ils ne font qu'une pause de quinze minutes.

82. (D) Les participants ont juste terminé d'écouter le rapport de Mme Johnson. La réponse (A) correspond à ce qu'ils vont faire lorsqu'ils reviendront après la pause. La réponse (B) correspond à ce qu'ils vont avoir maintenant. La réponse (C) joue sur la confusion entre les mots proches *résumé* (nom) et *resume* (verbe).

83. (A) Le niveau des eaux est monté très haut. La réponse (B) n'est pas mentionnée. La réponse (C) joue sur la confusion entre *more homes than families* et *families have been evacuated from their homes*. La réponse (D) joue sur la confusion entre *expensive property* et *expensive property damage*.

84. (A) Heureusement, aucune perte humaine n'est à déplorer. La réponse (B) correspond au niveau auquel l'eau est montée. La réponse (C) correspond au nombre de familles évacuées. La réponse (D) correspond au coût des pertes matérielles.

85. (C) Le président se rendra sur place vendredi. La réponse (A) joue sur la confusion entre les mots proches *Sunday* et *Monday*. La réponse (B) correspond au moment où l'eau a commencé à monter. La réponse (D) correspond au moment où le président s'adressera à la nation.

86. (B) Carlos est peintre en bâtiment. La réponse (A) joue sur la confusion entre *build new homes* et *make your home look like new*. La réponse (C) associe *designs interiors* et *decorating*. La réponse (D) joue sur la confusion entre *provides servants* et *provides services*.

87. (B) L'annonce dit *ask your neighbors (for references)*. La réponse (A) désigne les personnes dont les clients souhaiteraient avoir des références. La réponse (C) associe *decorators* et *decorating*. La réponse (D) associe *real estate agents* et *homes in this city*.

88. (C) Carlos est peintre en bâtiment depuis treize ans. La réponse (A) joue sur la confusion entre *four* et *for*. La réponse (B) joue sur la confusion entre les mots proches *eight* et *wait*. La réponse (D) ressemble à la bonne réponse.

89. (C) Les passagers de l'avion sont en train d'écouter le pilote. La réponse (A) joue sur la confusion entre *football captain* et *airline captain*. La réponse (B) joue sur la confusion entre les mots proches *hospital patients* et *be patient*. La réponse (D) associe *theater* et *ladies and gentlemen*.

90. (B) Le capitaine dit qu'ils peuvent s'attendre à stationner sur la piste pendant une bonne quinzaine de minutes environ. La réponse (A) joue sur la confusion entre *five* et *fifteen*. La réponse (C) correspond au nombre d'avions en attente d'autorisation de décollage. La réponse (D) joue sur la confusion entre les sons proches *fifty* et *fifteen*.

91. (D) La personne qui parle demande aux personnes qui l'écoutent de couper leurs téléphones portables. La réponse (A) joue sur la confusion entre les mots proches *eat* et *seats*. La réponse (B) joue sur la confusion avec *the no smoking sign*. La réponse (C) emploie le mot *sign* dans un contexte différent.

92. (B) Le Centre des arts du spectacle (*Center for Performing Arts*) est une organisation qui s'occupe de musique. La réponse (A) n'est pas liée aux arts du spectacle. La réponse (C) associe *youth* et *young*. La réponse (D) n'est pas liée aux arts du spectacle.

93. (A) Les personnes qui appellent doivent appuyer sur la touche 2 pour obtenir l'itinéraire leur permettant de se rendre au centre. La réponse (B) joue sur la confusion entre *four* et *for*. La réponse (C) joue sur la confusion entre les mots proches *nine* et *sign*. La réponse (D) correspond à ce que la personne qui appelle doit faire pour se faire inscrire sur la mailing list.

94. (C) Les personnes qui appellent doivent appuyer sur la touche 1 pour obtenir des informations concernant les billets. La réponse (A) correspond à ce qu'une personne obtient si elle appuie sur la touche 3. Les réponses (B) et (D) indiquent ce qu'une personne obtient si elle attend jusqu'à la fin du message.

95. (B) La tempête de neige débutera dans la soirée de vendredi. La réponse (A) correspond au moment où le bulletin météorologique est donné. La réponse (C) correspond au temps que durera la tempête de neige. La réponse (D) correspond au moment où la tempête de neige s'achèvera.

96. (D) On attend des chutes de neige pouvant atteindre une épaisseur de 25 à 30 centimètres (*10 to 12 inches*). La réponse (A) joue sur la confusion entre *two* et *four* et les mots proches *to* et *before*. La réponse (B) joue sur la confusion entre les mots proches *eight* et *late*. La réponse (C) ressemble à la bonne réponse.

97. (B) Il est conseillé aux auditeurs de *relax, stay home, and enjoy the snow*. La réponse (A) correspond à ce qui leur est conseillé de ne pas faire. La réponse (C) joue sur la confusion avec le conseil selon lequel il serait prudent de *to have flashlights in case of power outages*. La réponse (D) joue sur la confusion avec le conseil selon lequel il est plus prudent de *to have plenty of water and food on hand*.

98. (B) L'horaire de l'intervenante a été modifié et passe de 8 h 45 à 9 h 15. La réponse (A) correspond à l'horaire qui avait été initialement prévu pour elle. La réponse (C) joue sur la confusion avec *thirty minutes later*. La réponse (D) correspond à l'heure du déjeuner.

99. (C) Le diner sera servi au *Blue Mountain Room*. La réponse (A) correspond au lieu où la première personne interviendra. La réponse (B) correspond au lieu où le déjeuner sera servi. La réponse (D) joue sur la confusion avec le *Club Central*, où se déroulera la soirée dansante.

100. (D) L'activité qui vient juste d'être ajoutée est une soirée dansante au *Club Central*. La réponse (A) joue sur la confusion avec le *Blue Mountain Room*, où le dîner sera servi. Les réponses (B) et (C) correspondent aux activités qui avaient déjà été prévues.

PARTIE 5 (PAGES 138-141)

Remarque : la bonne réponse est signalée en premier.

101. (C) *Cost of living* est une expression d'affaires. La réponse (A) est un nom mais qui n'est pas utilisé dans cette expression. La réponse (B) est un verbe. La réponse (D) est un participe passé.

102. (A) *To call on* signifie *"passer voir"*. La réponse (B) signifie *to get someone's attention by shouting to them*. Les réponses (C) et (D) ne sont pas des verbes à préposition.

103. (B) Une action qui est accomplie avant une action passée se met au *past perfect*. La réponse (A) est au présent. La réponse (C) est au *present perfect*. La réponse (D) est au futur.

104. (C) Pour exprimer une condition réelle au présent, on peut employer le présent dans la proposition qui exprime le résultat de l'action. La réponse (A) est au conditionnel. La réponse (B) est au passé. La réponse (D) est au *present perfect* (conditionnel).

105. (D) Les ordinateurs seront installés par quelqu'un d'autre, c'est donc le participe passé qui est utilisé. La réponse (A) est au futur (passif). La réponse (B) est au participe présent. La réponse (C) est la base verbale.

106. (C) *However* indique un résultat inattendu. La réponse (A) indique un résultat inattendu mais n'est pas suivie d'un sujet et d'un verbe. La réponse (B) indique un résultat ou une conséquence. La réponse (D) indique un but.

107. (C) *Even though* indique un résultat inattendu. La réponse (A) signifie *anything*. La réponse (B) est un terme interrogatif. La réponse (D) indique un résultat inattendu.

Elle, pour être employée correctement, devrait être placée au début de la proposition exprimant le résultat de l'action.

108. (C) *On* est la préposition utilisée avec *conduct research*. La réponse (A) signifie *concerning*. La réponse (B) indique la source ou l'origine. La réponse (D) signifie *close to*.

109. (B) Les adverbes de fréquence définie peuvent se placer à la fin d'une phrase. Les réponses (A), (C) et (D) ne sont pas des emplacements valables pour ces adverbes.

110. (B) *Or* indique un choix entre des éléments. La réponse (A) indique un contraste entre des éléments. La réponse (C) est une négation, pas une conjonction. La réponse (D) est généralement employée avec *or*.

111. (D) *On* est utilisé avec les jours de la semaine. La réponse (A) indique la source ou l'origine. Les réponses (B) et (C) sont utilisées avec des lieux.

112. (C) *Until* indique un moment ou une action dont dépend une autre action. La réponse (A) est au conditionnel et n'est pas logique avec le reste de la phrase. La réponse (B) indique une relation de temps mais n'est pas logique avec le reste de la phrase. La réponse (D) est un pronom relatif.

113. (D) L'assistante est la personne qui a signé la note, c'est donc la base verbale qui est employée. La réponse (A) est un participe présent. La réponse (B) est un participe passé. La réponse (C) est au futur.

114. (C) Pour exprimer une condition réelle au présent, on peut mettre le présent dans la proposition qui exprime le résultat de l'action. La réponse (A) est au passé. La réponse (B) est au présent progressif. La réponse (D) est au futur.

115. (D) Une action qui s'est déroulée dans le passé et qui continue dans le présent peut se mettre au *present perfect* progressif. La réponse (A) est la base verbale. La réponse (B) est au passé. La réponse (C) est au *past perfect*.

116. (B) *To catch on* signifie *to become familiar with doing something*. Les réponses (A), (C) et (D) ne sont pas des verbes à préposition corrects.

117. (D) *Final* est un adjectif qui modifie *result*. La réponse (A) est un verbe. La réponse (B) est un adverbe. La réponse (C) est un nom qui fait référence à une personne.

118. (C) *Go through* signifie *to complete a transaction*. La réponse (A) signifie *to rise*. La réponse (B) signifie *to leave a place*. La réponse (D) signifie *to exceed*.

119. (C) L'inventaire sera terminé par quelqu'un d'autre, c'est donc le participe passé qui est employé. La réponse (A) est au futur (passif). La réponse (B) est la base verbale. La réponse (D) est un participe présent.

120. (B) *Were* est la forme de *be* utilisée dans la proposition introduite par *if* et qui exprime une condition irréelle. Les réponses (A), (C) et (D) ne sont pas utilisées dans la proposition introduite par *if* pour exprimer une condition irréelle.

121. (B) *Not only . . . but also* sont les termes que l'on associe pour dire « non seulement… mais aussi ». Les réponses (A), (C) et (D) ne peuvent pas être associées avec *not only*.

122. (D) Une action en cours est indiquée par le présent progressif ; il est ici à la forme passive. La réponse (A) est au présent progressif (actif). La réponse (B) est au présent (passif). La réponse (C) est la base verbale.

123. (C) *Should* est une forme modale qui indique l'obligation ou la préférence. Les réponses (A) et (D) sont des formes qui indiquent des actions accomplies et ne sont pas compatibles avec le futur. La réponse (B) est la base verbale.

124. (A) Les assistantes sont les personnes qui partent tôt, c'est donc la base verbale qui est employée. La réponse (B) est au présent. La réponse (C) est le participe présent. La réponse (D) est au passé.

125. (B) *Therefore* indique un résultat ou une conséquence. La réponse (A) indique un résultat inattendu. La réponse (C) sert à reprendre plusieurs points abordés. La réponse (D) indique un contraste.

126. (C) *One of* distingue un élément ou une personne par rapport à un groupe. La réponse (A) indique la source ou l'origine. La réponse (B) indique la manière. La réponse (D) est utilisée dans des comparaisons.

127. (C) *Identification number* est un terme d'affaires. La réponse (A) est un verbe. La réponse (B) est un nom qui fait référence à des choses. La réponse (D) est un participe passé.

128. (D) *Before* indique une relation temporelle séquentielle. La réponse (A) indique une relation temporelle simultanée. La réponse (B) indique un rapport de cause à effet. La réponse (C) indique une simultanéité mais elle n'est pas suivie d'un sujet et d'un verbe.

129. (A) Les adverbes de fréquence définie peuvent se placer à la fin de la phrase. La réponse (B) est un adverbe de fréquence indéfinie. La réponse (C) est utilisée avec une action accomplie. La réponse (D) indique un futur.

130. (B) *In spite of* indique un résultat inattendu. La réponse (A) doit être suivie d'un sujet et d'un verbe. Les réponses (C) et (D) sont des prépositions.

131. (C) *From . . . to* indique les limites d'une période. Les réponses (A) et (B) indiquent un lieu. La réponse (D) indique une manière.

132. (A) *For example* sert à introduire des exemples à partir d'une généralisation. La réponse (B) indique des informations supplémentaires. La réponse (C) indique un résultat inattendu. La réponse (D) indique un résultat ou une conséquence.

133. (C) *By* indique une voie passive, il faut donc mettre un participe passé. La réponse (A) est la base verbale. La réponse (B) est au présent. La réponse (D) est un participe présent.

134. (A) *Were* est la forme de *be* employée dans une proposition introduite par *if* pour exprimer une condition irréelle. Les réponses (B), (C), et (D) ne sont pas des formes de *be* utilisées dans la proposition introduite par *if* pour exprimer une condition irréelle.

135. (A) Il faut mettre du présent à la troisième personne. La réponse (B) ne s'accorde pas avec *who*. Les réponses (C) et (D) sont des formes progressives qui sont rarement employées avec des verbes d'état.

136. (C) *To take over* signifie *to obtain control of*. La réponse (A) signifie *to remove*. La réponse (B) signifie *to carry away*. La réponse (D) signifie *to leave*.

137. (B) *Briefing* est un nom qui signifie *a meeting to provide current information*. La réponse (A) est un adjectif. La réponse (C) est un adverbe. La réponse (D) est un verbe au passé.

138. (C) *Advisable* est un adjectif. Les réponses (A) et (D) sont des verbes. La réponse (B) est un nom.

139. (B) Il faut la base verbale pour former l'impératif. La réponse (A) est un nom. La réponse (C) est un verbe au passé. La réponse (D) est un verbe au présent progressif.

140. (A) *Either . . . or* sont les deux termes que l'on associe pour dire « soit… soit ». Les réponses (B), (C) et (D) ne peuvent pas être associées avec *either.*

PARTIE 6 (PAGES 142–146)

Remarque : la bonne réponse est signalée en premier.

141. (D) *This* sert de pronom faisant référence à la décision prise par Mme Michaels. La réponse (A) est un pronom possessif, mais il n'y a pas de nom auquel il pourrait renvoyer. Les réponses (B) et (C) sont des pronoms pluriels, mais ici il faut un mot singulier ; il n'y avait qu'une seule décision.

142. (C) Il faut mettre le verbe au *present perfect* ici pour faire référence à une action qui a commencé dans le passé mais qui est toujours vraie dans le présent. Les réponses (A), (B) et (D) ne sont pas à la forme correcte.

143. (C) *Think over* est un verbe à préposition qui signifie *reconsider* ; M. Jones n'est pas satisfait de la décision de Mme Michaels, il espère donc qu'elle reviendra dessus. La réponse (A) *think up* signifie *to get a new idea*. La réponse (B) *think of* signifie *to remember* et *call to mind*. La réponse (D) n'a pas de sens.

144. (C) Le verbe *consider* est suivi du gérondif. La réponse (A) est une base verbale. La réponse (B) est un verbe à l'infinitif. La réponse (D) est au futur.

145. (A) *While* introduit une proposition temporelle représentant une action qui se passe en même temps que l'action de la proposition principale. Les réponses (B) et (D) introduisent des actions qui se déroulent à un moment différent de l'action de la proposition principale. *During* signifie *at the same time as* mais ne peut pas être employée pour introduire une proposition temporelle.

146. (D) Junko aimerait voir son amie si celle-ci a un peu de temps à lui consacrer . Les réponses (A), (B) et (C) sont des mots qui pourraient être liés au fait de se retrouver pour déjeuner ou dîner, mais ils ne vont pas dans la phrase.

147. (C) Il faut le participe passé du verbe pour compléter la forme du *present perfect*. La réponse (A) est au présent. La réponse (B) est au passé à la forme simple. La réponse (D) est un participe présent.

148. (D) L'entreprise doit réduire les coûts car elle traverse des difficultés financières. Les réponses (A) et (B) donneraient à la phrase un sens inverse à celui de la bonne réponse. La réponse (C) joue sur la confusion avec *operating costs*, un autre type de dépenses auquel une entreprise doit faire face.

149. (A) L'expression *due to* signifie *because of*. Les réponses (B), (C) et (D) ne vont pas dans le contexte.

150. (B) L'objectif de cette lettre est d'expliquer à Mme Lerch comment passer une annnonce dans un journal. Les réponses (A), (C) et (D) sont liées au travail dans les journaux mais pas au sujet de la lettre.

151. (A) *These* est un démonstratif qui fait référence au mot *papers*. Les réponses (B), (C) et (D) sont des pronoms possessifs qui ne peuvent pas être utilisés en tant que démonstratifs.

152. (C) Il faut un verbe à la voie passive étant donné que le sujet *options* subit l'action. Les réponses (A), (B) et (D) sont toutes des formes actives.

Partie 7 (pages 147–163)

Remarque : la bonne réponse est signalée en premier.

153. (A) Le problème est qu'une personne du bureau de M. Gomez n'arrête pas de couper le thermostat. La réponse (B) est incorrecte car il y a un thermostat dans le bureau de M. Gomez. La réponse (C) joue sur la confusion entre *the other tenants want a thermostat* et *the other tenants are complaining about the lack of heat*. La réponse (D) est en contradiction avec *the tenants complaining about the lack of heat.*

154. (C) *We ask that you not touch the thermostat* signifie que *it should never be turned off.* Les réponses (A), (B) et (D) correspondent aux heures auxquelles les gens règlent généralement leurs thermostats.

155. (B) *Adjust* signifie *to alter* ou *change*. La réponse (A) joue sur la confusion avec le fait que les gens doivent payer le chauffage, mais ce message ne parle pas des factures de chauffage. La réponse (C) correspond à quelque chose que l'on fait par rapport à la température d'une pièce, mais elle ne convient pas avec le contexte. La réponse (D) est un mot qui ne peut pas être employé avec *temperature.*

156. (C) L'objectif de la note est de demander à M. Gomez de ne pas toucher le thermostat. La réponse (A) correspond à quelque chose que M. Gomez est susceptible de faire s'il veut obtenir une température plus élevée, mais cela n'est pas mentionné. La réponse (B) correspond à ce que la note demande à M. Gomez de ne pas faire. La réponse (D) joue sur la confusion avec *the other second-floor tenants are complaining.*

157. (B) L'annonce fait la promotion d'un kit de nettoyage pour chaussures blanches. La réponse (A) correspond à ce que le produit entretient. La réponse (C) joue sur la confusion entre *shoe repair* et *shoe care.* La réponse (D) n'est pas mentionnée.

158. (A) Le kit s'utilise en deux étapes et en deux minutes. La réponse (B) joue sur la confusion entre *five minutes* et *five dollars*, le prix du kit en cas de commande de chaussures. La réponse (C) joue sur la confusion entre *seven minutes* et *seven dollars*, le coût du kit. La réponse (D) n'est pas mentionnée.

159. (D) Le Kleen-Kit fait durer le blanc des chaussures blanches. La réponse (A) joue sur la confusion entre les mots proches *Wright* et *white*. La réponse (B) joue sur la confusion entre les mots proches *finishing* et *finishes*. La réponse (C) joue sur la confusion entre *staying handsome* et *white shoes are handsome.*

160. (A) L'e-mail parle d'horaires de travail. La réponse (B) n'est pas mentionnée. La réponse (C) joue sur la confusion entre les mots proches *observations* et *observes*. La réponse (D) reprend le mot *lunch*, mentionné comme partie des horaires quotidiens.

161. (C) L'entreprise applique la semaine des trente-cinq heures de travail. La réponse (A) correspond au jour où l'e-mail a été rédigé. La réponse (B) joue sur la confusion entre les mots proches *twenty-five* et *thirty-five*. La réponse (D) correspond à une semaine de travail type aux États-Unis.

162. (B) Les employés peuvent établir individuellement des horaires de travail différents avec l'accord de leur supérieur. La réponse (A) est en contradiction avec *with their supervisor's approval*. La réponse (C) correspond peut-être au poste de Mme Gibbons. La réponse (D) n'est pas mentionnée.

163. (B) La note est adressée à tous les employés. La réponse (A) joue sur la confusion entre *clients reading the memo* et *contracts with clients*. La réponse (C) correspond au sujet de la note. La réponse (D) désigne l'auteur de la note.

164. (C) Les visiteurs doivent être accompagnés car un certain nombre de contrats passés par l'entreprise avec ses clients sont de nature confidentielle. La réponse (A) n'est pas mentionnée. La réponse (B) correspond à la raison pour laquelle les visiteurs sont susceptibles de se rendre dans les bureaux de l'entreprise. La réponse (D) associe *visitors* et *guests*.

165. (D) Les visiteurs sont priés de se faire connaître à la réception. La réponse (A) correspond à ce que le réceptionniste fera. La réponse (B) n'est pas autorisée. La réponse (C) n'est pas mentionnée.

166. (B) Le réceptionniste appellera le bureau de l'employé afin de le prévenir de l'arrivée d'un visiteur. La réponse (A) est en contradiction avec *the receptionist will call*. La réponse (C) est incorrecte car ce sont les visiteurs, et non les employés, qui doivent attendre à la réception. La réponse (D) est incorrecte car les employés doivent venir pour accompagner leurs visiteurs.

167. (A) *Escort* signifie *to accompany*. Les visiteurs doivent être accompagnés par un membre du personnel, ce qui est indiqué dans le premier paragraphe de la note. La réponse (B) est l'inverse de la bonne réponse. La réponse (C) correspond à quelque chose qui doit être fait lorsqu'il y a un visiteur, mais elle ne convient pas au contexte. La réponse (D) joue sur la confusion avec *confidentiality*, le fait de garder les choses secrètes ou cachées.

168. (A) Les apparts-hôtels combinent les caractéristiques des appartements et des hôtels, d'où leur nom *apartment-hotels*. La réponse (B) est vraie pour les immeubles d'habitation mais pas des hôtels. La réponse (C) n'est pas mentionnée. La réponse (D) est vraie pour les hôtels mais pas pour les immeubles d'habitation.

169. (C) Un ingénieur en mission loin de chez lui pour une durée de dix semaines pourrait aller dans un appart-hôtel. Les réponses (A), (B) et (D) désignent des personnes susceptibles d'aller à l'hôtel pour des séjours d'une si courte durée.

170. (C) Les apparts-hôtels ne sont généralement pas situés en centre-ville. Les réponses (A), (B) et (D) ne sont pas mentionnées.

171. (D) Les apparts-hôtels sont souvent meilleur marché que les hôtels classiques. La réponse (A) joue sur la confusion entre les mots proches *larger* et *longer*. La réponse (B) est en contradiction avec *travelers often find it more comfortable to stay in an apartment-hotel*. La réponse (C) est en contradiction avec *they are run like hotels*.

172. (D) David Bikowski a été licencié de son poste dans une usine de production. La réponse (A) n'est pas mentionnée. La réponse (B) joue sur la confusion entre *being fired* et *being laid off*. La réponse (C) est en contradiction avec le fait qu'il reste à son nouveau poste, lequel est payé 100 dollars de moins par semaine.

173. (A) Le nouveau poste de M. Bikowski est rémunéré 100 dollars de moins par semaine que son ancien travail. La réponse (B) joue sur la confusion entre *a month* et *a week*. La réponse (C) joue sur la confusion entre les contraires *more* et *less*. La réponse (D) joue sur la confusion entre *month* et *week* et entre les contraires *more* et *less*.

174. (B) M. Bikowski a gardé son nouveau poste, même si on lui a proposé de revenir à son ancienne usine, car le travail dans cette société est moins stressant. La réponse (A) est en contradiction avec *the new job pays $100 less a week*. La réponse (C) n'est pas mentionnée. La réponse (D) joue sur la confusion entre *working close to home* et *finding a new job nearby*.

175. (A) Cette lettre accompagne un rapport d'évaluation. La réponse (B) joue sur la confusion entre *inquire about future job possibilities* et *look forward to working with you again in the future*. La réponse (C) associe *future projects* et *working with you again in the future*. La réponse (D) associe *payment* et *hired*.

176. (B) Le rapport que le consultant a préparé à l'attention de M. Thompson portait sur l'amélioration des performances des salariés. La réponse (A) est en contradiction avec *Mr. Thompson's hiring of Ms. Guess to write the report*. Les réponses (C) et (D) sont en contradiction avec *Mr. Thompson's hiring Guess Consulting to do the project evaluation.*

177. (D) Mme Guess a terminé le projet, qui est joint à la lettre. Les réponses (A), (B) et (C) sont mentionnées.

178. (A) M. Thompson doit être avocat à cause de la mention *Esq.* qui suit son nom. La réponse (B) associe *personnel director* et *employee performance evaluation*. La réponse (C) correspond à la profession de Mme Guess. La réponse (D) est en contradiction avec *I enjoyed working with your law firm.*

179. (D) L'annonce dit que la montre affiche *all twenty-four world time zones*. La réponse (A) joue sur la confusion entre *five time zones* et *five-year international warranty*. La réponse (B) joue sur la confusion entre les sons proches *twelve* et *twenty*. La réponse (C) joue sur la confusion entre *eighteen time zones* et *eighteen karat*.

180. (B) Une garantie internationale limitée de cinq ans est offerte. Les réponses (A) et (C) jouent sur la confusion entre *eighteen months*, *eighteen years* et *eighteen karats*. La réponse (D) associe *lifetime*, *tradition* et *since 1928.*

181. (C) Miller souhaite obtenir les brochures sur le marathon de juillet pour les personnes de son bureau. Les réponses (A), (B) et (D) sont liées à la discussion sur le marathon mais elles ne constituent pas l'objet de la lettre.

182. (B) La course de juillet est un semi-marathon. La réponse (A) joue sur la confusion avec la bonne réponse. La réponse (C) correspond à ce que Miller court chaque semaine. La réponse (D) correspond à la course de fond que Miller estime qu'elle devrait tenter.

183. (B) Wendel s'est fait une élongation à la jambe en jouant au golf. La réponse (A) joue sur la confusion avec les circonstances au cours desquelles elle s'est fait mal à la jambe. La réponse (C) joue sur la confusion avec le fait que ses collègues tirent beaucoup d'énergie du fait de courir. La réponse (D) est incorrecte car sa blessure est survenue en faisant du golf, et non en courant.

184. (B) Wendel pense qu'il faudra trois mois à Miller pour s'entraîner (la moitié des six mois que cela lui a pris à elle). Mars est dans trois mois à partir de janvier, le mois qui correspond à la date de la lettre. La réponse (A) correspond au moment où la lettre a été écrite. La réponse (C) correspond au temps d'entraînement qu'il a fallu à Wendel. La réponse (D) correspond à la date du marathon.

185. (C) Ils souhaitent collecter deux fois plus que les 400 000 dollars qu'ils ont collectés l'année dernière. La réponse (A) correspond à la moitié du montant collecté l'année dernière. La réponse (B) correspond au montant collecté l'année dernière. La réponse (D) correspond au triple du montant collecté l'année dernière.

186. (B) Althea mentionne *my brother's wedding*. La réponse (A) est vraie concernant le cousin d'Althea, Don Wade. La réponse (C) est incorrecte car c'est Althea, et non son frère, qui a remarqué l'annonce. La réponse (D) est vraie concernant Kathy.

187. (A) Althea écrit *I haven't heard from you in a few weeks, so maybe you have already found some work*. La réponse (B) n'est pas mentionnée. La réponse (C) est incorrecte car Althea écrit *the office is close to your apartment*. La réponse (D) est incorrecte car Althea dit que Don Wade sera présent au mariage.

188. (B) L'annonce dit que *no car is necessary*. Les réponses (A), (C) et (D) correspondent toutes à des conditions indispensables précisées dans l'annonce.

189. (C) L'annonce indique une expérience de deux ans comme faisant partie des exigences, et Althea écrit à Kathy *You have exactly the work experience they are looking for*. La réponse (A) est incorrecte car une voiture n'est pas nécessaire pour le poste.

La réponse (B) joue sur la confusion avec le fait qu'Althea connaisse le président du conseil d'administration. La réponse (D) n'est pas mentionnée.

190. (D) L'annonce dit qu'il faut copier-coller son CV, mais ne pas le mettre en pièce jointe. Les réponses (A), (B) et (C) correspondent à tous les éléments qui pourraient aider Kathy à obtenir le poste.

191. (B) Le message téléphonique d'Eva Pederson dit qu'elle a lu une note dans le hall d'entrée. La réponse (A) correspond à l'objet de la note. La réponse (C) joue sur la confusion avec la conférence que prévoit Eva. La réponse (D) correspond à un lieu où il serait possible d'afficher une note, mais n'est pas mentionnée.

192. (A) Eva a besoin d'idées pour résoudre son problème de parking, et la note recommande d'appeler la hotline de la ville pour obtenir des informations sur les parkings. La réponse (B) est incorrecte car les personnes qui assistent à la conférence n'ont pas accès au parking. La réponse (C) est incorrecte car les personnes qui assistent à la conférence ne sont pas des clients. La réponse (D) est incorrecte car les employés n'ont pas de passes.

193. (B) Seuls les clients actuels peuvent obtenir des passes. La réponse (A) est incorrecte car dans la mesure où ils ne sont pas clients, ils ne peuvent pas avoir accès au parking. La réponse (C) est incorrecte car les passes sont temporaires. La réponse (D) est incorrecte car le fait d'habiter en dehors de la ville est une condition préalable à l'obtention d'un passe.

194. (A) Le message d'Eva mentionne un lieu où les personnes qui assistent à la conférence pourront éventuellement garer leur voiture, ce lieu étant ouvert le week-end. La réponse (B) est incorrecte car la conférence a lieu à la mi-juin, non début juin. La réponse (C) joue sur la confusion entre *July* et *June*. La réponse (D) correspond au temps nécessaire pour marcher jusqu'au parking.

195. (C) Le message dit qu'Eva attend au moins soixante personnes. La réponse (A) joue sur la confusion avec les trente personnes qui n'ont pas répondu à l'invitation. La réponse (B) joue sur la confusion avec les cinquante personnes qui ont déjà répondu qu'elles seraient présentes. La réponse (D) correspond à trente plus cinquante.

196. (A) Le voyageur mentionne qu'il voulait voyager le week-end du 3, mais le site indique que ce n'est pas possible entre le 2 et le 4 octobre. La réponse (B) est en contradiction avec la bonne réponse. La réponse (C) n'est pas mentionnée. La réponse (D) est vraie, mais le voyageur ne s'excuse pas pour cela.

197. (D) Il dit *I will assume that one of you will meet me at the airport*. La réponse (A) joue sur la confusion avec la navette de bus mentionnée sur le site. La réponse (B) correspond à ce qu'il dit ne pas vouloir faire. La réponse (C) joue sur la confusion avec la *ten-minute walk from Tokyo International Airport* mentionnée sur le site.

198. (A) M. Lim discutera d'une franchise et aboutira à un accord éventuel, il s'agit donc d'un voyage d'affaires. Les réponses (B), (C) et (D) sont en contradiction avec la bonne réponse.

199. (C) L'annonce ne mentionne qu'une chambre simple, or M. Lim a réservé une chambre double. Les réponses (A) et (B) décrivent toutes deux l'hôtel et la chambre correspondant à la publicité et qui ont fait l'objet d'une réservation. La réponse (D) est incorrecte car la réservation de M. Lim a été faite *via* l'agence de voyages qui est propriétaire du site Internet.

200. (A) Selon les termes de la réservation, le voyage a été financé par des points voyage accumulés. Les réponses (B), (C) et (D) sont en contradiction avec la bonne réponse.

Grilles de réponses

ANSWER SHEET: Practice Test One

Listening Comprehension

Part 1		Part 2						Part 3						Part 4					
	Answer A B C D		Answer A B C		Answer A B C		Answer A B C		Answer A B C D		Answer A B C D		Answer A B C D		Answer A B C D		Answer A B C D		Answer A B C D
1	Ⓐ Ⓑ Ⓒ Ⓓ	11	Ⓐ Ⓑ Ⓒ	21	Ⓐ Ⓑ Ⓒ	31	Ⓐ Ⓑ Ⓒ	41	Ⓐ Ⓑ Ⓒ Ⓓ	51	Ⓐ Ⓑ Ⓒ Ⓓ	61	Ⓐ Ⓑ Ⓒ Ⓓ	71	Ⓐ Ⓑ Ⓒ Ⓓ	81	Ⓐ Ⓑ Ⓒ Ⓓ	91	Ⓐ Ⓑ Ⓒ Ⓓ
2	Ⓐ Ⓑ Ⓒ Ⓓ	12	Ⓐ Ⓑ Ⓒ	22	Ⓐ Ⓑ Ⓒ	32	Ⓐ Ⓑ Ⓒ	42	Ⓐ Ⓑ Ⓒ Ⓓ	52	Ⓐ Ⓑ Ⓒ Ⓓ	62	Ⓐ Ⓑ Ⓒ Ⓓ	72	Ⓐ Ⓑ Ⓒ Ⓓ	82	Ⓐ Ⓑ Ⓒ Ⓓ	92	Ⓐ Ⓑ Ⓒ Ⓓ
3	Ⓐ Ⓑ Ⓒ Ⓓ	13	Ⓐ Ⓑ Ⓒ	23	Ⓐ Ⓑ Ⓒ	33	Ⓐ Ⓑ Ⓒ	43	Ⓐ Ⓑ Ⓒ Ⓓ	53	Ⓐ Ⓑ Ⓒ Ⓓ	63	Ⓐ Ⓑ Ⓒ Ⓓ	73	Ⓐ Ⓑ Ⓒ Ⓓ	83	Ⓐ Ⓑ Ⓒ Ⓓ	93	Ⓐ Ⓑ Ⓒ Ⓓ
4	Ⓐ Ⓑ Ⓒ Ⓓ	14	Ⓐ Ⓑ Ⓒ	24	Ⓐ Ⓑ Ⓒ	34	Ⓐ Ⓑ Ⓒ	44	Ⓐ Ⓑ Ⓒ Ⓓ	54	Ⓐ Ⓑ Ⓒ Ⓓ	64	Ⓐ Ⓑ Ⓒ Ⓓ	74	Ⓐ Ⓑ Ⓒ Ⓓ	84	Ⓐ Ⓑ Ⓒ Ⓓ	94	Ⓐ Ⓑ Ⓒ Ⓓ
5	Ⓐ Ⓑ Ⓒ Ⓓ	15	Ⓐ Ⓑ Ⓒ	25	Ⓐ Ⓑ Ⓒ	35	Ⓐ Ⓑ Ⓒ	45	Ⓐ Ⓑ Ⓒ Ⓓ	55	Ⓐ Ⓑ Ⓒ Ⓓ	65	Ⓐ Ⓑ Ⓒ Ⓓ	75	Ⓐ Ⓑ Ⓒ Ⓓ	85	Ⓐ Ⓑ Ⓒ Ⓓ	95	Ⓐ Ⓑ Ⓒ Ⓓ
6	Ⓐ Ⓑ Ⓒ Ⓓ	16	Ⓐ Ⓑ Ⓒ	26	Ⓐ Ⓑ Ⓒ	36	Ⓐ Ⓑ Ⓒ	46	Ⓐ Ⓑ Ⓒ Ⓓ	56	Ⓐ Ⓑ Ⓒ Ⓓ	66	Ⓐ Ⓑ Ⓒ Ⓓ	76	Ⓐ Ⓑ Ⓒ Ⓓ	86	Ⓐ Ⓑ Ⓒ Ⓓ	96	Ⓐ Ⓑ Ⓒ Ⓓ
7	Ⓐ Ⓑ Ⓒ Ⓓ	17	Ⓐ Ⓑ Ⓒ	27	Ⓐ Ⓑ Ⓒ	37	Ⓐ Ⓑ Ⓒ	47	Ⓐ Ⓑ Ⓒ Ⓓ	57	Ⓐ Ⓑ Ⓒ Ⓓ	67	Ⓐ Ⓑ Ⓒ Ⓓ	77	Ⓐ Ⓑ Ⓒ Ⓓ	87	Ⓐ Ⓑ Ⓒ Ⓓ	97	Ⓐ Ⓑ Ⓒ Ⓓ
8	Ⓐ Ⓑ Ⓒ Ⓓ	18	Ⓐ Ⓑ Ⓒ	28	Ⓐ Ⓑ Ⓒ	38	Ⓐ Ⓑ Ⓒ	48	Ⓐ Ⓑ Ⓒ Ⓓ	58	Ⓐ Ⓑ Ⓒ Ⓓ	68	Ⓐ Ⓑ Ⓒ Ⓓ	78	Ⓐ Ⓑ Ⓒ Ⓓ	88	Ⓐ Ⓑ Ⓒ Ⓓ	98	Ⓐ Ⓑ Ⓒ Ⓓ
9	Ⓐ Ⓑ Ⓒ Ⓓ	19	Ⓐ Ⓑ Ⓒ	29	Ⓐ Ⓑ Ⓒ	39	Ⓐ Ⓑ Ⓒ	49	Ⓐ Ⓑ Ⓒ Ⓓ	59	Ⓐ Ⓑ Ⓒ Ⓓ	69	Ⓐ Ⓑ Ⓒ Ⓓ	79	Ⓐ Ⓑ Ⓒ Ⓓ	89	Ⓐ Ⓑ Ⓒ Ⓓ	99	Ⓐ Ⓑ Ⓒ Ⓓ
10	Ⓐ Ⓑ Ⓒ Ⓓ	20	Ⓐ Ⓑ Ⓒ	30	Ⓐ Ⓑ Ⓒ	40	Ⓐ Ⓑ Ⓒ	50	Ⓐ Ⓑ Ⓒ Ⓓ	60	Ⓐ Ⓑ Ⓒ Ⓓ	70	Ⓐ Ⓑ Ⓒ Ⓓ	80	Ⓐ Ⓑ Ⓒ Ⓓ	90	Ⓐ Ⓑ Ⓒ Ⓓ	100	Ⓐ Ⓑ Ⓒ Ⓓ

Reading

Part 5								Part 6				Part 7							
	Answer A B C D		Answer A B C D		Answer A B C D		Answer A B C D		Answer A B C D		Answer A B C D		Answer A B C D		Answer A B C D		Answer A B C D		Answer A B C D
101	Ⓐ Ⓑ Ⓒ Ⓓ	111	Ⓐ Ⓑ Ⓒ Ⓓ	121	Ⓐ Ⓑ Ⓒ Ⓓ	131	Ⓐ Ⓑ Ⓒ Ⓓ	141	Ⓐ Ⓑ Ⓒ Ⓓ	151	Ⓐ Ⓑ Ⓒ Ⓓ	161	Ⓐ Ⓑ Ⓒ Ⓓ	171	Ⓐ Ⓑ Ⓒ Ⓓ	181	Ⓐ Ⓑ Ⓒ Ⓓ	191	Ⓐ Ⓑ Ⓒ Ⓓ
102	Ⓐ Ⓑ Ⓒ Ⓓ	112	Ⓐ Ⓑ Ⓒ Ⓓ	122	Ⓐ Ⓑ Ⓒ Ⓓ	132	Ⓐ Ⓑ Ⓒ Ⓓ	142	Ⓐ Ⓑ Ⓒ Ⓓ	152	Ⓐ Ⓑ Ⓒ Ⓓ	162	Ⓐ Ⓑ Ⓒ Ⓓ	172	Ⓐ Ⓑ Ⓒ Ⓓ	182	Ⓐ Ⓑ Ⓒ Ⓓ	192	Ⓐ Ⓑ Ⓒ Ⓓ
103	Ⓐ Ⓑ Ⓒ Ⓓ	113	Ⓐ Ⓑ Ⓒ Ⓓ	123	Ⓐ Ⓑ Ⓒ Ⓓ	133	Ⓐ Ⓑ Ⓒ Ⓓ	143	Ⓐ Ⓑ Ⓒ Ⓓ	153	Ⓐ Ⓑ Ⓒ Ⓓ	163	Ⓐ Ⓑ Ⓒ Ⓓ	173	Ⓐ Ⓑ Ⓒ Ⓓ	183	Ⓐ Ⓑ Ⓒ Ⓓ	193	Ⓐ Ⓑ Ⓒ Ⓓ
104	Ⓐ Ⓑ Ⓒ Ⓓ	114	Ⓐ Ⓑ Ⓒ Ⓓ	124	Ⓐ Ⓑ Ⓒ Ⓓ	134	Ⓐ Ⓑ Ⓒ Ⓓ	144	Ⓐ Ⓑ Ⓒ Ⓓ	154	Ⓐ Ⓑ Ⓒ Ⓓ	164	Ⓐ Ⓑ Ⓒ Ⓓ	174	Ⓐ Ⓑ Ⓒ Ⓓ	184	Ⓐ Ⓑ Ⓒ Ⓓ	194	Ⓐ Ⓑ Ⓒ Ⓓ
105	Ⓐ Ⓑ Ⓒ Ⓓ	115	Ⓐ Ⓑ Ⓒ Ⓓ	125	Ⓐ Ⓑ Ⓒ Ⓓ	135	Ⓐ Ⓑ Ⓒ Ⓓ	145	Ⓐ Ⓑ Ⓒ Ⓓ	155	Ⓐ Ⓑ Ⓒ Ⓓ	165	Ⓐ Ⓑ Ⓒ Ⓓ	175	Ⓐ Ⓑ Ⓒ Ⓓ	185	Ⓐ Ⓑ Ⓒ Ⓓ	195	Ⓐ Ⓑ Ⓒ Ⓓ
106	Ⓐ Ⓑ Ⓒ Ⓓ	116	Ⓐ Ⓑ Ⓒ Ⓓ	126	Ⓐ Ⓑ Ⓒ Ⓓ	136	Ⓐ Ⓑ Ⓒ Ⓓ	146	Ⓐ Ⓑ Ⓒ Ⓓ	156	Ⓐ Ⓑ Ⓒ Ⓓ	166	Ⓐ Ⓑ Ⓒ Ⓓ	176	Ⓐ Ⓑ Ⓒ Ⓓ	186	Ⓐ Ⓑ Ⓒ Ⓓ	196	Ⓐ Ⓑ Ⓒ Ⓓ
107	Ⓐ Ⓑ Ⓒ Ⓓ	117	Ⓐ Ⓑ Ⓒ Ⓓ	127	Ⓐ Ⓑ Ⓒ Ⓓ	137	Ⓐ Ⓑ Ⓒ Ⓓ	147	Ⓐ Ⓑ Ⓒ Ⓓ	157	Ⓐ Ⓑ Ⓒ Ⓓ	167	Ⓐ Ⓑ Ⓒ Ⓓ	177	Ⓐ Ⓑ Ⓒ Ⓓ	187	Ⓐ Ⓑ Ⓒ Ⓓ	197	Ⓐ Ⓑ Ⓒ Ⓓ
108	Ⓐ Ⓑ Ⓒ Ⓓ	118	Ⓐ Ⓑ Ⓒ Ⓓ	128	Ⓐ Ⓑ Ⓒ Ⓓ	138	Ⓐ Ⓑ Ⓒ Ⓓ	148	Ⓐ Ⓑ Ⓒ Ⓓ	158	Ⓐ Ⓑ Ⓒ Ⓓ	168	Ⓐ Ⓑ Ⓒ Ⓓ	178	Ⓐ Ⓑ Ⓒ Ⓓ	188	Ⓐ Ⓑ Ⓒ Ⓓ	198	Ⓐ Ⓑ Ⓒ Ⓓ
109	Ⓐ Ⓑ Ⓒ Ⓓ	119	Ⓐ Ⓑ Ⓒ Ⓓ	129	Ⓐ Ⓑ Ⓒ Ⓓ	139	Ⓐ Ⓑ Ⓒ Ⓓ	149	Ⓐ Ⓑ Ⓒ Ⓓ	159	Ⓐ Ⓑ Ⓒ Ⓓ	169	Ⓐ Ⓑ Ⓒ Ⓓ	179	Ⓐ Ⓑ Ⓒ Ⓓ	189	Ⓐ Ⓑ Ⓒ Ⓓ	199	Ⓐ Ⓑ Ⓒ Ⓓ
110	Ⓐ Ⓑ Ⓒ Ⓓ	120	Ⓐ Ⓑ Ⓒ Ⓓ	130	Ⓐ Ⓑ Ⓒ Ⓓ	140	Ⓐ Ⓑ Ⓒ Ⓓ	150	Ⓐ Ⓑ Ⓒ Ⓓ	160	Ⓐ Ⓑ Ⓒ Ⓓ	170	Ⓐ Ⓑ Ⓒ Ⓓ	180	Ⓐ Ⓑ Ⓒ Ⓓ	190	Ⓐ Ⓑ Ⓒ Ⓓ	200	Ⓐ Ⓑ Ⓒ Ⓓ

ANSWER SHEET: Practice Test Two

Listening Comprehension

Part 1		Part 2						Part 3						Part 4					
	Answer		Answer		Answer		Answer		Answer		Answer		Answer		Answer		Answer		Answer
	A B C D		A B C		A B C		A B C		A B C D		A B C D		A B C D		A B C D		A B C D		A B C D
1	Ⓐ Ⓑ Ⓒ Ⓓ	11	Ⓐ Ⓑ Ⓒ	21	Ⓐ Ⓑ Ⓒ	31	Ⓐ Ⓑ Ⓒ	41	Ⓐ Ⓑ Ⓒ Ⓓ	51	Ⓐ Ⓑ Ⓒ Ⓓ	61	Ⓐ Ⓑ Ⓒ Ⓓ	71	Ⓐ Ⓑ Ⓒ Ⓓ	81	Ⓐ Ⓑ Ⓒ Ⓓ	91	Ⓐ Ⓑ Ⓒ Ⓓ
2	Ⓐ Ⓑ Ⓒ Ⓓ	12	Ⓐ Ⓑ Ⓒ	22	Ⓐ Ⓑ Ⓒ	32	Ⓐ Ⓑ Ⓒ	42	Ⓐ Ⓑ Ⓒ Ⓓ	52	Ⓐ Ⓑ Ⓒ Ⓓ	62	Ⓐ Ⓑ Ⓒ Ⓓ	72	Ⓐ Ⓑ Ⓒ Ⓓ	82	Ⓐ Ⓑ Ⓒ Ⓓ	92	Ⓐ Ⓑ Ⓒ Ⓓ
3	Ⓐ Ⓑ Ⓒ Ⓓ	13	Ⓐ Ⓑ Ⓒ	23	Ⓐ Ⓑ Ⓒ	33	Ⓐ Ⓑ Ⓒ	43	Ⓐ Ⓑ Ⓒ Ⓓ	53	Ⓐ Ⓑ Ⓒ Ⓓ	63	Ⓐ Ⓑ Ⓒ Ⓓ	73	Ⓐ Ⓑ Ⓒ Ⓓ	83	Ⓐ Ⓑ Ⓒ Ⓓ	93	Ⓐ Ⓑ Ⓒ Ⓓ
4	Ⓐ Ⓑ Ⓒ Ⓓ	14	Ⓐ Ⓑ Ⓒ	24	Ⓐ Ⓑ Ⓒ	34	Ⓐ Ⓑ Ⓒ	44	Ⓐ Ⓑ Ⓒ Ⓓ	54	Ⓐ Ⓑ Ⓒ Ⓓ	64	Ⓐ Ⓑ Ⓒ Ⓓ	74	Ⓐ Ⓑ Ⓒ Ⓓ	84	Ⓐ Ⓑ Ⓒ Ⓓ	94	Ⓐ Ⓑ Ⓒ Ⓓ
5	Ⓐ Ⓑ Ⓒ Ⓓ	15	Ⓐ Ⓑ Ⓒ	25	Ⓐ Ⓑ Ⓒ	35	Ⓐ Ⓑ Ⓒ	45	Ⓐ Ⓑ Ⓒ Ⓓ	55	Ⓐ Ⓑ Ⓒ Ⓓ	65	Ⓐ Ⓑ Ⓒ Ⓓ	75	Ⓐ Ⓑ Ⓒ Ⓓ	85	Ⓐ Ⓑ Ⓒ Ⓓ	95	Ⓐ Ⓑ Ⓒ Ⓓ
6	Ⓐ Ⓑ Ⓒ Ⓓ	16	Ⓐ Ⓑ Ⓒ	26	Ⓐ Ⓑ Ⓒ	36	Ⓐ Ⓑ Ⓒ	46	Ⓐ Ⓑ Ⓒ Ⓓ	56	Ⓐ Ⓑ Ⓒ Ⓓ	66	Ⓐ Ⓑ Ⓒ Ⓓ	76	Ⓐ Ⓑ Ⓒ Ⓓ	86	Ⓐ Ⓑ Ⓒ Ⓓ	96	Ⓐ Ⓑ Ⓒ Ⓓ
7	Ⓐ Ⓑ Ⓒ Ⓓ	17	Ⓐ Ⓑ Ⓒ	27	Ⓐ Ⓑ Ⓒ	37	Ⓐ Ⓑ Ⓒ	47	Ⓐ Ⓑ Ⓒ Ⓓ	57	Ⓐ Ⓑ Ⓒ Ⓓ	67	Ⓐ Ⓑ Ⓒ Ⓓ	77	Ⓐ Ⓑ Ⓒ Ⓓ	87	Ⓐ Ⓑ Ⓒ Ⓓ	97	Ⓐ Ⓑ Ⓒ Ⓓ
8	Ⓐ Ⓑ Ⓒ Ⓓ	18	Ⓐ Ⓑ Ⓒ	28	Ⓐ Ⓑ Ⓒ	38	Ⓐ Ⓑ Ⓒ	48	Ⓐ Ⓑ Ⓒ Ⓓ	58	Ⓐ Ⓑ Ⓒ Ⓓ	68	Ⓐ Ⓑ Ⓒ Ⓓ	78	Ⓐ Ⓑ Ⓒ Ⓓ	88	Ⓐ Ⓑ Ⓒ Ⓓ	98	Ⓐ Ⓑ Ⓒ Ⓓ
9	Ⓐ Ⓑ Ⓒ Ⓓ	19	Ⓐ Ⓑ Ⓒ	29	Ⓐ Ⓑ Ⓒ	39	Ⓐ Ⓑ Ⓒ	49	Ⓐ Ⓑ Ⓒ Ⓓ	59	Ⓐ Ⓑ Ⓒ Ⓓ	69	Ⓐ Ⓑ Ⓒ Ⓓ	79	Ⓐ Ⓑ Ⓒ Ⓓ	89	Ⓐ Ⓑ Ⓒ Ⓓ	99	Ⓐ Ⓑ Ⓒ Ⓓ
10	Ⓐ Ⓑ Ⓒ Ⓓ	20	Ⓐ Ⓑ Ⓒ	30	Ⓐ Ⓑ Ⓒ	40	Ⓐ Ⓑ Ⓒ	50	Ⓐ Ⓑ Ⓒ Ⓓ	60	Ⓐ Ⓑ Ⓒ Ⓓ	70	Ⓐ Ⓑ Ⓒ Ⓓ	80	Ⓐ Ⓑ Ⓒ Ⓓ	90	Ⓐ Ⓑ Ⓒ Ⓓ	100	Ⓐ Ⓑ Ⓒ Ⓓ

Reading

Part 5								Part 6				Part 7							
	Answer		Answer		Answer		Answer		Answer		Answer		Answer		Answer		Answer		Answer
	A B C D		A B C D		A B C D		A B C D		A B C D		A B C D		A B C D		A B C D		A B C D		A B C D
101	Ⓐ Ⓑ Ⓒ Ⓓ	111	Ⓐ Ⓑ Ⓒ Ⓓ	121	Ⓐ Ⓑ Ⓒ Ⓓ	131	Ⓐ Ⓑ Ⓒ Ⓓ	141	Ⓐ Ⓑ Ⓒ Ⓓ	151	Ⓐ Ⓑ Ⓒ Ⓓ	161	Ⓐ Ⓑ Ⓒ Ⓓ	171	Ⓐ Ⓑ Ⓒ Ⓓ	181	Ⓐ Ⓑ Ⓒ Ⓓ	191	Ⓐ Ⓑ Ⓒ Ⓓ
102	Ⓐ Ⓑ Ⓒ Ⓓ	112	Ⓐ Ⓑ Ⓒ Ⓓ	122	Ⓐ Ⓑ Ⓒ Ⓓ	132	Ⓐ Ⓑ Ⓒ Ⓓ	142	Ⓐ Ⓑ Ⓒ Ⓓ	152	Ⓐ Ⓑ Ⓒ Ⓓ	162	Ⓐ Ⓑ Ⓒ Ⓓ	172	Ⓐ Ⓑ Ⓒ Ⓓ	182	Ⓐ Ⓑ Ⓒ Ⓓ	192	Ⓐ Ⓑ Ⓒ Ⓓ
103	Ⓐ Ⓑ Ⓒ Ⓓ	113	Ⓐ Ⓑ Ⓒ Ⓓ	123	Ⓐ Ⓑ Ⓒ Ⓓ	133	Ⓐ Ⓑ Ⓒ Ⓓ	143	Ⓐ Ⓑ Ⓒ Ⓓ	153	Ⓐ Ⓑ Ⓒ Ⓓ	163	Ⓐ Ⓑ Ⓒ Ⓓ	173	Ⓐ Ⓑ Ⓒ Ⓓ	183	Ⓐ Ⓑ Ⓒ Ⓓ	193	Ⓐ Ⓑ Ⓒ Ⓓ
104	Ⓐ Ⓑ Ⓒ Ⓓ	114	Ⓐ Ⓑ Ⓒ Ⓓ	124	Ⓐ Ⓑ Ⓒ Ⓓ	134	Ⓐ Ⓑ Ⓒ Ⓓ	144	Ⓐ Ⓑ Ⓒ Ⓓ	154	Ⓐ Ⓑ Ⓒ Ⓓ	164	Ⓐ Ⓑ Ⓒ Ⓓ	174	Ⓐ Ⓑ Ⓒ Ⓓ	184	Ⓐ Ⓑ Ⓒ Ⓓ	194	Ⓐ Ⓑ Ⓒ Ⓓ
105	Ⓐ Ⓑ Ⓒ Ⓓ	115	Ⓐ Ⓑ Ⓒ Ⓓ	125	Ⓐ Ⓑ Ⓒ Ⓓ	135	Ⓐ Ⓑ Ⓒ Ⓓ	145	Ⓐ Ⓑ Ⓒ Ⓓ	155	Ⓐ Ⓑ Ⓒ Ⓓ	165	Ⓐ Ⓑ Ⓒ Ⓓ	175	Ⓐ Ⓑ Ⓒ Ⓓ	185	Ⓐ Ⓑ Ⓒ Ⓓ	195	Ⓐ Ⓑ Ⓒ Ⓓ
106	Ⓐ Ⓑ Ⓒ Ⓓ	116	Ⓐ Ⓑ Ⓒ Ⓓ	126	Ⓐ Ⓑ Ⓒ Ⓓ	136	Ⓐ Ⓑ Ⓒ Ⓓ	146	Ⓐ Ⓑ Ⓒ Ⓓ	156	Ⓐ Ⓑ Ⓒ Ⓓ	166	Ⓐ Ⓑ Ⓒ Ⓓ	176	Ⓐ Ⓑ Ⓒ Ⓓ	186	Ⓐ Ⓑ Ⓒ Ⓓ	196	Ⓐ Ⓑ Ⓒ Ⓓ
107	Ⓐ Ⓑ Ⓒ Ⓓ	117	Ⓐ Ⓑ Ⓒ Ⓓ	127	Ⓐ Ⓑ Ⓒ Ⓓ	137	Ⓐ Ⓑ Ⓒ Ⓓ	147	Ⓐ Ⓑ Ⓒ Ⓓ	157	Ⓐ Ⓑ Ⓒ Ⓓ	167	Ⓐ Ⓑ Ⓒ Ⓓ	177	Ⓐ Ⓑ Ⓒ Ⓓ	187	Ⓐ Ⓑ Ⓒ Ⓓ	197	Ⓐ Ⓑ Ⓒ Ⓓ
108	Ⓐ Ⓑ Ⓒ Ⓓ	118	Ⓐ Ⓑ Ⓒ Ⓓ	128	Ⓐ Ⓑ Ⓒ Ⓓ	138	Ⓐ Ⓑ Ⓒ Ⓓ	148	Ⓐ Ⓑ Ⓒ Ⓓ	158	Ⓐ Ⓑ Ⓒ Ⓓ	168	Ⓐ Ⓑ Ⓒ Ⓓ	178	Ⓐ Ⓑ Ⓒ Ⓓ	188	Ⓐ Ⓑ Ⓒ Ⓓ	198	Ⓐ Ⓑ Ⓒ Ⓓ
109	Ⓐ Ⓑ Ⓒ Ⓓ	119	Ⓐ Ⓑ Ⓒ Ⓓ	129	Ⓐ Ⓑ Ⓒ Ⓓ	139	Ⓐ Ⓑ Ⓒ Ⓓ	149	Ⓐ Ⓑ Ⓒ Ⓓ	159	Ⓐ Ⓑ Ⓒ Ⓓ	169	Ⓐ Ⓑ Ⓒ Ⓓ	179	Ⓐ Ⓑ Ⓒ Ⓓ	189	Ⓐ Ⓑ Ⓒ Ⓓ	199	Ⓐ Ⓑ Ⓒ Ⓓ
110	Ⓐ Ⓑ Ⓒ Ⓓ	120	Ⓐ Ⓑ Ⓒ Ⓓ	130	Ⓐ Ⓑ Ⓒ Ⓓ	140	Ⓐ Ⓑ Ⓒ Ⓓ	150	Ⓐ Ⓑ Ⓒ Ⓓ	160	Ⓐ Ⓑ Ⓒ Ⓓ	170	Ⓐ Ⓑ Ⓒ Ⓓ	180	Ⓐ Ⓑ Ⓒ Ⓓ	190	Ⓐ Ⓑ Ⓒ Ⓓ	200	Ⓐ Ⓑ Ⓒ Ⓓ

ANSWER SHEET: Practice Test Three

Listening Comprehension

Part 1		Part 2						Part 3						Part 4					
	Answer		Answer		Answer		Answer		Answer		Answer		Answer		Answer		Answer		Answer
	A B C D		A B C		A B C		A B C		A B C D		A B C D		A B C D		A B C D		A B C D		A B C D
1	Ⓐ Ⓑ Ⓒ Ⓓ	11	Ⓐ Ⓑ Ⓒ	21	Ⓐ Ⓑ Ⓒ	31	Ⓐ Ⓑ Ⓒ	41	Ⓐ Ⓑ Ⓒ Ⓓ	51	Ⓐ Ⓑ Ⓒ Ⓓ	61	Ⓐ Ⓑ Ⓒ Ⓓ	71	Ⓐ Ⓑ Ⓒ Ⓓ	81	Ⓐ Ⓑ Ⓒ Ⓓ	91	Ⓐ Ⓑ Ⓒ Ⓓ
2	Ⓐ Ⓑ Ⓒ Ⓓ	12	Ⓐ Ⓑ Ⓒ	22	Ⓐ Ⓑ Ⓒ	32	Ⓐ Ⓑ Ⓒ	42	Ⓐ Ⓑ Ⓒ Ⓓ	52	Ⓐ Ⓑ Ⓒ Ⓓ	62	Ⓐ Ⓑ Ⓒ Ⓓ	72	Ⓐ Ⓑ Ⓒ Ⓓ	82	Ⓐ Ⓑ Ⓒ Ⓓ	92	Ⓐ Ⓑ Ⓒ Ⓓ
3	Ⓐ Ⓑ Ⓒ Ⓓ	13	Ⓐ Ⓑ Ⓒ	23	Ⓐ Ⓑ Ⓒ	33	Ⓐ Ⓑ Ⓒ	43	Ⓐ Ⓑ Ⓒ Ⓓ	53	Ⓐ Ⓑ Ⓒ Ⓓ	63	Ⓐ Ⓑ Ⓒ Ⓓ	73	Ⓐ Ⓑ Ⓒ Ⓓ	83	Ⓐ Ⓑ Ⓒ Ⓓ	93	Ⓐ Ⓑ Ⓒ Ⓓ
4	Ⓐ Ⓑ Ⓒ Ⓓ	14	Ⓐ Ⓑ Ⓒ	24	Ⓐ Ⓑ Ⓒ	34	Ⓐ Ⓑ Ⓒ	44	Ⓐ Ⓑ Ⓒ Ⓓ	54	Ⓐ Ⓑ Ⓒ Ⓓ	64	Ⓐ Ⓑ Ⓒ Ⓓ	74	Ⓐ Ⓑ Ⓒ Ⓓ	84	Ⓐ Ⓑ Ⓒ Ⓓ	94	Ⓐ Ⓑ Ⓒ Ⓓ
5	Ⓐ Ⓑ Ⓒ Ⓓ	15	Ⓐ Ⓑ Ⓒ	25	Ⓐ Ⓑ Ⓒ	35	Ⓐ Ⓑ Ⓒ	45	Ⓐ Ⓑ Ⓒ Ⓓ	55	Ⓐ Ⓑ Ⓒ Ⓓ	65	Ⓐ Ⓑ Ⓒ Ⓓ	75	Ⓐ Ⓑ Ⓒ Ⓓ	85	Ⓐ Ⓑ Ⓒ Ⓓ	95	Ⓐ Ⓑ Ⓒ Ⓓ
6	Ⓐ Ⓑ Ⓒ Ⓓ	16	Ⓐ Ⓑ Ⓒ	26	Ⓐ Ⓑ Ⓒ	36	Ⓐ Ⓑ Ⓒ	46	Ⓐ Ⓑ Ⓒ Ⓓ	56	Ⓐ Ⓑ Ⓒ Ⓓ	66	Ⓐ Ⓑ Ⓒ Ⓓ	76	Ⓐ Ⓑ Ⓒ Ⓓ	86	Ⓐ Ⓑ Ⓒ Ⓓ	96	Ⓐ Ⓑ Ⓒ Ⓓ
7	Ⓐ Ⓑ Ⓒ Ⓓ	17	Ⓐ Ⓑ Ⓒ	27	Ⓐ Ⓑ Ⓒ	37	Ⓐ Ⓑ Ⓒ	47	Ⓐ Ⓑ Ⓒ Ⓓ	57	Ⓐ Ⓑ Ⓒ Ⓓ	67	Ⓐ Ⓑ Ⓒ Ⓓ	77	Ⓐ Ⓑ Ⓒ Ⓓ	87	Ⓐ Ⓑ Ⓒ Ⓓ	97	Ⓐ Ⓑ Ⓒ Ⓓ
8	Ⓐ Ⓑ Ⓒ Ⓓ	18	Ⓐ Ⓑ Ⓒ	28	Ⓐ Ⓑ Ⓒ	38	Ⓐ Ⓑ Ⓒ	48	Ⓐ Ⓑ Ⓒ Ⓓ	58	Ⓐ Ⓑ Ⓒ Ⓓ	68	Ⓐ Ⓑ Ⓒ Ⓓ	78	Ⓐ Ⓑ Ⓒ Ⓓ	88	Ⓐ Ⓑ Ⓒ Ⓓ	98	Ⓐ Ⓑ Ⓒ Ⓓ
9	Ⓐ Ⓑ Ⓒ Ⓓ	19	Ⓐ Ⓑ Ⓒ	29	Ⓐ Ⓑ Ⓒ	39	Ⓐ Ⓑ Ⓒ	49	Ⓐ Ⓑ Ⓒ Ⓓ	59	Ⓐ Ⓑ Ⓒ Ⓓ	69	Ⓐ Ⓑ Ⓒ Ⓓ	79	Ⓐ Ⓑ Ⓒ Ⓓ	89	Ⓐ Ⓑ Ⓒ Ⓓ	99	Ⓐ Ⓑ Ⓒ Ⓓ
10	Ⓐ Ⓑ Ⓒ Ⓓ	20	Ⓐ Ⓑ Ⓒ	30	Ⓐ Ⓑ Ⓒ	40	Ⓐ Ⓑ Ⓒ	50	Ⓐ Ⓑ Ⓒ Ⓓ	60	Ⓐ Ⓑ Ⓒ Ⓓ	70	Ⓐ Ⓑ Ⓒ Ⓓ	80	Ⓐ Ⓑ Ⓒ Ⓓ	90	Ⓐ Ⓑ Ⓒ Ⓓ	100	Ⓐ Ⓑ Ⓒ Ⓓ

Reading

Part 5								Part 6				Part 7							
	Answer		Answer		Answer		Answer		Answer		Answer		Answer		Answer		Answer		Answer
	A B C D		A B C D		A B C D		A B C D		A B C D		A B C D		A B C D		A B C D		A B C D		A B C D
101	Ⓐ Ⓑ Ⓒ Ⓓ	111	Ⓐ Ⓑ Ⓒ Ⓓ	121	Ⓐ Ⓑ Ⓒ Ⓓ	131	Ⓐ Ⓑ Ⓒ Ⓓ	141	Ⓐ Ⓑ Ⓒ Ⓓ	151	Ⓐ Ⓑ Ⓒ Ⓓ	161	Ⓐ Ⓑ Ⓒ Ⓓ	171	Ⓐ Ⓑ Ⓒ Ⓓ	181	Ⓐ Ⓑ Ⓒ Ⓓ	191	Ⓐ Ⓑ Ⓒ Ⓓ
102	Ⓐ Ⓑ Ⓒ Ⓓ	112	Ⓐ Ⓑ Ⓒ Ⓓ	122	Ⓐ Ⓑ Ⓒ Ⓓ	132	Ⓐ Ⓑ Ⓒ Ⓓ	142	Ⓐ Ⓑ Ⓒ Ⓓ	152	Ⓐ Ⓑ Ⓒ Ⓓ	162	Ⓐ Ⓑ Ⓒ Ⓓ	172	Ⓐ Ⓑ Ⓒ Ⓓ	182	Ⓐ Ⓑ Ⓒ Ⓓ	192	Ⓐ Ⓑ Ⓒ Ⓓ
103	Ⓐ Ⓑ Ⓒ Ⓓ	113	Ⓐ Ⓑ Ⓒ Ⓓ	123	Ⓐ Ⓑ Ⓒ Ⓓ	133	Ⓐ Ⓑ Ⓒ Ⓓ	143	Ⓐ Ⓑ Ⓒ Ⓓ	153	Ⓐ Ⓑ Ⓒ Ⓓ	163	Ⓐ Ⓑ Ⓒ Ⓓ	173	Ⓐ Ⓑ Ⓒ Ⓓ	183	Ⓐ Ⓑ Ⓒ Ⓓ	193	Ⓐ Ⓑ Ⓒ Ⓓ
104	Ⓐ Ⓑ Ⓒ Ⓓ	114	Ⓐ Ⓑ Ⓒ Ⓓ	124	Ⓐ Ⓑ Ⓒ Ⓓ	134	Ⓐ Ⓑ Ⓒ Ⓓ	144	Ⓐ Ⓑ Ⓒ Ⓓ	154	Ⓐ Ⓑ Ⓒ Ⓓ	164	Ⓐ Ⓑ Ⓒ Ⓓ	174	Ⓐ Ⓑ Ⓒ Ⓓ	184	Ⓐ Ⓑ Ⓒ Ⓓ	194	Ⓐ Ⓑ Ⓒ Ⓓ
105	Ⓐ Ⓑ Ⓒ Ⓓ	115	Ⓐ Ⓑ Ⓒ Ⓓ	125	Ⓐ Ⓑ Ⓒ Ⓓ	135	Ⓐ Ⓑ Ⓒ Ⓓ	145	Ⓐ Ⓑ Ⓒ Ⓓ	155	Ⓐ Ⓑ Ⓒ Ⓓ	165	Ⓐ Ⓑ Ⓒ Ⓓ	175	Ⓐ Ⓑ Ⓒ Ⓓ	185	Ⓐ Ⓑ Ⓒ Ⓓ	195	Ⓐ Ⓑ Ⓒ Ⓓ
106	Ⓐ Ⓑ Ⓒ Ⓓ	116	Ⓐ Ⓑ Ⓒ Ⓓ	126	Ⓐ Ⓑ Ⓒ Ⓓ	136	Ⓐ Ⓑ Ⓒ Ⓓ	146	Ⓐ Ⓑ Ⓒ Ⓓ	156	Ⓐ Ⓑ Ⓒ Ⓓ	166	Ⓐ Ⓑ Ⓒ Ⓓ	176	Ⓐ Ⓑ Ⓒ Ⓓ	186	Ⓐ Ⓑ Ⓒ Ⓓ	196	Ⓐ Ⓑ Ⓒ Ⓓ
107	Ⓐ Ⓑ Ⓒ Ⓓ	117	Ⓐ Ⓑ Ⓒ Ⓓ	127	Ⓐ Ⓑ Ⓒ Ⓓ	137	Ⓐ Ⓑ Ⓒ Ⓓ	147	Ⓐ Ⓑ Ⓒ Ⓓ	157	Ⓐ Ⓑ Ⓒ Ⓓ	167	Ⓐ Ⓑ Ⓒ Ⓓ	177	Ⓐ Ⓑ Ⓒ Ⓓ	187	Ⓐ Ⓑ Ⓒ Ⓓ	197	Ⓐ Ⓑ Ⓒ Ⓓ
108	Ⓐ Ⓑ Ⓒ Ⓓ	118	Ⓐ Ⓑ Ⓒ Ⓓ	128	Ⓐ Ⓑ Ⓒ Ⓓ	138	Ⓐ Ⓑ Ⓒ Ⓓ	148	Ⓐ Ⓑ Ⓒ Ⓓ	158	Ⓐ Ⓑ Ⓒ Ⓓ	168	Ⓐ Ⓑ Ⓒ Ⓓ	178	Ⓐ Ⓑ Ⓒ Ⓓ	188	Ⓐ Ⓑ Ⓒ Ⓓ	198	Ⓐ Ⓑ Ⓒ Ⓓ
109	Ⓐ Ⓑ Ⓒ Ⓓ	119	Ⓐ Ⓑ Ⓒ Ⓓ	129	Ⓐ Ⓑ Ⓒ Ⓓ	139	Ⓐ Ⓑ Ⓒ Ⓓ	149	Ⓐ Ⓑ Ⓒ Ⓓ	159	Ⓐ Ⓑ Ⓒ Ⓓ	169	Ⓐ Ⓑ Ⓒ Ⓓ	179	Ⓐ Ⓑ Ⓒ Ⓓ	189	Ⓐ Ⓑ Ⓒ Ⓓ	199	Ⓐ Ⓑ Ⓒ Ⓓ
110	Ⓐ Ⓑ Ⓒ Ⓓ	120	Ⓐ Ⓑ Ⓒ Ⓓ	130	Ⓐ Ⓑ Ⓒ Ⓓ	140	Ⓐ Ⓑ Ⓒ Ⓓ	150	Ⓐ Ⓑ Ⓒ Ⓓ	160	Ⓐ Ⓑ Ⓒ Ⓓ	170	Ⓐ Ⓑ Ⓒ Ⓓ	180	Ⓐ Ⓑ Ⓒ Ⓓ	190	Ⓐ Ⓑ Ⓒ Ⓓ	200	Ⓐ Ⓑ Ⓒ Ⓓ

ANSWER SHEET: Practice Test Four

Listening Comprehension

Part 1		Part 2						Part 3						Part 4					
	Answer A B C D		Answer A B C		Answer A B C		Answer A B C		Answer A B C D		Answer A B C D		Answer A B C D		Answer A B C D		Answer A B C D		Answer A B C D
1	Ⓐ Ⓑ Ⓒ Ⓓ	11	Ⓐ Ⓑ Ⓒ	21	Ⓐ Ⓑ Ⓒ	31	Ⓐ Ⓑ Ⓒ	41	Ⓐ Ⓑ Ⓒ Ⓓ	51	Ⓐ Ⓑ Ⓒ Ⓓ	61	Ⓐ Ⓑ Ⓒ Ⓓ	71	Ⓐ Ⓑ Ⓒ Ⓓ	81	Ⓐ Ⓑ Ⓒ Ⓓ	91	Ⓐ Ⓑ Ⓒ Ⓓ
2	Ⓐ Ⓑ Ⓒ Ⓓ	12	Ⓐ Ⓑ Ⓒ	22	Ⓐ Ⓑ Ⓒ	32	Ⓐ Ⓑ Ⓒ	42	Ⓐ Ⓑ Ⓒ Ⓓ	52	Ⓐ Ⓑ Ⓒ Ⓓ	62	Ⓐ Ⓑ Ⓒ Ⓓ	72	Ⓐ Ⓑ Ⓒ Ⓓ	82	Ⓐ Ⓑ Ⓒ Ⓓ	92	Ⓐ Ⓑ Ⓒ Ⓓ
3	Ⓐ Ⓑ Ⓒ Ⓓ	13	Ⓐ Ⓑ Ⓒ	23	Ⓐ Ⓑ Ⓒ	33	Ⓐ Ⓑ Ⓒ	43	Ⓐ Ⓑ Ⓒ Ⓓ	53	Ⓐ Ⓑ Ⓒ Ⓓ	63	Ⓐ Ⓑ Ⓒ Ⓓ	73	Ⓐ Ⓑ Ⓒ Ⓓ	83	Ⓐ Ⓑ Ⓒ Ⓓ	93	Ⓐ Ⓑ Ⓒ Ⓓ
4	Ⓐ Ⓑ Ⓒ Ⓓ	14	Ⓐ Ⓑ Ⓒ	24	Ⓐ Ⓑ Ⓒ	34	Ⓐ Ⓑ Ⓒ	44	Ⓐ Ⓑ Ⓒ Ⓓ	54	Ⓐ Ⓑ Ⓒ Ⓓ	64	Ⓐ Ⓑ Ⓒ Ⓓ	74	Ⓐ Ⓑ Ⓒ Ⓓ	84	Ⓐ Ⓑ Ⓒ Ⓓ	94	Ⓐ Ⓑ Ⓒ Ⓓ
5	Ⓐ Ⓑ Ⓒ Ⓓ	15	Ⓐ Ⓑ Ⓒ	25	Ⓐ Ⓑ Ⓒ	35	Ⓐ Ⓑ Ⓒ	45	Ⓐ Ⓑ Ⓒ Ⓓ	55	Ⓐ Ⓑ Ⓒ Ⓓ	65	Ⓐ Ⓑ Ⓒ Ⓓ	75	Ⓐ Ⓑ Ⓒ Ⓓ	85	Ⓐ Ⓑ Ⓒ Ⓓ	95	Ⓐ Ⓑ Ⓒ Ⓓ
6	Ⓐ Ⓑ Ⓒ Ⓓ	16	Ⓐ Ⓑ Ⓒ	26	Ⓐ Ⓑ Ⓒ	36	Ⓐ Ⓑ Ⓒ	46	Ⓐ Ⓑ Ⓒ Ⓓ	56	Ⓐ Ⓑ Ⓒ Ⓓ	66	Ⓐ Ⓑ Ⓒ Ⓓ	76	Ⓐ Ⓑ Ⓒ Ⓓ	86	Ⓐ Ⓑ Ⓒ Ⓓ	96	Ⓐ Ⓑ Ⓒ Ⓓ
7	Ⓐ Ⓑ Ⓒ Ⓓ	17	Ⓐ Ⓑ Ⓒ	27	Ⓐ Ⓑ Ⓒ	37	Ⓐ Ⓑ Ⓒ	47	Ⓐ Ⓑ Ⓒ Ⓓ	57	Ⓐ Ⓑ Ⓒ Ⓓ	67	Ⓐ Ⓑ Ⓒ Ⓓ	77	Ⓐ Ⓑ Ⓒ Ⓓ	87	Ⓐ Ⓑ Ⓒ Ⓓ	97	Ⓐ Ⓑ Ⓒ Ⓓ
8	Ⓐ Ⓑ Ⓒ Ⓓ	18	Ⓐ Ⓑ Ⓒ	28	Ⓐ Ⓑ Ⓒ	38	Ⓐ Ⓑ Ⓒ	48	Ⓐ Ⓑ Ⓒ Ⓓ	58	Ⓐ Ⓑ Ⓒ Ⓓ	68	Ⓐ Ⓑ Ⓒ Ⓓ	78	Ⓐ Ⓑ Ⓒ Ⓓ	88	Ⓐ Ⓑ Ⓒ Ⓓ	98	Ⓐ Ⓑ Ⓒ Ⓓ
9	Ⓐ Ⓑ Ⓒ Ⓓ	19	Ⓐ Ⓑ Ⓒ	29	Ⓐ Ⓑ Ⓒ	39	Ⓐ Ⓑ Ⓒ	49	Ⓐ Ⓑ Ⓒ Ⓓ	59	Ⓐ Ⓑ Ⓒ Ⓓ	69	Ⓐ Ⓑ Ⓒ Ⓓ	79	Ⓐ Ⓑ Ⓒ Ⓓ	89	Ⓐ Ⓑ Ⓒ Ⓓ	99	Ⓐ Ⓑ Ⓒ Ⓓ
10	Ⓐ Ⓑ Ⓒ Ⓓ	20	Ⓐ Ⓑ Ⓒ	30	Ⓐ Ⓑ Ⓒ	40	Ⓐ Ⓑ Ⓒ	50	Ⓐ Ⓑ Ⓒ Ⓓ	60	Ⓐ Ⓑ Ⓒ Ⓓ	70	Ⓐ Ⓑ Ⓒ Ⓓ	80	Ⓐ Ⓑ Ⓒ Ⓓ	90	Ⓐ Ⓑ Ⓒ Ⓓ	100	Ⓐ Ⓑ Ⓒ Ⓓ

Reading

Part 5								Part 6				Part 7							
	Answer A B C D		Answer A B C D		Answer A B C D		Answer A B C D		Answer A B C D		Answer A B C D		Answer A B C D		Answer A B C D		Answer A B C D		Answer A B C D
101	Ⓐ Ⓑ Ⓒ Ⓓ	111	Ⓐ Ⓑ Ⓒ Ⓓ	121	Ⓐ Ⓑ Ⓒ Ⓓ	131	Ⓐ Ⓑ Ⓒ Ⓓ	141	Ⓐ Ⓑ Ⓒ Ⓓ	151	Ⓐ Ⓑ Ⓒ Ⓓ	161	Ⓐ Ⓑ Ⓒ Ⓓ	171	Ⓐ Ⓑ Ⓒ Ⓓ	181	Ⓐ Ⓑ Ⓒ Ⓓ	191	Ⓐ Ⓑ Ⓒ Ⓓ
102	Ⓐ Ⓑ Ⓒ Ⓓ	112	Ⓐ Ⓑ Ⓒ Ⓓ	122	Ⓐ Ⓑ Ⓒ Ⓓ	132	Ⓐ Ⓑ Ⓒ Ⓓ	142	Ⓐ Ⓑ Ⓒ Ⓓ	152	Ⓐ Ⓑ Ⓒ Ⓓ	162	Ⓐ Ⓑ Ⓒ Ⓓ	172	Ⓐ Ⓑ Ⓒ Ⓓ	182	Ⓐ Ⓑ Ⓒ Ⓓ	192	Ⓐ Ⓑ Ⓒ Ⓓ
103	Ⓐ Ⓑ Ⓒ Ⓓ	113	Ⓐ Ⓑ Ⓒ Ⓓ	123	Ⓐ Ⓑ Ⓒ Ⓓ	133	Ⓐ Ⓑ Ⓒ Ⓓ	143	Ⓐ Ⓑ Ⓒ Ⓓ	153	Ⓐ Ⓑ Ⓒ Ⓓ	163	Ⓐ Ⓑ Ⓒ Ⓓ	173	Ⓐ Ⓑ Ⓒ Ⓓ	183	Ⓐ Ⓑ Ⓒ Ⓓ	193	Ⓐ Ⓑ Ⓒ Ⓓ
104	Ⓐ Ⓑ Ⓒ Ⓓ	114	Ⓐ Ⓑ Ⓒ Ⓓ	124	Ⓐ Ⓑ Ⓒ Ⓓ	134	Ⓐ Ⓑ Ⓒ Ⓓ	144	Ⓐ Ⓑ Ⓒ Ⓓ	154	Ⓐ Ⓑ Ⓒ Ⓓ	164	Ⓐ Ⓑ Ⓒ Ⓓ	174	Ⓐ Ⓑ Ⓒ Ⓓ	184	Ⓐ Ⓑ Ⓒ Ⓓ	194	Ⓐ Ⓑ Ⓒ Ⓓ
105	Ⓐ Ⓑ Ⓒ Ⓓ	115	Ⓐ Ⓑ Ⓒ Ⓓ	125	Ⓐ Ⓑ Ⓒ Ⓓ	135	Ⓐ Ⓑ Ⓒ Ⓓ	145	Ⓐ Ⓑ Ⓒ Ⓓ	155	Ⓐ Ⓑ Ⓒ Ⓓ	165	Ⓐ Ⓑ Ⓒ Ⓓ	175	Ⓐ Ⓑ Ⓒ Ⓓ	185	Ⓐ Ⓑ Ⓒ Ⓓ	195	Ⓐ Ⓑ Ⓒ Ⓓ
106	Ⓐ Ⓑ Ⓒ Ⓓ	116	Ⓐ Ⓑ Ⓒ Ⓓ	126	Ⓐ Ⓑ Ⓒ Ⓓ	136	Ⓐ Ⓑ Ⓒ Ⓓ	146	Ⓐ Ⓑ Ⓒ Ⓓ	156	Ⓐ Ⓑ Ⓒ Ⓓ	166	Ⓐ Ⓑ Ⓒ Ⓓ	176	Ⓐ Ⓑ Ⓒ Ⓓ	186	Ⓐ Ⓑ Ⓒ Ⓓ	196	Ⓐ Ⓑ Ⓒ Ⓓ
107	Ⓐ Ⓑ Ⓒ Ⓓ	117	Ⓐ Ⓑ Ⓒ Ⓓ	127	Ⓐ Ⓑ Ⓒ Ⓓ	137	Ⓐ Ⓑ Ⓒ Ⓓ	147	Ⓐ Ⓑ Ⓒ Ⓓ	157	Ⓐ Ⓑ Ⓒ Ⓓ	167	Ⓐ Ⓑ Ⓒ Ⓓ	177	Ⓐ Ⓑ Ⓒ Ⓓ	187	Ⓐ Ⓑ Ⓒ Ⓓ	197	Ⓐ Ⓑ Ⓒ Ⓓ
108	Ⓐ Ⓑ Ⓒ Ⓓ	118	Ⓐ Ⓑ Ⓒ Ⓓ	128	Ⓐ Ⓑ Ⓒ Ⓓ	138	Ⓐ Ⓑ Ⓒ Ⓓ	148	Ⓐ Ⓑ Ⓒ Ⓓ	158	Ⓐ Ⓑ Ⓒ Ⓓ	168	Ⓐ Ⓑ Ⓒ Ⓓ	178	Ⓐ Ⓑ Ⓒ Ⓓ	188	Ⓐ Ⓑ Ⓒ Ⓓ	198	Ⓐ Ⓑ Ⓒ Ⓓ
109	Ⓐ Ⓑ Ⓒ Ⓓ	119	Ⓐ Ⓑ Ⓒ Ⓓ	129	Ⓐ Ⓑ Ⓒ Ⓓ	139	Ⓐ Ⓑ Ⓒ Ⓓ	149	Ⓐ Ⓑ Ⓒ Ⓓ	159	Ⓐ Ⓑ Ⓒ Ⓓ	169	Ⓐ Ⓑ Ⓒ Ⓓ	179	Ⓐ Ⓑ Ⓒ Ⓓ	189	Ⓐ Ⓑ Ⓒ Ⓓ	199	Ⓐ Ⓑ Ⓒ Ⓓ
110	Ⓐ Ⓑ Ⓒ Ⓓ	120	Ⓐ Ⓑ Ⓒ Ⓓ	130	Ⓐ Ⓑ Ⓒ Ⓓ	140	Ⓐ Ⓑ Ⓒ Ⓓ	150	Ⓐ Ⓑ Ⓒ Ⓓ	160	Ⓐ Ⓑ Ⓒ Ⓓ	170	Ⓐ Ⓑ Ⓒ Ⓓ	180	Ⓐ Ⓑ Ⓒ Ⓓ	190	Ⓐ Ⓑ Ⓒ Ⓓ	200	Ⓐ Ⓑ Ⓒ Ⓓ

Conversion des scores aux tests

Comment convertir vos scores aux tests

Pour convertir vos scores aux tests , utilisez le tableau de la page 260.
Suivez les étapes indiquées ci-dessous.

1. Faites un test complet.
2. Faites le total de vos bonnes réponses pour la section compréhension orale.
3. Faites correspondre le nombre total de vos bonnes réponses pour la section compréhension orale avec le score correspondant figurant dans le tableau.
4. Faites le total de vos bonnes réponses pour la section compréhension écrite.
5. Faites correspondre le nombre total de vos bonnes réponses pour la section compréhension écrite avec le score correspondant figurant dans le tableau.
6. Additionnez les deux scores. Vous obtiendrez ainsi votre score total au test.

Exemple

Nombre de réponses correctes pour l'oral	56	= Score pour l'oral		290
Nombre de réponses correctes pour l'écrit	82	= Score pour l'écrit	+	405
Estimation du score total				695

Votre score au test n° 1

Nombre de réponses correctes pour l'oral	___	= Score pour l'oral		_____
Nombre de réponses correctes pour l'écrit	___	= Score pour l'écrit	+	_____
Estimation du score total				_____

Votre score au test n° 2

Nombre de réponses correctes pour l'oral	___	= Score pour l'oral		_____
Nombre de réponses correctes pour l'écrit	___	= Score pour l'écrit	+	_____
Estimation du score total				_____

Votre score au test n° 3

Nombre de réponses correctes pour l'oral	___	= Score pour l'oral		_____
Nombre de réponses correctes pour l'écrit	___	= Score pour l'écrit	+	_____
Estimation du score total				_____

Votre score au test n° 4

Nombre de réponses correctes pour l'oral	___	= Score pour l'oral		_____
Nombre de réponses correctes pour l'écrit	___	= Score pour l'écrit	+	_____
Estimation du score total				_____

Tableau de conversion des tests

	SCORE	
# BONNES RÉPONSES	ORAL	ÉCRIT
0	5	5
1	5	5
2	5	5
3	5	5
4	5	5
5	5	5
6	5	5
7	10	5
8	15	5
9	20	5
10	25	5
11	30	5
12	35	5
13	40	5
14	45	5
15	50	5
16	55	10
17	60	15
18	65	20
19	70	25
20	75	30
21	80	35
22	85	40
23	90	45
24	95	50
25	100	60
26	110	65
27	115	70
28	120	80
29	125	85
30	130	90
31	135	95
32	140	100
33	145	110
34	150	115
35	160	120
36	165	125
37	170	130
38	175	140
39	180	145
40	185	150
41	190	160
42	195	165
43	200	170
44	210	175
45	215	180
46	220	190
47	230	195
48	240	200
49	245	210
50	250	215

	SCORE	
# BONNES RÉPONSES	ORAL	ÉCRIT
51	255	220
52	260	225
53	270	230
54	275	235
55	280	240
56	290	250
57	295	255
58	300	260
59	310	265
60	315	270
61	320	280
62	325	285
63	330	290
64	340	300
65	345	305
66	350	310
67	360	320
68	365	325
69	370	330
70	380	335
71	385	340
72	390	350
73	395	355
74	400	360
75	405	365
76	410	370
77	420	380
78	425	385
79	430	390
80	440	395
81	445	400
82	450	405
83	460	410
84	465	415
85	470	420
86	475	425
87	480	430
88	485	435
89	490	445
90	495	450
91	495	455
92	495	465
93	495	470
94	495	480
95	495	485
96	495	490
97	495	495
98	495	495
99	495	495
100	495	495

Contenu des CD audio

CD1

Test complet n° 1

Piste	Activité
1	Introduction
2	Part 1: Consignes
3	Part 1: Questions 1-10
4	Part 2: Consignes
5	Part 2: Questions 11-25
6	Part 2: Questions 26-40
7	Part 3: Consignes
8	Part 3: Questions 41-43
9	Part 3: Questions 44-46
10	Part 3: Questions 47-49
11	Part 3: Questions 50-52
12	Part 3: Questions 53-55
13	Part 3: Questions 56-58
14	Part 3: Questions 59-61
15	Part 3: Questions 62-64
16	Part 3: Questions 65-67
17	Part 3: Questions 68-70
18	Part 4: Consignes
19	Part 4: Questions 71-73
20	Part 4: Questions 74-76
21	Part 4: Questions 77-79
22	Part 4: Questions 80-82
23	Part 4: Questions 83-85
24	Part 4: Questions 86-88
25	Part 4: Questions 89-91
26	Part 4: Questions 92-94
27	Part 4: Questions 95-97
28	Part 4: Questions 98-100

CD2

Test complet n° 2

Piste	Activité
1	Part 1: Consignes
2	Part 1: Questions 1-10
3	Part 2: Consignes
4	Part 2: Questions 11-25
5	Part 2: Questions 26-40
6	Part 3: Consignes
7	Part 3: Questions 41-43
8	Part 3: Questions 44-46
9	Part 3: Questions 47-49
10	Part 3: Questions 50-52
11	Part 3: Questions 53-55
12	Part 3: Questions 56-58
13	Part 3: Questions 59-61
14	Part 3: Questions 62-64
15	Part 3: Questions 65-67
16	Part 3: Consignes
17	Part 4: Questions
18	Part 4: Questions 71-73
19	Part 4: Questions 74-76
20	Part 4: Questions 77-79
21	Part 4: Questions 80-82
22	Part 4: Questions 83-85
23	Part 4: Questions 86-88
24	Part 4: Questions 89-91
25	Part 4: Questions 92-94
26	Part 4: Questions 95-97
27	Part 4: Questions 98-100

CD3

Test complet n° 3

Piste	Activité
1	Part 1: Consignes
2	Part 1: Questions 1-10
3	Part 2: Consignes
4	Part 2: Questions 11-25
5	Part 2: Questions 26-40
6	Part 3: Consignes
7	Part 3: Questions 41-43
8	Part 3: Questions 44-46
9	Part 3: Questions 47-49
10	Part 3: Questions 50-52
11	Part 3: Questions 53-55
12	Part 3: Questions 56-58
13	Part 3: Questions 59-61
14	Part 3: Questions 62-64
15	Part 3: Questions 65-67
16	Part 3: Consignes
17	Part 4: Questions
18	Part 4: Questions 71-73
19	Part 4: Questions 74-76
20	Part 4: Questions 77-79
21	Part 4: Questions 80-82
22	Part 4: Questions 83-85
23	Part 4: Questions 86-88
24	Part 4: Questions 89-91
25	Part 4: Questions 92-94
26	Part 4: Questions 95-97
27	Part 4: Questions 98-100

CD4

TEST COMPLET N° 4

Piste	Activité
1	Part 1: Consignes
2	Part 1: Questions 1-10
3	Part 2: Consignes
4	Part 2: Questions 11-25
5	Part 2: Questions 26-40
6	Part 3: Consignes
7	Part 3: Questions 41-43
8	Part 3: Questions 44-46
9	Part 3: Questions 47-49
10	Part 3: Questions 50-52
11	Part 3: Questions 53-55
12	Part 3: Questions 56-58
13	Part 3: Questions 59-61
14	Part 3: Questions 62-64
15	Part 3: Questions 65-67
16	Part 3: Questions 68-70
17	Part 4: Consignes
18	Part 4: Questions 71-73
19	Part 4: Questions 74-76
20	Part 4: Questions 77-79
21	Part 4: Questions 80-82
22	Part 4: Questions 83-85
23	Part 4: Questions 86-88
24	Part 4: Questions 89-91
25	Part 4: Questions 92-94
26	Part 4: Questions 95-97
27	Part 4: Questions 98-100

Welcome to *Longman English Interactive!*

Nous vous indiquons ici une description simplifiée de la procédure d'inscription. Un guide complet pour l'inscription et l'utilisation du programme est disponible en français sur le site :
http://www.longmanenglishinteractive.com/manuals/LEI_StudentManual_FR.pdf

Comment s'inscrire à *Longman English Interactive*

Le code d'accès sous la languette permet de vous inscrire puis d'utiliser le programme pendant un an. Vous n'aurez à saisir ce code que lors de votre première connexion.

Note : si la languette a déjà été soulevée, il se peut que le code ne soit plus valable. Si c'est le cas, vous pouvez acquérir un nouveau code à l'adresse suivante :
http://www.LongmanEnglishInteractive.com
Cliquez sur **Students** dans la fenêtre **First-Time users.** Puis cliquez sur **I need to buy access.**

Pour activer votre code d'accès

S'inscrire à *Longman English Interactive* est simple et rapide. Vous n'aurez à procéder à l'inscription qu'une seule fois. Prenez soin de vérifier la configuration de votre ordinateur (voir plus bas), puis munissez-vous de votre code d'accès à 31 lettres.

1. Rendez-vous sur le site http://www.longmanenglishinteractive.com et cliquez sur le bouton **Students** dans la fenêtre **First-Time users.**
2. Cliquez sur **I already have an access code**.
3. Cliquez sur **I accept** pour accepter les conditions d'utilisation.
4. Indiquez si vous avez déjà un compte Pearson Education en cochant **Yes**, **No** (ou **Not sure** si vous ne savez pas).
5. Si vous cliquez sur **No**, l'étape suivante vous invite à créer votre *login* (nom d'utilisateur) et votre *password* (mot de passe). **Il est fortement conseillé d'utiliser votre adresse email comme login car elle est unique.**
6. Mot de passe : il doit être composé d'un minimum de 8 caractères et contenir au moins un chiffre.
7. L'écran suivant vous invite à saisir vos coordonnées personnelles et à choisir une question de sécurité.
8. Saisissez votre code d'accès à 31 lettres.
9. A la fin de votre inscription, une page de confirmation s'affiche. Votre compte est activé. Conservez précieusement vos *login* et *password* car vous en aurez besoin à chaque utilisation de *Longman English Interactive*. Vous recevrez également un e-mail de confirmation.

Une fois inscrit, vous pouvez accéder à *Longman English Interactive* et commencer à étudier, à votre rythme.

Comment accéder au programme *Longman English Interactive*

1. A la fin de l'inscription, cliquez sur **Log in now**, puis sur **Join another course**. Le cours *Longman English Interactive* s'affiche.
2. Cochez la case **Work on your own**.
3. Lors de vos visites ultérieures, rendez-vous sur le site http://www.longmanenglishinteractive.com et cliquez sur le bouton **Log in** dans la fenêtre **Registered User**.
4. Saisissez le login et le password que vous avez créés lors de votre inscription.

Configuration pour utiliser *Longman English Interactive*

PC (configuration minimum): Windows® 2000 et ultérieur, Internet Explorer® 6.x OU Firefox® 2.0, Adobe® Reader 7, Adobe® Flash Player 8, Java™ 1.4.2

Mac (configuration minimum) : OS X 10.3.9, Safari® 2.0 OU Firefox® 2.0, Adobe® Reader 7, Adobe® Flash Player8, Java ™ 1.4.2

Pour tous les ordinateurs :
Ecouteurs ou enceintes et micro, intégrés à l'ordinateur ou externes, connexion Internet à haut débit, 256 Mb RAM, résolution écran 1024 x 768

Besoin d'aide ?
Envoyez un e-mail (en anglais) à EPSupport@pearsoned.com
ou contactez-nous en ligne à http://www.PearsonLongmanSupport.com
En cas de difficulté vous pouvez nous contacter à longman.fr@pearson.com